Israel and Its Bible

GARLAND REFERENCE LIBRARY OF SOCIAL SCIENCE
VOLUME 1031

Israel and Its Bible

A Political Analysis

Ira Sharkansky

Garland Publishing, Inc.
New York and London
1996

Library of Congress Cataloging-in-Publication Data

Sharkansky, Ira.
Israel and its Bible : a political analysis / Ira Sharkansky.
p. cm. — (Garland reference library of social science ; vol. 1031)
Includes bibliographical references and index.
ISBN 0-8153-2021-3 (alk. paper)
1. Politics in the Bible. 2. Bible. O.T.—Criticism, interpretation, etc. 3. Bible. O.T.—Influence. 4. Judaism—20th century. 5. Israel—Politics and government. I. Title. II. Series.
BS1199.P6S53 1996
221.6—dc20 95-48104
CIP

Printed on acid-free, 250-year-life paper
Manufactured in the United States of America

For Mattan, Tamar, Erica, and Stefan

Contents

Preface

This book began its life shortly after the birth of our youngest child. We called him Mattan (gift), on account of our age, and our hope for his future. Then a Bible dictionary led me to one Mattan who was a priest of Baal slain in an episode of regime change (*II Kings* 11:18), and a more tantalizing story in *Jeremiah* 38 that mentioned another Mattan. His son was among the princes who accused the prophet of treason and sought to kill him.

It did not take long for the political character of these stories to lead me through the rest of *Kings* and *Jeremiah* and then back and forth to the whole of the Hebrew Bible and into the vast literature of commentaries and scholarship. At about the same time I began to perceive the significance of biblical work done by friends who I had known via my other interests in political science, i.e., Steven Brams, Daniel J. Elazar, and Aaron Wildavsky. An early conclusion was that the political situation of ancient Israel bore great resemblance to that of the modern country. After I wrote *Ancient and Modern Israel: An Exploration of Political Parallels* (State University of New York Press, 1991), I realized that I had not done justice to the numerous perspectives on politics that were apparent in the Bible and the literature about it.

Much of the Bible is written with far greater beauty than is found in modern social science. Yet its use of metaphor, allegory, poetry, allusion, and hyperbole as well as its vast breadth in historical period and existential concerns render it difficult to define its meanings in ancient contexts or its messages for the present. What one scholar wrote about *Ecclesiastes* is applicable to much of the Bible: "My reading . . . is not necessarily the right one, and certainly not the only possible one."[1] With all of the limitations, it is my intentions to portray politically relevant episodes and themes of the Hebrew Bible that appear to shed light on the continued vitality of Judaism and the character of modern Israel. In this light I seek to develop the following themes:

- The Bible's composition and compilation over perhaps a millennium reflect the development of a people with a strong sense of national identity but generally small in population, weak in economic resources and military power, and dependent on more powerful regimes that had an interest in the land the Jews considered their own.
- This produced a situation of universal political relevance: a community whose aspirations were chronically greater than its achievements. The Bible reveals a skepticism about power holders as well as a sensitivity to their problems and a pragmatic willingness to adjust goals to reality.
- The literary richness of the Bible has generated scholarship from the perspectives of numerous varieties of religious doctrine, secular humanism, and social science. There is much in this scholarship for its insight into the Bible and modern society, but lack of certainty is endemic to any scholarship associated with the Bible.
- It is a great leap to see connections between ancient and modern cultures. This is especially the case with cultural entities as rich in their complexities as the Hebrew Bible, Judaism, and Israel. Yet the insights seem worth the risks. The disputatious character of Judaism and the noisy criticism among Israeli elites seem to emerge from roots that produced books like *Job* and *Ecclesiastes* and the prophet Jeremiah. Ancient conditions remain to reinforce these traits: i.e., weakness and dependence, aspirations that cannot be attained, along with a strong sense of communal identity, creative perceptions of alternative ways for dealing with communal security, and a willingness to argue about perceptions, visions, and plans.

Along the way to this book, I have benefited greatly from the advice and criticism of numerous Jews and non-Jews, clerics, secular scholars and others, believers, agnostics, and committed atheists. Our mutual fascination with the Bible reflects its many sides and its capacity to attract and provoke. If this book has any merit, it will attract more of the disputes that are at the heart of its enterprise. And if I have perceived the style of biblical scholarship correctly, some of the comments will be harsh.

Specialists may object to the freedom with which the substantive chapters of this book mix materials taken from different modes of scholarship. Rabbis and Christian clerics, each from their own perspective, will assert that passages in the following chapters overlook or misunderstand biblical interpretations developed in post-biblical sources. Scholars who specialize in the Bible and Jewish history may perceive that there is nothing new. Some introductory comments by C. S. Lewis to his *Reflections on the Psalms* may be suitable for this book as well: "I am no Hebraist, no higher critic, no ancient historian, no archaeologist. I write for the unlearned about things in which I am unlearned myself."[2]

It is also appropriate to paraphrase the prophet Amos (Amos 7:14). I am neither a rabbi, a biblical scholar, nor even a political philosopher, nor the son of these. My perspectives are those of a political scientist with primary interests in political behavior, public policy, and public administration. This background has prepared me to focus on how the Bible describes God and humans; its proclamations, laws, and other expressions of norms indicating how they should have acted; and its reports of their failures as well as accomplishments.

AN AFTERWORD

This book went into production in September, 1995. It reached the stage of final page proofs in November, shortly after the assassination of Prime Minister Yitzhak Rabin. In the week after the assassination the Israeli media provided one extended discussion, often at an impressive intellectual level, concerned with the various individuals, groups, and social conditions that contributed to the killing, and its implications.

Hatred against the Israeli government, and especially the prime minister expressed by certain religious and nationalist Jews derived from arrangements made with the Palestinian Authority. Much of the discussion in the period following the killing dealt with the significance of the biblical Land of Israel, how much of that imprecise landscape could be bargained away to those perceived as recent terrorists for the promise of peace, and how Jews should conduct their disputes about these issues. The assassination and the soul searching that followed showed the passions that Jews can allocate to political issues with biblical roots.

At this point it is too early to express serious conclusions about the killing and its implications for the future of Judaism and Israel. Among the crucial questions are: Can Israel's rabbis and secular leaders dissuade their followers from violence and lead them to conduct disputes via persuasion? And can Israel's security forces deal adequately with those who would not be persuaded to desist from violence?

NOTES

[1]James L. Crenshaw, *Ecclesiastes: A Commentary* (London: SCM Press Ltd., 1988), p. 53.

[2] C. S. Lewis, *Reflections on the Psalms* (London: Fontana Books, 1961), p. 9.

Israel and Its Bible

Part I
On the Political Significance of the Bible

It is the theme of this book that the character of politics in the Hebrew Bible explains something about the nature of Israeli politics as well as the intellectual plurality that is Judaism. Yet the Bible complicates the analysis. Its reputation derives from spiritual qualities. The classic works of philosophy and political science began elsewhere, in the culture of the Greeks that was anathema to many ancient Jews. However, there is much of political relevance in the Bible. At its center are the Israelites who aspired to rule themselves, their struggles against powerful others, and God who they saw as their patron and the source of their laws.

If modern readers do not find the politics in the Bible by themselves, they may be led to them by political activists who have sought to justify their programs by reference to biblical episodes or by the increasing number of scholars who examine the Bible for its political significance. All of these politicians and scholars are limited, whether they recognize it or not, by the nature of the Bible. The political messages of the Bible are rich and even profound, but they are not straightforward in our terms. They differ, contrast, and even contradict one another and lend themselves to distortion and exploitation by those who want the Bible's legitimacy for their own purposes. Commentaries on the Bible are no less diverse. It could not be otherwise, given the contents of the Bible and multiplicity of themes that they present.

The diversity of political themes and norms that appear in the Bible may have something to do with the culture of the ancient writers. Unlike the Greeks and modern academics who trace their intellectual lineage to Greece, the people called Hebrews, then Israelites, and then Jews were not preoccupied with a clear enunciation of general principles and the specification of implications logically subordinate to those principles. The Bible includes stories, laws, moral precepts, bits of theology, social criticism, and other wisdom collected over the centuries. The people who produced this material had a sense of their own distinctiveness but encountered one challenge after another to their survival. In tales of their ups and downs and many other observations preserved as sacred text, they show that a plurality of perspectives and other political skills could compensate, in part, for a lack of sheer power. For us, the multiplicity of themes and the confusion of political ideas in the Bible are not annoying, but features that seem to be valuable in their own right. They suggest one source of the richness in Judaic culture and the democracy that has developed in modern Israel.

A modern political scientist who writes in this way about the Hebrew Bible is on ground that is made slippery by the huge time span involved as well as the nature of the Bible. In the pages that follow we will be viewing biblical stories and passages through eyes trained in the thought of the Greeks and their European successors rather than that of the ancient Jews. The heavy presence of the Bible in our culture justifies the effort. It appears that more people quote the Bible than read it. That by itself is reason for looking closely at the Bible in order to warn against a simplistic reliance on part of the text to represent the whole.

Chapter 1
Israel and the Diversity of Biblical Politics

There appears to be a connection between the character of Israeli politics and the Hebrew Bible.[1] This is not a messianic vision of God-ordained Israel or a justification of Israel's behavior on the basis of religious doctrines. It reflects a secular reading of the way politics is described in the Bible and the way it is practiced in modern Israel.

At the very beginning of this book, I ask the reader's indulgence for "a bit of a stretch."[2] The argument is not buttoned down in all of its particulars. It is that the political culture of modern Israel reflects certain traits of the politics apparent in the Bible. A related line of argument is that the character of Judaism draws on biblical traits; and Judaism adds its own explanation to politics in the Jewish state.

Two kinds of material that appear in the Bible contribute to these themes. One includes those institutions and behaviors that are mentioned in the Bible that serve to limit the power of rulers. Another is the very diversity of politically relevant themes, which suggest that authors or compilers of the Holy Book were open to a diversity of perspectives, and did not produce a statement of strict orthodoxy closed in the face of argument.

There are no clear lines of development described in this book for the millennia that intervened between the composition of the Bible and the emergence of modern Israel. Occasional references to the long middle period of Jewish history demonstrate the reasonable nature of the larger argument, but the middle period is not covered with anything like the thoroughness devoted to the biblical text or the period after 1948.

Why should the reader accept an argument that is not fully specified? The lacuna may be greater than that left in other works about political culture, but political culture is a problematic concept in any case. Political scientists and sociologists have used it to develop insights to the explanation of various behaviors in different contexts, but they often fail to specify or explain all the details.[3] In the case at hand, the intellectual reward seems to justify the risk. We are dealing with important features of modern Israel's political culture, which seem to have roots deep in the nation's history and help to explain the character of the country's regime.

The polities described in the Bible were not democracies, and Israel falls short of the norm that a democracy should provide for majority rule where all citizens have equal opportunities. All democracies are imperfect according to the strict criteria of equality, but Israel is more explicit than others in this regard. Its declaration of being a Jewish state generates criticism that is not overcome by its declarations in behalf of equal rights.

The biblical polities proclaimed that their laws came from a god that was not approachable for dialogue with the common people, and they existed in a milieu of autocratic despots. However, they had some traits associated with democracy despite conditions that were anything but democratic. The laws of the biblical polities at least formally limited the rulers and protected those who were economically weak. Episodes concerned with the prophets reveal great reverence devoted to critics of political elites. One incident in the career of Jeremiah depicts that he expressed more severe criticism of policy than has been allowed in democracies of the twentieth century.

Several characteristics of modern Israel would appear to have worked against a democratic regime. Most of the population came from societies of central and eastern Europe or the Middle East where democracy was weakly established, if it existed at all. The first years of the new state were marked by a difficult war and mass immigration. Almost all of the immigrants were desperately poor, in need of housing and social services. The economy was so short of resources that it could barely pay for imports of basic foods. Such conditions are typically cited as explanations for *coups d'etat* engineered by military officers or other cancellations of democratic procedures. Yet Israel ranks along with the 20 or 30 democracies among the more than 150 countries of the world. Its political parties are competitive and implement peaceful turnovers of power after elections. The country tolerates and even honors sharp criticism of government officials. Few countries that came on the world's scene along with Israel in the decade after World War II fulfilled their proclamations of democracy with anything close to Israel's achievements.[4]

ON POLITICS AND POLITIES

It is appropriate at this point to describe briefly the traits associated with different kinds of politics and polities. These concepts will return several times in connection with later discussions of the political cultures apparent in the Hebrew Bible as well as Judaism and modern Israel.

Politics has been defined as collective decision-making or a determination of *who gets what* in a polity.[5] A *polity* or *regime* includes the institutions and practices in which politics occurs. Polities may be arrayed along a spectrum that ranges from authoritarian or dictatorial to those labeled liberal, pluralist, polyarchic, or democratic. Important in the placement of a regime along such a spectrum is the manner of selecting leaders, including provisions for competition, the nature of elections, and an orderly turning over of power to those who win an election; the inclination of office holders to dominate or to engage in dialogue with adversaries and constituents; and assurances for diversity, individual liberty, and freedom.

One should be wary of expecting neat divisions between authoritarian and democratic polities. Actual regimes, including those described in the Hebrew Bible, have mixtures of traits. There is also dispute among scholars as to what should be called authoritarian and what democratic, liberal, or pluralist.[6] The complexities inherent in the concept of democracy are apparent across several sub-fields of political science. Democracy involves elements of governmental structure and procedure, as well as characteristics of political behavior and the workings of political parties, interest groups, and mass media, plus social and economic traits that affect the opportunities of individuals and communities for political access and policy benefits.[7]

There are minimum expectations about the traits that a democratic regime should display along with a recognition that national experiences have produced some dispersion around the norms. As will be shown below, modern Israel scores well on many of these traits but not in the eyes of its critics. Biblical polities do not score well on any of the traits associated with democracy, although they show some features that will be described as "proto-democratic."

Democracies are expected to have competitive elections open to all contenders or at least those who did not threaten its democratic character. Voting rights should be available to all adult citizens, with opportunities to speak freely, and they should have reasonable access to information about governmental activities. Electoral procedures and legislative districting should provide fair representation of perspectives and communities. There should be a peaceful turnover of governmental positions from the losers to the winners.

Political parties and interest groups should facilitate the representative character of the regime, and they should be able to oppose the personnel and policies of the current government. This may entail some assurances of the rights of individuals within such organizations, but there are also values associated with the discipline of party affiliates and the officials elected as party representatives. Politicians who campaign as advocates of one party's program and then shift loyalties when in office limit the voters' capacity to shape the policies of government.

Electronic and print media should reflect a wide spectrum of perspectives. They should be free to express themselves on issues of importance. Decision making in a democracy generally occurs by means of persuasion and voting. Democratic states employ violence against those citizens or residents who do not obey the rules. There may be emergency procedures that allow a suspension of normal conditions, as well as opportunities to remove the civil rights of individuals as a result of judicial proceedings. The free expression of individuals and media may be constrained with respect to the protection of state secrets, libel, and incitement of mass hatreds.

Elements of political culture may be the essential ingredients that allow the institutions of competitive elections and free discussion to take root. Among the important features of a democratic culture may be an openness to a diversity of perspective, along with skepticism in the face of claims made by elites. Closely related to these traits may be flexibility and pragmatism with respect to the pursuit of solutions rather than an acceptance of the one sure way propounded by ideologues; an assumption that leaders are likely to be imperfect; and a tolerance of public criticism directed at key figures. While there is no indication that ancient Israelite or Judean polities were consistent in providing anything like modern concepts of freedom of speech, the Bible compiled in those polities provides an honored place for prophets who were shrill in criticizing the moral lapses and other policy choices of their regimes.

Related to a democratic culture may be the availability of sufficient resources to avoid the mass poverty that can open the way to demagoguery. An alternative to abundant resources may be ethical norms that support a sharing of the resources that are available. Countries identified as democracies provide for the private acquisition of resources, and typically have differences in economic and political opportunities associated with class, ethnicity, race, region, and gender. To the extent that population sectors diverge greatly in the direction of inequalities, they may threaten the democratic nature of the regime. Democratic polities deal with this danger by offering constitutional or statutory assurances of equal political opportunities, progressive rates of taxation, education, and other social services that seek to level economic opportunities.

A variety of moral standards may be used by leaders to select a course of action or by their critics to judge those courses of action. A tolerance for diverse standards is an important element of a regime's character. Polities toward the authoritarian end of the political spectrum are less tolerant of multiple standards than polities toward the democratic end. A multiplicity of normative standards is likely to generate dispute. While pluralistic, polyarchic, or democratic regimes respect dispute, authoritarian or autocratic regimes prize the leader's choice of policies and have little tolerance for anything else.[8] The moral standards identified by political scientists include:

- an *egoistic, communal*, or *nationalistic* standard (what's good for me or my people);
- an *egalitarian* standard that esteems the equal treatment of all individuals and communities;
- an *altruistic* standard that values a concern for the weaker individuals or nations;
- a *utilitarian* standard (e.g., the greatest good for the greatest number or the greatest benefits for the least cost);
- a *pragmatic* standard or an esteem for proposals that promise to achieve some success amidst difficult surroundings;
- a *procedural* standard (e.g., a concern to follow rules that require democratic selection of key officials, the agreements of certain officials for a policy to go forward, or the public's ratification of major decisions);

- a *legal* standard that requires or forbids particular actions as defined in law that itself has been legislated or proclaimed according to official procedures;
- a *religious* standard (as perceived by *A*, God demands *X*);
- norms of *justice* or *righteousness*, which are complex in expressing a people's sense as to what is right, proper, or fair and may encompass several of the standards listed above.

Most of these moral standards can be perceived in one section or another of the Hebrew Bible, as will be shown in subsequent chapters. The mixture of standards may confuse modern readers who expect the Bible to proclaim authoritative truth. The Bible offers no systematic discussion of what is more or less important or why one perspective should be chosen over another in a given situation. Yet the very variety of standards and the lack of authoritative priorities suggests a flexibility or openness in the face of diversity and a willingness to adjust normative aspirations to realities. If this trait is not democratic, per se, it is consistent with the pragmatism that goes along with democracy.

Polities also differ in their power. A polity may be strong or weak with respect to how it relates to its own population. It may be domineering or dependent with respect to other polities or co-exist with them on terms that are more or less equal. The elements of power are the resources available to regime leaders: the size and skills of the population and its willingness to serve the regime plus money, raw materials, technology, and the infrastructures of industry, transportation arteries, and communications. On these dimensions the biblical polities were weaker than several neighboring regimes. A preoccupation with their weakness may have contributed to moral concerns for the weak and a preoccupation with community survival. The Bible articulates standards of justice and righteousness that include altruism toward the weak. It also endorses norms of nationalism, piety with respect to the Almighty, and a pragmatic concern to achieve what is possible.

POLITICS IN THE BIBLE AND ISRAEL

The polities of the Hebrews, Israelites, or Jews portrayed in the Hebrew Bible were small and generally dominated by powerful empires. The biblical polities were on the authoritarian end of the spectrum. However, they tantalize a political scientist by traits associated with democracies. There was a concern for legality and the more complex moral standards of righteousness and justice. There was also skepticism in the face of authority and self-doubt. The authors and editors of the Bible seemed to be acutely aware of their people's weakness and dependence on others. By some views, this awareness helps to explain their recognition of diverse moral norms and a degree of tolerance for individuals who behave at different times according to different standards. But we must guard against being carried away by an enthusiasm for biblical openness to diversity. The text gives expression to a great variety of political norms. In numerous passages, however, it also expresses a shrill *intolerance* for anything other than conventional orthodoxy. And some passages show something like *political correctness.* Alongside book-length expressions of doubt and skepticism, *Job* and *Ecclesiastes* conclude with affirmations of pious reverence.

The first generation of Israeli politicians may not have come from democratic societies. However, they came from circles where ideas of democracy mingled with Zionism and socialism. Israel's first prime minister, David Ben Gurion, was an archetype of the Jew who passed through youth movements in eastern Europe and then a kibbutz in Palestine. Like many others of his generation, Ben Gurion had little time for formal academic training. Yet he read widely and engaged the leading scientists and scholars of Israel in disputes over issues of philosophy, science, and biblical interpretation. Many of the controversies dealt with state building: the appropriate limits of state authority, the nature of democracy, and the contributions to be expected from intellectuals in creating symbols and institutions for the new nation. Especially relevant for the argument of this book was the fascination of Ben Gurion and other Zionists with the Bible. They cited biblical roots in behalf of democracy, social justice, and the criticism of established elites as well as their re-conquest of the Land of Israel.[9] Michael Keren describes one argument in which the prime minister perceived support in the prophets for his style of political foresight, while the distinguished scholar Ephraim Urbach responded that the prophets were noted for their criticism of political leaders no less than for being visionaries.[10]

Israel earns its place in the list of democratic regimes by means of free and open elections, proportional representation in the national parliament (Knesset) and local councils, and the peaceful transfer of power from incumbents who lose elections. Typically about 20 parties compete in national elections, with about 10 passing the minimum electoral requirements for gaining a seat in the Knesset. The ideological variety represented in the Knesset has ranged from Communists and Arab-dominated parties on the left to free-enterprise, Jewish religious, and nationalist parties on the right, with Islamic religious parties winning places in some local councils. Both Jews and non-Jews have credible records of voter turnout at about 80 percent in national elections. The major parties now employ primaries open to all dues-paying members to select nominees for major offices. The ultra-Orthodox Jewish religious parties, which together represent about 10 percent of the electorate and occasionally exercise swing weight in the make up of government coalitions, are headed by councils of elderly rabbis who do not stand for popular election.

The multiplicity of political parties and an electoral system of proportional representation both reflects and reinforces a tendency toward a diversity of options without clear choice between them. No party has ever won a majority at an Israeli national election. All Cabinets have been coalitions between parties whose leaders continue to quarrel even while they govern.

The political economy is mixed, with a strong tilt to state intervention. Israel ranks at or near the top of democracies with respect to the government's control of economic resources.[11] Programs of the government or quasi-governmental organizations provide numerous free or subsidized social services, including child allowances, schooling, medical care, housing, and mass transportation. There is a wide spectrum of print media and no lack of controversial material on government operated radio and television. Severe threats against the state and its people are cited to explain procedures of censorship and other legal provisions associated with national security that are severe by comparison with other democracies.[12]

There is no intention here to offer a defense or apology for the character of Israeli government and politics or to assess the numerous criticisms of the regime.[13] Likewise, there is no claim that any of the polities described in the Hebrew Bible would qualify as democracies as that term is generally understood. The concern is, rather, to focus on those elements of the Israeli polity that seem to reflect aspects of Jewish culture that also make their appearance in the biblical text. The author accepts the view of other political scientists who list Israel along with other modern democracies as well as numerous criticisms that point to the imperfections in the democracies of Israel and other countries.

The most sensitive questions concerning the quality of Israel's democracy involve the relations between the Jewish majority (83 percent of the population)[14] and non-Jews. No democracy is truly egalitarian in its political opportunities, but Israel departs from that standard more clearly than others. The 1948 Declaration of Independence proclaimed Israel as a Jewish state, even while it assured an equality of rights regardless of religion, ethnicity, or sex. Israeli intellectuals (Jews and non-Jews) and governmental reports have conceded that Jews receive the major portions of political opportunities and policy benefits. They have argued various sides of the question as to whether those distributions are justified or not by the threats of security or Arab disinclination to recognize the legitimacy of the Israeli regime. A subset of these arguments focuses on Israeli practices in the territories occupied as a result of the 1967 war, where the non-Jews do not benefit from a number of legal protections available to Israeli citizens.[15] Civil libertarians also criticize Israel for giving to religious authorities (Jewish, Moslem, Christian, and Druze) a near monopoly to deal with sensitive issues of personal status in their communities, especially marriage and divorce according to religious law.

Israel is a feisty society. Its capacity for self-criticism is prominent among the traits that grant it status as a democracy. Loud critics of the regime are widely read and occasionally honored. Some prominent Israelis censure government policy in ways that resemble the shrill pronouncements of biblical prophets.[16] Unlike the biblical prophets, modern critics who have won respect in Israel do not claim to be speaking for the Lord. Like the prophets, however, their declarations are extreme and intense. They employ historic Jewish themes in criticizing existing policy, and they evoke dire threats for those who resist their message.

The late Yehoshafat Harkabi was head of military intelligence and became Professor of International Relations at the Hebrew University of Jerusalem. He was especially critical of Israelis who revered the heroic religiosity and nationalism of the Bar Kokhba Rebellion against the Romans in 131-35 CE.[17] According to Harkabi, Bar Kokhba was guilty of irrational warfare that was bound to end in disaster. Harkabi compared Bar Kokhba to modern extremists who insist that the West Bank should be Israel's possession. Harkabi predicted disaster, perhaps even the destruction of the Jewish people, if the zealots do not stop or if they are not stopped by more reasonable Israelis. Harkabi was among the first prominent Israelis who urged the government to deal openly with the Palestine Liberation Organization (PLO), at a time when it was conventional to view that organization as terrorist and beyond the pale of political discourse.[18]

Meron Benvenisti was deputy mayor of Jerusalem and worked unsuccessfully in behalf of creating ethnic boroughs that would contribute to the city's stability. He earned a doctorate at Harvard's Kennedy School, returned to Israel and dedicated himself to the West Bank Data Project, concerned with investigating Jewish settlements in the occupied territories. Benvenisti has referred to the Israelis as conquerors and parasites and compared them to medieval autocrats who plundered the lands they occupied. Like Harkabi, he predicts national disaster if his warnings are not heeded.[19]

The late Yeshayahu Leibowitz was a religious Jew and professor of chemistry at the Hebrew University. He appeared frequently on Israeli television, usually in rumpled clothes with his eyeglasses and skullcap askew. Soon after the end of the six-day war in June 1967, Leibowitz began to warn Israelis about the moral costs of military occupation. In his view, it was impossible to realize Jewish values in a bi-national state, especially where the Jews are military occupiers. The scenario that he projected is a brutalization of the Jewish state by those who will achieve an upper hand by force and put people like him in concentration camps.[20]

Each of these critics has had regular access to the most prestigious of Israel's newspapers as well as radio and television forums. Harkabi and Leibowitz were designated recipients of Israel Prizes for 1993 by the Ministry of Education and Culture. The public accepted Harkabi's award routinely but Leibowitz's evoked surprise and condemnation as well as praise. The censure was directed at his use of the term *Nazi* to describe Israel's actions.[21] For a society built on the ashes of the Holocaust, that was inaccurate and intolerable criticism. After a few days of controversy, Leibowitz resolved the issue by declining the award.

Domestic as well as foreign critics have accused Israel of the illegal occupation of territory, the repression of a conquered population, illegal detentions, torture, censoring the media, and piracy.[22] Officials reject these charges and explain their actions as legitimate self defense that falls within Israeli law or Israeli interpretations of international law. They admit that some personnel exceed formal norms but assert that such actions are subject to investigation and discipline. Local and overseas commentators ponder the vexatious issues, occasionally in language that is appropriate to a seminar, sometimes with the noise of public demonstration.

There is much dispute about Israeli policies that proceeds at a tone only a bit lower than that of the prophets. Comparative research finds that Israelis are more likely to engage in public demonstrations than the citizens of other western democracies and are less likely to protest government actions by individual letters of complaint.[23]

Part of Israel's story is a congestion of moral dilemmas. In this trait modern Israel resembles the Israelites at several points during the Exodus and at other difficult times in their history. Only slightly unusual was the period July 29-August 2, 1993, when four issues with intense emotional content crowded the nation's agenda.

1. The Israel Defense Forces were engaged in a week-long artillery, naval, and air bombardment of southern Lebanon. According to leading members of the Cabinet, the operation was directed at pushing residents of the region from their homes in order to pressure the Lebanese government to stop rocket attacks on northern Israel that originated with groups in southern Lebanon. Israeli authorities and commentators were aware of the imbalance in force employed and the moral problems in directing force against villagers in order to win concessions from authorities in Beirut. Against some 273 rockets that landed in Israel or the Israeli-controlled "security zone" of southern Lebanon during the week of the operation, Israeli forces fired 22,238 artillery shells into Lebanon and dropped some 1,000 aerial bombs.[24]
2. The Israeli Knesset, by a vote of 54 to 50, with 8 abstentions, defeated a proposal by the State Prosecutor to remove the parliamentary immunity of Knesset Member Raphael Pinchasi of

the Sephardi ultra-Orthodox party known by its Hebrew acronym of SHAS. The Prosecutor wanted to bring Pinchasi to trial for the alleged crimes of forging documents, filing false claims, and receiving things of value by deceit. The operation in Lebanon was connected with the Knesset vote against removing Pinchasi's immunity. Left-wing parties that had supported the government on the basis of its peace efforts indicated that they would withdraw their support because of the heavy bombardment. All this occurred as the Prime Minister and Foreign Minister were secretly approaching an agreement with the PLO. With a threat to the coalition from the left, it was not a time when a Prime Minister wanted to be distracted by a matter of government ethics and the possibility that SHAS would leave his coalition. He signaled to his Labor Party colleagues to preserve Pinchasi's immunity in order to avoid offending SHAS.

3. A five-judge panel of the Israeli Supreme Court ordered the release of John Demjanjuk, who had appealed his conviction and death sentence for crimes against the Jewish people. The Court ruled that the alleged identity of the accused as a sadistic killer in a Nazi death camp could not be established beyond a reasonable doubt. The Court further indicated that, despite *prima facie* evidence that Demjanjuk was guilty of serious alternate charges, those charges should not now be considered in the judgment because Demjanjuk had not been given a chance in the trial to defend himself against them. This decision produced international praise for Israel's rule of law and outrage about the injustice involved in the Jewish state's releasing a person who appeared to have participated in the Holocaust.

4. Israeli media reported that in 1983 Professor Marcus Klingberg had been secretly tried and sentenced to 18 years on charges of espionage. Klingberg had been an internationally-known scientist, chair of the Tel Aviv University Department of Preventive Medicine, and a researcher at a government laboratory. After he disappeared in 1983, neither his wife nor daughter responded to inquiries about him. Some of his departmental colleagues at the University of Tel Aviv refused to answer journalists' inquiries about him, and others denied knowing him.[25] Under Israeli law, the Legal Advisor to the Government can decide to withhold details of an indictment and evidence from the accused in certain

cases involving national security and to forbid news reports about a trial and incarceration.[26]

These issues reflected a number of Israel's chronic problems. The polity aspires to democracy but cannot free itself from vexatious issues that defy resolution by simple standards of right and wrong. It was on the verge of a breakthrough in negotiations with its Palestinian adversaries but had ongoing problems with terrorists. It was troubled by political party scandals affected by religious-secular and Ashkenazi-Sephardi tensions. It still had some problems left over from the Cold War. And it could not free itself from the trauma of the Holocaust.

Among the provocative questions that Israel presents for a political scientist are, *Why is the country democratic?* and *Why the high incidence of factions?* The second question recalls epigrams about Jews, such as, *where there are two Jews there will be at least three opinions*; and *each community must have at least two synagogues: one for those Jews who will not attend the other.* Factionalism may be a cultural trait of Jews and seems to supply at least part of the answer to the first question. That is, Israel is democratic because Jews have acquired a capacity for living with numerous perspectives.[27]

From where does the capacity to live with numerous perspectives come? Part of the answer may be the high level of literacy that has characterized Jews (or at least Jewish men) for centuries and even millennia. Jewish communities over the centuries have not relied on small groups of literate elites. There is also the community's sense of being different, which reflects the biblical heritage of being the Chosen People, as well as Gentiles' desire to keep their own distance from the Jews. Whether the source of being distinct comes from inside or outside, it has produced a lot of Jewish thought about *What is good for the Jews? What is the implications of one or another event in the Gentile world for the Jews?* and *What should the Jews do?* This thinking appears in several episodes in the Hebrew Bible and numerous Jewish writings since the Bible's composition. Norman F. Cantor's *The Sacred Chain* portrays the varieties of Jewish culture throughout history and the numerous ways, often contentious, that Jews responded to their diversity.[28]

Part of the explanation for Jewish tolerance of factions may lie with the bloody intolerance that marked the later part of the biblical period, and the early post biblical period. Josephus describes the gory details of Jewish civil wars. During the rebellion against Rome of 66-73 C.E, Jews fought among themselves within Jerusalem and eased the city's conquest and destruction.[29] These events are the subject of numerous rabbinical homilies concerned with the sin and the folly of violence among Jews.

Jewish factions also have something to do with dispersion among many lands and Jews' different ways of looking at themselves and their neighbors. The history of European Jews in the nineteenth century (i.e., the background for much of the Israeli population) is one of multiplying intellectual and political options as Jews left the isolation of closed religious communities for the experience of the Enlightenment. Competing Jewish organizations sprang up to advocate the learning of Gentile languages and a greater integration into one or another European homeland, the learning of Hebrew to prepare for migration to Palestine, and the promotion of Yiddish to keep the Jews where they were but as a distinct community that would pursue its national interests within the framework of a European nation. Many Jews became socialists or communists, while others were attracted to liberalism or remained steadfastly aloof from secular issues. Orthodox Jews could choose from Hasidic or anti-Hasidic congregations or those that sought to remain outside of that dispute. A great number of European Jews sought change through migration. Some went to Palestine, but the great majority traveled west. As they reached western Europe or North America, they found opportunities to integrate themselves into the political parties available to the general population as well as to affiliate with a variety of Orthodox, Reform, or Conservative congregations.[30]

The following description pertains only to Bukowina in the last quarter of the nineteenth century. It was a tiny corner of the Jewish world on the border between Ukraine and Romania. Its general message of disputes is relevant to much of Jewish history:

> Among the Hasidim, Bojan abhorred Sadgora . . . Sadgora detested Bojan back . . . both abhorred the Maskilim (secularized intellectuals) who betrayed Tradition . . . The Maskilim, in their turn, were divided amongst those who were content to participate in the bourgeois Christian parties and those who felt it useful to be more Jewish . . . (One of the

> Maskilim) turned his most intense fire . . .against Zionism, insisting that Jews should build their future . . . in central Europe . . . and that they should do so in the prevailing German tongue. . . he spent his last years in bitter personal struggle with those elements of Habsburg Jewry who felt one could only get through to the Jewish masses by using Yiddish.[31]

Moving backward in time from the nineteenth century, one also finds diversity in Jewish communities. It is significant that Jews failed to establish a single Rabbinical hierarchy. There were separate developments in the many locales where Jews established communities. Several disputes continued for decades or centuries. Some have not subsided even now. The mystical school of *kabbalah* began to cause arguments among Jews in the twelfth century. There were arguments surrounding Maimonides' writings from the thirteenth century. The seventeenth century saw contention about the messianic claims for Sabbatai Sevi and the rise of Hasidism. There was also the Amsterdam community's lack of patience with intellectual creativity and its banishment of Baruch Spinoza in 1656.

ON THE BIBLE AND THIS BOOK

It is important to emphasize that this book *does not* claim that the Hebrew Bible is primarily a political book or that the politics apparent in the Bible or practiced in Jewish communities from ancient to modern times were democratic. The following chapters focus on the politically relevant portions of the Bible. These are extensive, but they do not clearly outweigh the elements of the text that can be described as spiritual, religious, or apolitical expressions of faith, piety, and devotion.

Some political scientists have found signs of democracy, republicanism, and federalism in the Bible.[32] The meaning of politically relevant episodes in the Hebrew Bible is too obscure, ambiguous, cryptic, and unclear to substantiate claims of such certainty. However, several traits of the Bible suggest that facets of ancient Judaic culture were similar to traits that have been described as important features of modern democracies. The Bible gives expression to a diversity of politically relevant perspectives. It also includes episodes that provide support for the values of skepticism with respect to figures of authority, the legitimacy of criticizing elites, and a pragmatic acceptance of what can be achieved even if it falls short of aspirations. Modern Israelis cite biblical sources for justification of political actions. Often such claims provoke accusations of exploiting sacred sources for legitimating controversial postures in contemporary affairs. They also lead opponents to offer contrary ways of interpreting the same biblical materials.[33]

Authoritarian concepts like monarchy, theocracy, oligarchy, and plutocracy (used to describe rule by the rich or by the relatively well-off in poor communities) are more useful than democracy in summarizing what is known about Jewish governance from biblical times until the twentieth century. It is also the case that prominent sectors in modern Israel do not subscribe to democracy. Ultra-Orthodox parties follow the decisions of elderly rabbis who do not stand for popular election. Other groups that take extreme positions on issues of Jewish control of the Land of Israel have put their own goals above the requirements of democracy.[34]

Many will quarrel with the interpretations in subsequent chapters. The Bible's stories, laws, and commentaries are brimming over with political detail, yet its style complicates any effort to define their meaning in modern terms. Stories, proclamations, allusions, metaphors, hyperbole, and contradictions assure a continuing supply of creative commentators. What one reader sees as dominant themes another may overlook altogether or define as insignificant. The very attempt to define the Bible's doctrine is Greek in its nature, and many ancient Jews looked at the Greeks as loathsome foreigners.

There are few topics in modern political science that do not appear in the Holy Book: motivations for power and restraint, emotions of revenge and mercy, strategies of national development and military victory, assertions of what must be done and assessments of what can be accomplished, a fickle population and individuals who would climb to power by rousing popular appetites, expressions of support and opposition to the monarchical form of government, the selection of kings and subordinate officers, international relations and local government, the admiration of great figures and criticism of personal weakness, governmental events that seem readily explainable and others that defy analysis.

The Bible portrays how individuals responded to severe pressures. It expresses the values of piety, justice, righteousness, and equity and describes ambivalence, avarice, and dishonesty in the face of impossible demands and strong temptations. Survival was a prime value, heightened by a reluctance to take the easy route of postponing gratification to a life after death. Leaders coped within the opportunities available to them and paid the price of imperfect decisions.

The failure of the Bible to define clear principles of governing suggests the pragmatism of a weak people who prized national independence but who could seldom realize their aspiration in the midst of powerful empires that coveted their land. The Holy Book indicates that a regime should be just and responsive but may have to be cruel and arbitrary. A political scientist will find no indication given as to when a government should be one or the other. Perhaps the ultimate message is that individuals must ponder the circumstances and judge wisely.

The candid telling of heroes' stories suggests either that the Bible's writers were not puritans or that they were able to put their puritanism in perspective. Great leaders behaved badly and still retained their offices. Not even God is beyond reproach. Abraham and Moses questioned his justice and persuaded him to moderate punishment of sinners. God's reputation of omnipotence and omniscience did not protect him from an unreliable people. Time and again the Israelites violated what God described as the most basic of his laws, i.e., those which forbid idolatry. None of the leaders God chose for his people were without blemish. One scholar uses the term "dissonance" to emphasize a trait of the Bible that is especially prominent in the *Book of Job,* where Almighty God appears to be insecure and unjust.[35]

Subsequent chapters portray a wide diversity of politically-relevant norms in the Hebrew Bible. The word "norm" is useful for our purposes. Its meanings include *typical, average, rule, standard, expectation, ideal, and principle.* Thus, *norms* may be descriptions of *reality* (i.e., normal or average behavior) or statements of *ideals.* We use the concept of norms to indicate what appears to be legitimized by the Bible as stated explicitly or inferred from the words or actions of major characters. Whether thought of as descriptions of what is typical, or expressions of ideals, the norms with political significance that appear in the Bible are diverse, contrasting, and contradictory when viewed through modern eyes. The diversity by itself is an important trait about the politically relevant features of the Bible. It suggests a culture that was not possessed by a simple or inflexible orthodoxy. A prominent element of that diversity, i.e., the openness to self-doubt and criticism, seems likely to reinforce itself by supporting a continuing elaboration of numerous perspectives and norms.

For some of the Bible's writers and editors, there was too much variety in the Holy Books. Those who produced *Chronicles* took out some episodes about David in earlier books and added other details in order to make the great king less earthy and more pious. Rabbis and other commentators of ancient and modern times have had even less tolerance for the human frailties of biblical leaders. For readers looking for morally pure heroes, the place to look is Jewish legends and not the Bible itself.[36]

The diversity of themes in the Hebrew Bible touches more than politics. Its variety of religious norms has supported the development of three major faiths and numerous factions of each.[37] It is common to say that both Rabbinical Judaism and Christianity developed from the Hebrew Bible but that both have departed from it.[38] The doctrines of the Hebrew Bible are so diverse that no evolving faith could be described simply as "biblical."

This description of political diversity as portrayed in the Hebrew Bible may be a surprise to some readers and disturbing to those who ascribe to one or another orthodoxy. However, it should not be viewed negatively. Its significance for Israel and elsewhere is that it bestows biblical legitimacy upon a tolerance of diversity, an honesty about political reality, and a justification of dispute about basic issues.

There is also a glaring paradox in this view of the Hebrew Bible. While numerous, different, and even contrasting political norms appear in the biblical text, the Bible does not clearly express tolerance. Its acceptance of diversity is implied by its failure to order according to any explicit system all the political norms that are apparent in its books. The Bible is often intolerant. Penalties for violating laws were severe. God, kings, and prophets were autocratic. They proclaimed more often than they argued or reasoned. They cursed opponents and killed many of them.

The explanation of the paradox may lie in the authors' and editors' lack of concern for the explicit definition of political norms and the priorities among them. Or the explanation may rest with the rabbis who accepted the Bible as finally compiled. They showed a greater tolerance for diverse messages than the authors of individual episodes. The *Book of Ecclesiastes* appears to be one of the latest of the biblical books, and it approaches an explicit tolerance for diversity. However, *Ecclesiastes* has its own paradox. It supports pious reverence along with skepticism. Insofar as we are asking Greek questions of a Hebrew text, we should not expect clear answers. Yet the picture available is important. It sheds a Hebrew insight on our Greek view of politics: it is possible to exist without being dominated by harsh categories and crisp logic. Indeed, such a world view is more humanly political than one that insists on clear concepts and orderly syllogism.

There is also a problem with the argument that links diversity in the political norms in the Hebrew Bible with the vitality of Judaism and the democracy of modern Israel. During the periods of Greek and Roman rule at the end of the biblical period, Judeans fought one another in ways that showed anything but a tolerance for diversity. Some Israelis today perceive that a modern civil war is imminent, perhaps as zealots with an attachment to the Land of Israel fight against those who would withdraw from parts of the Land for the sake of peace.[39]

Against these reservations it may be said that ancient bloodshed among Jews may have coincided with the work of other Jews who were compiling a Bible with numerous perspectives about God, secular authorities, and the relations between Jews and foreigners. The pressures of Greek and Roman occupation and the clash of loyalties among Jews seem to have produced both warfare and intellectual creativity in the same community. The disasters of the civil wars figure prominently in subsequent Jewish traditions as horrible lessons of what may occur if Jewish conflict surpasses the boundaries of sharp dispute. Right- and left-wing Israelis of secular as well as religious communities have warned against the possibilities of domestic warfare that may expose the nation once again to foreign conquest and subjugation.

As has been noted above, concepts of political culture are not so rigorous as to support precise hypotheses between cultural feature *A* and political behaviors *B*. This book claims no more than the ancient Judean capacity to produce writing of great variety, rich with nuance and subtlety, seems to have contributed to subsequent developments in the direction of intellectual vitality among Jews and a capacity among the Jews of Israel to create a democracy despite their severe problems.

Much biblical commentary is concerned with explaining apparent differences in norms or outright contradictions in the text. The talents of orthodox commentators are to make the confusing appear understandable, according to the orthodoxy that they endorse. Readers strain, extrapolate, eliminate counter examples, or otherwise distort the text to find a biblical endorsement for one or another form of government or one or another posture with respect to public policy.[40] This book accepts and embraces the diversity of biblical norms. It suggests a capacity to express ideal principles while admitting that situations may determine which must apply. The Bible's articulation of diverse norms and perception of good and bad in the same individual are traits of political flexibility and sophistication that contribute to communal survival.[41]

Scholars who specialize in biblical analysis categorize their numerous approaches with the following terms:

- *textual criticism*: examining the biblical text as presented in order to discern the meaning or to resolve problems involving passages or episodes;
- *source criticism*: seeking to discern the various layers of composition and editing (redaction), including indications of underlying oral traditions (whose identification is sometimes identified separately as "form criticism"); source and form criticism are concerned to determine when passages were composed, with an eye to discerning the motives behind the compositions;
- *historical criticism*: using the biblical text, together with archaeological findings and other non-biblical sources, to discern what really happened in biblical periods or episodes.

Political scientists who write about the Bible use their own closely parsed terms. *Norms, principles, laws, values, commandments, rules, covenants, agreements, policy,* and *implementation* have distinct meanings, in part depending on their context. There are different connotations between the Hebrew and English versions for some of these words, which has special importance when dealing with the Bible. I have selected words with an eye to their technical as well as their conventional meanings, while minimizing discussions that do not add to the argument.

It is also the case that originality is elusive in dealing with topics that have been examined for two thousand years. What claims to be distinctive in this book is the emphasis on the variety of political themes in the Bible, and the connections between this variety and the character of Judaism and Israel.

Several additional perspectives on the Bible also guided the writing of this book.

1. It helps to lay aside the concept of biblical truth or reliability on the one hand and unrelieved cynicism on the other hand. More appropriate postures are skepticism as to the historic reliability of any particular episode and an openness to political insights from a great work of literature.
2. The Bible was compiled, edited, and re-edited over the course of many years. It is helpful to recognize the changing perspectives inherent in it. However, efforts to identify the various layers are no less problematic than the text itself. The full text presently available has value in its own right and will be analyzed for what it can tell us about the political perspectives that can be perceived in the Bible as finally edited and compiled.
3. Writings about the Bible are no less diverse and intellectually rich than the Bible itself. No one should insist on the certainty of detailed interpretations for biblical statements or episodes. The original text and commentaries invite contending views at just about every point. There are many quarrels among the scholars who specialize in the Bible and related issues of history, language, and archaeology. It is also the case that disputes between scholars, and the supporters of one or another perspective are nasty in the extreme. For an outsider who comes to biblical scholarship from social science, the shrillness of some disputes seems inconsistent with the lack of firm and obvious support for any of the positions at stake. The existence of these debates is important in pointing to the limits of certainty with respect to the issues involved. This book makes no effort to resolve these disputes. Most seem to be unresolvable with anything like the certainty that is desirable.
4. The complexities of the Bible and other ancient sources require an approach that is skeptical and self-critical. It is appropriate to recognize the pervasive disputes, to check interpretations against

the biblical text, and to rely only on the most obvious of conclusions. In seeking guidance to the interpretation of the biblical text, I have taken what I perceive to be good ideas and reasonable commentaries from recognized scholars associated with different points of view as well as from religious commentators and writers for general audiences. I have also cited some extreme and even incredible interpretations to illustrate the creativity with which writers on the Bible may seek to explain one or another statement or allusion in the text.

5. This book does not claim to describe fully politics and the activities of governments that are mentioned in the Bible. It is doubtful if anyone can do that with the materials at hand or likely to be unearthed. Rather than trying to be comprehensive, this book is an extended essay about major political themes in the Hebrew Bible that are important for understanding modern Judaism and Israel.
6. The multifaceted character of the Bible is part of its political meaning and its elemental honesty. It does not offer simplistic political descriptions that are said to prevail for once and all times. It includes ambiguities and contradictions that reflect the experiences of God's people in various settings or how they viewed their history as conditions changed over the years. The complexity of the Bible matches that of ongoing politics, where there is competition over how to deal with difficult problems and how to evaluate the choices made by others.

SUBSEQUENT CHAPTERS

Chapter 2 considers the geopolitical context of the Bible's composition. A tolerance of diversity may have derived, in part, from the weakness of the people that produced the Bible. They did not have the power to enforce a simple orthodoxy on powerful neighbors who intervened in their affairs. The diverse nature of the text has supported, in its turn, a great variety of commentaries.

Part II includes five chapters that focus on major characters and themes of political significance: Moses, David, Jeremiah, a chapter that combines *Job* and *Ecclesiastes*, and God. Moses was leader of the exodus and creator of the nation. David established the Israelite state and began a dynasty that ruled for more than 400 years. Jeremiah was among the most overtly political of the prophets. His book describes sharper criticism of regime leaders and policies than has been allowed in modern countries, especially in times of national crisis. God pervades the Hebrew Bible. He was creator, supreme authority, lawgiver, and source of numerous political initiatives. God is the omniscient and omnipotent expression of monotheism, yet his character is problematic. He is firmly autocratic in some episodes but vacillates, deceives, and bargains elsewhere, and on occasion may even be a target of derision. The regimes depicted in the Bible were authoritarian but softened by traits associated with modern democracies: power holders were constrained by legal provisions and moral norms; there were dialogues among elites and critics; and alongside it all is the skepticism of *Job* and *Ecclesiastes.* The stories of Moses, David, Jeremiah, and God also show that the Chosen People could be craving and thankless, testing the capacities of those who would be their leaders. Part II also conveys the features of the Bible that make it great literature: its irony, its honest portrayal of complex figures, and its capacity to raise tantalizing questions that defy resolution.

Part III includes three chapters that explore the modern relevance of biblical politics. Chapter 8 describes a range of postures that can claim biblical legitimacy with respect to power, law, justice, ethnocentrism, the Promised Land, the monarchy, and historic progress. It explains the diversity that others find in the Bible and warns that the Holy Book is an unreliable source for legitimizing specific political behaviors, policies, or governments. Chapter 9 links the politics of the Hebrew Bible to continuing traits of Judaism, and Chapter 10 links them to the politics of modern Israel. The connections between the Bible, Jewish vitality, and Israeli democracy are not detailed with scientific precision. The lack of simple linkages is inherent in each element. The diversity of the Bible and Judaism defy analysis that does not equivocate. Israel is so beset by turbulence as to challenge conceptions of political science developed for more conventional countries. A high density of moral quandaries and pragmatic coping is prominent in modern Israel as well as the polities described in the Bible. Also prominent are a cluster of traits that help to explain these characteristics: weakness, external threat, turbulence and uncertainty along with a sense of communal worth that justifies a struggle of survival.

NOTES

[1] For a discussion of the suitability of the terms "Hebrew Bible" and "Old Testament," see Robert Alter, "Introduction to the Old Testament," in R. Alter and F. Kermode, *The Literary Guide to the Bible* (Cambridge, MA: Harvard University Press, 1987); and Burton L. Visotzky, *Reading the Book: Making the Bible a Timeless Text* (New York: Anchor Books, 1991 Chapter 2.

[2] See Steven Heydemann's comments on my chapter as part of his review of Bernard Reich and Gershon R. Kieval, eds., *Israeli Politics in the 1990s: Key Domestic and Foreign Policy Factors* (Westport, CT: Greenwood Press, 1991) in *Israel Studies Bulletin*, Volume 9, Number 1, Fall 1993, pp. 16-18.

[3] See, for example, Daniel J. Elazar and Stuart A. Cohen, *The Jewish Polity: Jewish Political Organization from Biblical Times to the Present* (Bloomington, Indiana: Indiana University Press, 1985); Gabriel A. Almond and Sidney Verba, *The Civic Culture: Political Attitudes and Democracy in Five Nations,* (Newbury Park, CA: Sage Publications, 1989); Daniel J. Elazar, *American Federalism: A View from the States* (New York: Harper & Row, 1984); and Ira Sharkansky, *Regionalism in American Politics* (Indianapolis: Bobbs-Merrill, 1970).

[4] See, for example, Arend Lijphart, *Democracies: Patterns of Majoritarian and Consensus Government in Twenty-one Countries* (New Haven: Yale University Press, 1984); G. Bingham Powell, Jr., *Contemporary Democracies: Participation, Stability, and Violence* (Cambridge: Harvard University Press, 1982); and Peter Y. Medding, *The Founding of Israeli Democracy 1948-1967* (New York: Oxford University Press, 1990).

[5] The literature of democracy is richly diverse, detailed, and often quarrelsome. The material to be included in this section reflects the work of countless writers over many centuries. The brevity of the treatment here is not equivalent to the richness of the scholarship concerned with these concepts. However, it may be sufficient as an introduction to issues that will be treated in later chapters. Among the

items that provided the stimuli of this discussion are: Giovanni Sartori, *The Theory of Democracy Revisited* (Chatham, NJ.: Chatham House Publishers, Inc.: 1987); Harold D. Lasswell, *Who Gets What, When, How?* (New York: McGraw-Hill, 1936); David Louis Cingranelli, *Ethics, American Foreign Policy, and the Third World* (New York: St. Martin's Press, 1993).

[6]Charles H. McIlwain, *Constitutionalism, Ancient and Modern* (Ithaca, NY.: Cornell University Press, 1947); J. Ronald Pennock and John W. Chapman, eds., *Constitutionalism* (New York: New York University Press, 1977); John Patrick Kirscht, *Dimensions of Authoritarianism: A Review of Research and Theory* (Lexington: University of Kentucky Press, 1967); Amos Permutter, *Modern Authoritarianism: A Comparative Institutional Analysis* (New Haven: Yale University Press, 1981).

[7] Powell; Lijphart; and Samuel Huntington, *Understanding Political Development : An Analytic Study*. Boston: Little, Brown: 1987.

[8] See, for example, David Louis Cingrannelli, ed., *Human Rights: Theory and Measurement* (New York: St. Martin's Press, 1988); John Martin Gillroy and Maurice Wade, eds., *The Moral Dimensions of Public Policy Choice: Beyond the Market Paradigm* (Pittsburgh: University of Pittsburgh Press, 1992); and Charles Fried, "Difficulties in the Economic Analysis of Rights," in Gillroy and Wade; James S. Fishkin, *The Limits of Obligation* (New Haven: Yale University Press, 1982); R. M. Hare, *Essays on Political Morality* (Oxford: Clarendon Press, 1989), especially p. 78; Michael Walzer, *Obligations: Essays on Disobedience, War, and Citizenship* (Cambridge, MA: Harvard University Press, 1970); Michael Walzer, *Just and Unjust Wars: A Moral Argument with Historical Illustrations* (New York: Basic Books, 1977); and Nancy L. Rosenblum, ed., *Liberalism and the Moral Life* (Cambridge: Harvard University Press, 1989).

[9] Abraham Wolfensohn, *From the Bible to the Labor Movement* (Tel Aviv: Am Oved, 1975). Hebrew.

[10] Michael Keren, *Ben Gurion and the Intellectuals: Power, Knowledge, and Charisma.* (Dekalb, IL: Northern Illinois University Press: 1983)..

[11]Israel ranked highest among a group of 43 highly and moderately developed countries in 1990 with respect to the percentage of Gross Domestic Product represented by government consumption expenditures. Selected percentages are Israel: 30.3; Sweden: 27.2; Denmark: 25.2; United States: 21.7; and Japan: 9.1. See *International Financial Statistics* (Washington: International Monetary Fund, October 1992).

[12] Menachem Hofnung, *Israel - State Security Against the Rule of Law 1948-1991* (Jerusalem: Nevo Publisher, 1991), pp. 110-37. Hebrew.

[13]See, for example, Meron Benvenisti, *The Shepherds' War: Collected Essays (1981-1989)* (Jerusalem: The Jerusalem Post, 1989); Benvenisti, *The West Bank Data Project: A Survey of Israel's Policies* (Washington: American Enterprise Institute, 1984); Benvenisti, *The Sling and the Club* (Jerusalem: Keter, 1988), Hebrew; Avner Yaniv, ed., *National Security and Democracy in Israel*, (Boulder, CO: Lynne Rienner Publishers, 1993); Michael Shalev, *Labour and the Political Economy in Israel* (New York: Oxford University Press, 1992); Baruch Kimmerling, ed., *The Israeli State and Society: Boundaries and Frontiers* (Albany: State University of New York Press, 1989); Michael Romann and Alex Weingrod, *Living Together Separately: Arabs and Jews in Contemporary Jerusalem* (Princeton: Princeton University Press, 1991); M. A. Aamiry, *Jerusalem: Arab Origin and Heritage* (London: Longman, 1978); Islamic Council of Europe. *Jerusalem: The Key to World Peace* (London: Islamic Council of Europe, 1980); Walid Khalidi, *From Haven to Conquest: Readings in Zionism and the Palestine Problem until 1948* (Beirut: Institute for Palestine Studies, 1971); George T. Abed, "The Economic Viability of a Palestinian State," *Journal of Palestine Studies*, XIX, 2, Winter 1990, 3-28; Edward W. Said, "Reflections on Twenty Years of Palestinian His-

tory," *Journal of Palestine Studies*, XX, 4, Summer 1991, 5-22; Elia Zureik, "Prospects of the Palestinians in Israel: I", *Journal of Palestine Studies*, XXII, 2, Winter 1993, 90-109.

[14] Not counting the non-Jews of the occupied territories, outside of East Jerusalem.

[15] Avner Yaniv, ed., *National Security and Democracy in Israel* (Boulder, CO: Lynne Rienner Publishers, 1993).

[16] This section relies on the author's *Ancient and Modern Israel: An Exploration of Political Parallels* (Albany: State University of New York Press, 1991), especially Chapter 4.

[17] See his *The Bar Kokhba Syndrome: Risk and Realism in International Relations*, Translated by Max D. Ticktin; Edited by David Altshuler (Chappaqua, NY.: Rossel Books, 1983); and his *Israel's Fateful Hour*, translated by Lenn Schramm (New York: Harper & Row, 1988).

[18] Harkabi, *Bar Kokhba*, pp. 113-14.

[19] Meron Benvenisti, *The West Bank Data Project: A Survey of Israel's Policies* (Washington: American Enterprise Institute for Policy Research, 1984), p. 34; also his *The Sling and the Club: Territories, Jews and Arabs* (Jerusalem: Keter Publishing House, Ltd., 1988), Hebrew; and *The Shepherds' War: Collected Essays (1981-1989)* (Jerusalem: The Jerusalem Post, 1989).

[20] Yeshayahu Leibowitz, *On Just About Everything: Talks with Michael Shashar* (Jerusalem: Keter Publishing House, Ltd., 1988), Hebrew, p. 24.

[21] For example, Leibowitz, p. 78.

[22] Gregg Barak, "Toward a Criminology of State Criminality," in Barak, ed., *Crimes by the Capitalist State: An Introduction to State Criminality* (Albany: State University of New York Press), pp. 3-16;

and Daniel E. Georges-Abeyie, "Piracy, Air Piracy, and Recurrent U.S. and Israeli Civilian Aircraft Interceptions" in Barak, pp. 129-44.

[23] Gadi Wolfsfeld, *The Politics of Provocation* (Albany: State University of New York Press, 1988).

[24] *Ma'ariv,* 1.8.1993; 2.8.1993; 5.8.1993. Hebrew; *International Herald Tribune*, August 7-8, 1993.

[25] *Ma'ariv,* August 4, 1993. Hebrew.

[26] Hofnung.

[27] This section draws on Ezra Mendelsohn, *On Modern Jewish Politics* (New York: Oxford University Press, 1993); Jonathan Frankel, *Prophecy and Politics: Socialism, Nationalism, and the Russian Jews, 1862-1917* (Cambridge: Cambridge University Press, 1981); Zvi Gitelman, ed., *The Quest for Utopia: Jewish Political Ideas and Institutions Through the Ages* (Armonk, NY: M.E. Sharpe, Inc., 1992); and Eli Lederhandler, *The Road to Modern Jewish Politics: Political Tradition and Political Reconstruction in the Jewish Community of Tsarist Russia* (New York: Oxford University Press, 1989).

[28]Norman F. Cantor, *The Sacred Chain: The History of the Jews* (New York: Harper Collins, 1994).

[29] Josephus, *The Jewish War* (New York: Penguin Books, 1970). See Nachman Ben-Yehuda, *Political Assassinations by Jews: A Rhetorical Device for Justice* (Albany: State University Press of New York, 1993).

[30] A sample of the relevant literature appears in Ezra Mendelsohn, *On Modern Jewish Politics* (New York: Oxford University Press, 1993); Jonathan Frankel, *Prophecy and Politics: Socialism, Nationalism, and the Russian Jews, 1862-1917* (Cambridge: Cambridge University Press, 1981); Zvi Gitelman, ed., *The Quest for Utopia: Jewish Political Ideas and Institutions Through the Ages* (Armonk, NY: M.E. Sharpe, Inc., 1992); and Eli Lederhandler, *The Road to Modern Jew-*

ish Politics: Political Tradition and Political Reconstruction in the Jewish Community of Tsarist Russia (New York: Oxford University Press, 1989).

[31] O. I. McCagg, Jr., *A History of Habsburg Jews, 1670-1918* (Bloomington: Indiana University Press, 1989), pp. 173-74.

[32] Daniel J. Elazar and Stuart A. Cohen, *The Jewish Polity: Jewish Political Organization from Biblical Times to the Present* (Bloomington: Indiana University Press, 1985); Elazar, "The Book of Joshua as a Political Classic," *Jewish Political Studies Review*, Vol. 1, No. 1-2, 1989, pp. 93-150.

[33] Keren, Chapter 3.

[34] Ehud Sprinzak, *The Ascendance of Israel's Radical Right* (New York: Oxford University Press, 1991).

[35] David Penchansky, *The Betrayal of God: Ideological Conflict in Job* (Louisville, KY: Westminster/John Knox Press, 1990).

[36] Louis Ginzberg, *The Legends of the Jews* (Philadelphia: The Jewish Publication Society of America, 1911).

[37] James A. Sanders estimates that 600 denominations emerged from what he calls the pluralism of the Bible. See his "The Integrity of Biblical Pluralism," in Jason P. Rosenblatt and Joseph C. Sitterson, Jr., *"Not in Heaven" Coherence and Complexity in Biblical Narrative* (Bloomington: Indiana University Press, 1991), pp. 154-69.

[38] Bloom.

[39] Ehud Sprinzak, *The Ascendance of Israel's Radical Right.*

[40] Among the items to be discussed in subsequent chapters are Elazar and Cohen, *The Jewish Polity*; Elazar, "The Book of Joshua as a Political Classic"; Robert B. Coote and Mary P. Coote, *Power, Politics,*

and the Making of the Bible: An Introduction (Minneapolis: Fortress Press, 1990); Richard Elliott Friedman, *Who Wrote the Bible?* (New York: Harper and Row, 1987); Norman K. Gottwald, *The Tribes of Yahweh: A Sociology of the Religion of Liberated Israel, 1250-1050 BCE* (Maryknoll, NY: Orbis Books, 1979); Gottwald, *The Hebrew Bible: A Socio-Literary Introduction* (Philadelphia: Fortress Press, 1985); and Aaron Wildavsky, *The Nursing Father: Moses as a Political Leader* (University: University of Alabama Press, 1984). Other recent works dealing with the politics in the Hebrew Bible include Steven J. Brams, *Biblical Games: A Strategic Analysis of Stories in the Old Testament* (Cambridge, Massachusetts: M.I.T. Press, 1980); Brams, *Superior Beings: If They Exist, How Would We Know?* (New York: Springer-Verlag, 1983); Michael Walzer, *Exodus and Revolution* (New York: Basic Books, 1985); Stuart A. Cohen, *The Three Crowns: Structures of Communal Politics in Early Rabbinic Jewry* (Cambridge: Cambridge University Press, 1990); H. Mark Roelofs, "Hebraic-Biblical Political Thinking," *Polity* XX, 4 (Summer 1988), 572-97; and Roelofs, "Liberation Theology: The Recovery of Biblical Radicalism," *American Political Science Review* 82, 2, June 1988, pp. 549-66; Morton Smith, *Palestinian Parties and Politics That Shaped the Old Testament* (London: SCM Press, 1987); and Giovanni Garbini, *History and Ideology in Ancient Israel* (New York: Crossroad Publishing Company, 1988). For a description of how ideologues throughout the ages have used its stories and characters for their own purposes, see Walzer, plus Harold Bloom, *The American Religion: The Emergence of the Post-Christian Nation* (New York: Simon and Schuster, 1992; and Leo Strauss and Joseph Cropsey, eds., *History of Political Philosophy* (Chicago: Rand McNally, 1963).

[41] Robert Alter uses similar terms with reference to the literary skills of those who wrote and/or edited the Bible. These skills led them to convey their messages with irony and ambiguity and to reveal the many sides of the characters they described. *The World of Biblical Literature* (New York: Basic Books, 1992).

Chapter 2
Reading the Bible Politically

The Hebrew Bible provides a treasure of political material, but it does not yield easily to analysis in modern terms. It comes to us in 39 books. Some were combined or organized differently in previous versions. Most seem to be compilations gathered from several oral and written sources. Portions of the text may have been written as early as the period of David and Solomon, several hundred years after the Israelites were said to have settled in the land. The material was added to, edited, and re-edited during the next 1,000 years or so.

Some readers may view this chapter as a detour from the main argument of the book. Those familiar with biblical scholarship will view it as elementary. It is conceived as a second introductory chapter that is meant to focus on the structure of the Bible and commentaries about it. It deals with the great diversity both in the Bible's contents and scholarly views of its contents. It emphasizes the political themes that can be perceived in the composition, compilation, and editing of the Bible's books, and the subsequent scholarship about the Bible.

The diversity of politically relevant material in the Hebrew Bible says something about its composition. Some episodes seem to have been composed in order to make a regime look good by describing its ancestors in reverent terms or its actions as rooted in laws that came from the Almighty. Yet the available studies of the Bible's composition are speculative. They are not proven beyond the capacity of rival scholars to doubt the details. Some biblical books express sentiments sharply at odds with those in other books. In certain cases, they reflect contrasting perspectives on controversial issues. How all of this came to be canonized as part of Holy Text is only one of the mysteries that the Hebrew Bible offers for modern scholars. To call the material inspiring, rich, complex, and confusing only begins the inquiry. It is little wonder that schools of commentary are no less diverse than the Bible itself, and that some biblical scholars denounce one another in terms like the prophets' condemnations of blasphemy. The purpose of this chapter is to review the character of the Hebrew Bible for the insights shed on ancient politics and the problems of finding clear meaning in those insights.

THE POLITICS OF COMPILING THE HEBREW BIBLE

The editing of the Hebrew Bible was a long process that seems to have occasioned numerous quarrels as to what to include or exclude and how to edit what was included. None of this is clearly documented. Modern scholars argue about who contributed what, when, and for what reason.[1]

Orthodox rabbinical commentators differ on numerous details. However, they tend to agree on the following: the Pentateuch (Genesis through Deuteronomy) was provided to Moses by God; the Book of Joshua was composed largely by Joshua; the Books of Judges, Ruth, and Samuel were composed by Samuel and his students; the prophets or their students composed the books attributed to them by name; Jeremiah also composed the Book of Kings and Lamentations; Solomon composed Ecclesiastes and Song of Songs; the scribe Ezra composed the book that carries his name as well as the Book of Chronicles; and Nehemiah composed the book that carries his name.[2]

Secular scholars have struggled with detailed analysis of the text and artful hypotheses in order to identify who wrote or edited various books and passages. One critic of their work calls it an

> exercise in futility . . . detective ventures . . . kept going only by recourse to unwarranted assumptions, ad hoc epicycling, non sequiturs, and other offenses against logic and common sense that could provide matter for a textbook on fallacies.[3]

The timing of the final edition of the biblical canon is also a subject of dispute. According to one legend, the contents of the Bible were finally decided at a conference of rabbis at Yavneh in 90 C.E.[4] Yet the Talmud refers to later controversies about the inclusion of various books.[5]

> The period immediately after the destruction of the Second Temple is one of the obscurest chapters in Jewish history. From this crucial era, which determined the fate of Judaism and molded its image for

> many generations . . . there have been preserved only a few fragmentary sources, insufficient to furnish data for a chapter of history. Hence we sometimes struggle with basic questions and cannot solve them.[6]

The contents and order of the Hebrew Bible that is used by Jews differs from that used by Christians. Jews arrange the Bible according to the order of *Torah* (the five books said to be authored by God and Moses), *Prophets* (Joshua, Judges, Samuel, Kings, plus the books identified by the names of the prophets), and *Writings* (the remaining books accepted into the Jewish Canon). The Jewish Bible ends with *Daniel, Ezra, Nehemiah*, and *Chronicles*. The order of the Christians' Old Testament shows the influence of the Greek translation of the Hebrew text, begun in the third century B.C.E., before the rabbis settled on what became the order accepted among Jews. It departs from the Jewish order after the Book of Judges, and ends with the prophets Hosea through Malachi. The Old Testament of the Roman Catholic and Greek Orthodox Churches ends with the *First* and *Second Books of Maccabees* and includes some Apocryphal materials within some of the other books.

Scholars have questioned the inclusion of some books in the Bible and the exclusion of others. For some of these exclusions, it seems that the rabbis were troubled by ideas that approached too closely the doctrines of the Christians. The *Books of Maccabees* add important dimensions of Judaic history but may have offered too much legitimacy to the Hasmoneans whose behaviors were flawed in the eyes of numerous rabbis.[7]

The *Books of Job* and *Ecclesiastes* found their place in the Hebrew Bible even though they were suspect for ideas considered heretical by virtue of their questioning of faith and the justice of God. Both *Job* and *Ecclesiastes* have statements of faith that seem odd in combination with the skepticism they express more prominently. According to some critics, the statements of faith were added to appease the rabbis who decided on canonization. The *Book of Ecclesiastes* also benefited from the claim that Solomon was its author.

The *Book of Ezekiel* was troublesome for its mysticism and its explicit descriptions of God. Some rabbis prohibited anyone under the age of thirty from reading certain portions.[8] The *Song of Songs* appeared to some readers then, as now, as too worldly, if not downright pornographic. It benefited from the argument that Solomon was the author and that its proclamations of love were not so much carnal descriptions as an allegory for the love between God and Israel.[9]

The *Book of Esther* offered several problems related to its inclusion in the Bible. Its shrill nationalism was problematic for the rabbis when they were suffering from the losses to Rome and working out the posture of passivity with respect to secular powers.[10] The Book has been faulted for not mentioning God. Esther did not act like a nice Jewish girl when she participated in the contest to select a member of the king's harem. Yet she used her charms for the sake of Israel.[11] No less a commentator than Maimonides wrote that only the *Book of Esther* has the same status as the Books of the Torah. Rabbi David Hartman argues that *Esther* shows how intrigue, manipulation, and pure chance may determine whether the Jewish people will be preserved or destroyed.[12] Perhaps nothing more profound than the Book's connection with the children's holiday of Purim assures its place in Jewish tradition.[13]

Some modern analysts see lines of clear purpose in the Bible's composition. However, these claims provoke many questions that they leave unanswered. *Deuteronomy, Joshua, Judges, First* and *Second Samuel,* and *First* and *Second Kings* (the so-called Deuteronomic history) are said to glorify a line of development from Moses to the Davidic kings of Judah. They describe the southern dynasty of David as chosen by God. The northern Kingdom of Israel is portrayed as an apostate for its break-away from the holy dynasty and the holy city of Jerusalem. The history of the northern kingdom is contaminated further by its involvement with non-Israelites and their gods.

The Deuteronomic history is thought to have been compiled from existing materials during the period of the final kings of Judah and into the exile of Judeans to Babylon (c 640-540 B.C.E.).[14] The period of compilation is said to explain the glorification of the community in an earlier period when it was united in the observance of God's holy law, and resistant to foreign deities. It may have been the editors' intention to portray for the Babylonian exiles the disunity and faithlessness that caused national tragedy and to show the road to national survival via unity amidst other people and their gods.

Those who advocate a holistic view of the Deuteronomic history must concede that it did not touch up everything in *Joshua* through *Kings*. Perhaps the editors left some ambiguities in history to speak for themselves. They describe in detail Solomon's foreign wives and his honoring of their idols. The biblical explanation is that because of old age foreign wives "turned his heart to follow other gods, and he did not remain wholly loyal to the Lord. . ."[15] Some modern commentators suggest that Solomon's many weddings and diverse religious behavior were part of his wisdom: i.e., efforts to cement together a society that was not homogeneous as well as to firm up his overseas alliances. By this view, Solomon was head of state as well as king of the Jews. He preferred to make love rather than war.[16]

David Noel Freedman concludes that the whole of the Hebrew Bible was compiled from a unitary perspective on the basis of numerous written and oral materials composed at different times. Freedman describes a pessimism that pervades the first part of the Bible (i.e., a message of judgment and punishment), followed by a theme of return from exile, rebuilding the Temple, seeing God intervening in behalf of his people and providing hope for the future. Freedman provides support for the theme of this book in conceding that biblical compilers left a number of contradictions within the larger themes that he identifies. The history described was not uni-directional, and the norms were not spelled out in simplistic fashion without ambiguities.

There is much for the readers to ponder at the interface of the aspiration and reality shown by the Bible's authors and editors. Not the least of Freedman's unanswered questions deals with the *Book of Daniel*. It seems to have been compiled substantially after the remainder of the biblical text and to focus on a later set of problems produced by the confrontation of Judaic and Greek civilizations.[17]

Richard Elliott Friedman provides another integrated view of the Bible's editing and compilation, which is explicitly political. He concludes that competing groups of priests (those descended from Moses as opposed to those descended from Aaron) sought to protect their interests by the way they each depicted biblical figures reputed to be their ancestors.[18] Like David Noel Freedman, however, Richard Elliott Friedman relies on some speculations that seem fanciful. This book's chapter on Jeremiah is critical of key points in Friedman's work that do not compare well with the biblical text.

Giovanni Garbini offers a view of biblical compilation that is less holistic than those of David Noel Freedman or Richard Elliott Friedman.[19] He hypothesizes numerous motives of biblical authors and editors who wrote, compiled, and re-wrote oral and written materials in response to events that surrounded them into the early Christian era. He reasons that there were Jerusalem-centered, Babylonian-centered, and Egyptian-centered Judaisms as well as priests of different family loyalties, sects centered in Jerusalem and at other shrines within Israel and Judea, pro- and anti-monarchists, cosmopolitans, and ethno-centrics, all of whom left their mark on the Holy Book.

When dealing with modern analyses of biblical compositions and their motives, it is important to realize that there is much dispute among the experts. Scholars are more likely to agree in opposing an interpretation of biblical text than agree about an alternative interpretation.[20] One view about the story of Abraham is that it was composed during the periods of exile or post-exile (i.e., after 586 B.C.E.), and reflects the efforts of a despairing community to create ancient roots for itself.[21] Another view is that the Abraham stories were created during the time of David (about 1000 B.C.E.) in order to create a common ancestor myth that would support the monarchy's efforts to build a unified national society against the background of tribal divisions.[22]

THE GEOPOLITICAL CONTEXT OF BIBLICAL POLITICS

The diversity of political behaviors and norms apparent in the Hebrew Bible seem appropriate to the unenviable setting in which it was produced. Its authors and compilers were preoccupied by their own survival amidst a chronic condition of invasion and foreign domination.[23] Their Promised Land was small and poor, had a substantial foreign population, and was desired by nearby great powers.[24] The demands of physical and cultural survival may have fostered a capacity to recognize and cope with numerous perspectives and severe threats. National heroes had to develop their capacity to think, express themselves, and behave flexibly. Simple ideas or rigid intellectual categories would not last for long as national guidance in the shifting and dangerous environment.

The stylized maps that put Jerusalem at the center of the world were not far wrong. The ancient country of the Jews was in the same place as modern Israel, more or less. It was on a land bridge between Asia Minor, Mesopotamia, Africa, and Arabia, "a meeting place between continents and civilizations."[25] Israel sat astride the routes of trade and invasion between major empires. At various times it was the corridor by which Egypt attacked Assyria, Babylon, or Persia, or by which Egypt was invaded by those powers. It was on the route that the Phoenicians used in trading with Africa, Arabia, and India via the Red Sea. Caravans crossed the land from Mesopotamia to Egypt and from Arabia to Asia Minor.[26]

The description recorded in the *Book of Numbers* of a land "flowing with milk and honey"[27] was a judgment made by spies who had come from the desert. The land came to be known for its production of grains, fruit, olive oil, and resins used in making perfumes that were taken from balsam trees grown around the Dead Sea. However, it lacked an abundance of fresh water and rich soils. It never developed the agricultural wealth or the large populations associated with the Nile River of Egypt or the Tigris and Euphrates Rivers of eastern empires.

The Israelites lagged behind the great powers in the sophistication of their government. The early dynasties of Mesopotamia and Egypt preceded the Davidic kings of the Israelites by more than 2,000 years.[28] Egypt had an elaborate court and established border controls whereas the Hebrew patriarchs are described as wandering in their poor land and occasionally having to go down to Egypt in order to find grain for themselves and their animals.

The 31 royal city-states mentioned by Joshua indicated the ethnic diversity and political fragmentation of the Promised Land at the time the Israelites were said to have arrived from slavery in Egypt. The Israelites may have imposed greater unity on the Promised Land than its previous occupiers.[29] However, even they were troubled by the problems built into a land sitting astride international routes and the divisive geography of mountains and valleys, coastal plain and desert, and enclaves of non-Israelites that remained among the Israelite tribes.

The Israelites aspired to rule themselves but were usually dominated by others. International relations were a constant preoccupation of Israelite leaders. Usually they paid tribute to an imperial capital. Occasionally they sought to play off one empire against another. This led to national disaster on more than one occasion.

The northern kingdom of Israel was destroyed by Assyria in 722 B.C.E. The southern kingdom of Judah became a province of Babylon in 586 B.C.E. and passed to Persia 50 years later. Alexander added Judea to his Greek Empire in the 4th century B.C.E. From the 2nd century B.C.E., Rome viewed Judea as an outpost on its eastern frontier.

> It is not too much to say that the geographical position of this little land has always dominated its history.[30]

It is too much to say that geography *determined* the political traits of the Israelites without allowing for other cultural influences and the choices made by individual leaders.[31] However, the Israelites seldom overcame the constraints associated with their location and its limited economic potential.

The traits of being chronically marginal and threatened left their mark on the writings of ancient Israelites.[32] The Bible gives a prominent role to notions of justice, which often meant the protection of the weak.[33] However, the central characters of the Bible were pragmatic as well as concerned with ideals. They were willing to compromise in order to achieve what they could. The self-criticism that permeates the story of the Exodus, *Joshua* through *Kings*, plus the books of prophecy reflects Israelite quarrels about what they should compromise, and what should be their essential goals. The *Books of Job* and *Ecclesiastes* express the self-doubt of a people that recognized their marginality and dependence on forces they could not control.

DOES THE BIBLE DEPICT POLITICAL REALITY?

Quarrels about the dating of various sections of the Bible and their historical accuracy complicate any effort to assert that the Bible provides reliable descriptions of what occurred in various periods.

> . . . the material contained in the Hebrew Bible has been selected and edited according to specific and ideological criteria . . . this fact must be borne in mind by anyone who wishes to use it for the purpose of historical reconstruction.[34]

In other words, historical Israel is not the Israel of the Hebrew Bible. Historical Israel produced biblical Israel.[35] Among the questions derived from this is whether a scholar should use the biblical material to portray the politics of the time when it was composed or compiled, or politics of the earlier period being described?

Attorneys and political scientists who know the problems of discerning the intentions of the men who wrote the United States Constitution should appreciate this point about the meaning of biblical phrases. The authors of the Bible were ten or more times distant from us than the authors of the Constitution. Moreover, the identities of the biblical authors are not known for sure, and they were not inclined to articulate views about political institutions with anything like the clarity that is available in the records of the Constitutional Convention and other writings of the framers.

The Bible includes descriptions of ancient social and political conditions that have been accepted as credible reports of reality as well as fantastic tales that seem no more reliable than those of Odysseus.[36] There are numerous gaps and contradictions in its reports of ancient history. Few non-biblical sources corroborate the biblical record. Serious scholars concede that they must speculate about important points. Some commentators rely for important conclusions on what they describe as common sense.

> We cannot know any of these things, but it lies within the realm of the possible . . . from what we were able to piece together . . .[37]

This passage refers to the period of the exodus from Egypt, which is especially problematic due to the absence of sources independent of the Bible. There are more sources for later periods. Even these leave a great deal to the interpolations and interpretations of modern writers.

A modern historian writes that "the study of Israelite antiquity (is) . . . a cross fire . . . a cacophony of historical approaches, a scramble to make an end run around the problem of interpreting text." The scholar quoted here makes his own heroic effort to find credibility in biblical stories. With respect to some episodes, he makes the modest claim that "Proof that the narrative is historical cannot be adduced. But evidence that it is historical can."[38]

Previous assessments of the Bible as myth or the distortions of Jewish editors have been replaced by modern views that it contains much that is useful to a professional historian.

> Something in us rebels . . . at the notion that the materials . . . are *not* history. The material seems too specific in factors of personality and locale . . . by its concern for chronology; its interest in political and military events . . . in the wielding of power and the conditions of justice; by its . . . claim . . . to historical witness; by the realism and sobriety of its narrative style . . .[39]

A British historian has written that no ancient nation surveyed its history, and none analyzed its goals and its records with the same quality and thoroughness as the Israelites.[40] Leo Oppenheim compared the Hebrew Bible favorably with the materials preserved from ancient Mesopotamia: ". . . the cuneiform texts fail by far to reach the degree of superb objectivity, the empathic understanding and sense for history which is displayed in the story of David as told in the books of Samuel."[41] Such sentiments still allow sharp controversies about what can be accepted as fact, when various passages were composed, or how biblical comments about social, economic, or political conditions should be interpreted.

Modern scholars tend to view the stories of Moses and Joshua as mythical but as revealing Israelite ideals at the time they were written and edited. One scholar is willing to accept the *Book of Judges* for the general conditions it describes, while viewing its details as "hero stories."[42] Some extend the mythic era of the Bible through Saul and David[43] and even to the later events depicted in the *Book of Ezra,*[44] while others conclude that materials in the Books of *Samuel* and *Kings* recount some events that can be accepted as realistic along with mythic elements.[45]

Some scholars concede their inability to verify the Bible and view it not so much as a narrative of history but as a witness to history or as a use of historical materials to explain God's relations with his people.[46] One scholar terms the details of biblical episodes as "historicized fiction."[47] Another emphasizes that biblical authors and editors revered God's relationship with his people; that they returned to stories from earlier periods of time and again to revise them in light of the changing meanings that they saw in history.[48]

In a situation where there is much missing information, it is impossible to *prove* a biblical description of historical events. Archaeological findings that are counter to the biblical record may allow moderns to *disprove* a biblical rendition of history. However, archaeological findings are clouded by the possibility that what has been found to date does not represent the full extent of ancient artifacts. Also, physical remains may provide only the vaguest hints about the social conditions, the behaviors, or the attitudes of people who lived in the ruins or who used the pottery. According to a skeptical view, "most discussions of biblical archaeology remain inconclusive or controversial . . ."[49] A more positive view is that the field of biblical archaeology has not unearthed any findings that contradict in a prominent way the historical details of the Bible.[50] One scholar sees archaeological research as endorsing biblical accounts for a general sense of accuracy even if they do not verify the specifics:

> The witness of archaeology is indirect. It has lent to the picture of Israel's origins as drawn in Genesis a flavor of probability, and has provided the background for understanding it, but it has not proved the stories true in detail, and cannot do so.[51]

Religious belief can affect one's view of archaeology. Orthodox Jews tend to oppose the granting of licenses for digs. One ostensible reason is that ancient Jewish graves are about to be defiled. Behind this may lay the belief that established Rabbinical commentaries on the Bible contain all that should be known about ancient Israel. Religious Christians and secular Israeli Jews, in contrast, have been ardent supporters of archaeology in the Holy Land. They seek proof of biblical events.[52]

The archaeological record of the biblical period is partial at best, especially for the period before David. The lack of ruins or documentary evidence may reflect the poverty and marginality of the people at the center of the biblical record. For only a short time in their ancient history, if at all, were the Israelites a real power to be reckoned with among the other empires of the world. About the archaeological findings that illuminate Solomon's building program, one modern source states

> . . . his accomplishments . . . were rather modest, certainly when compared to the works of the monarchs of the great empires of Mesopotamia and Egypt, but even when compared with the building remains of the later Omride period of Israel's history.[53]

Where the Israelites do figure in the discovered records of great empires, the material testifies to their weakness and dependence. The stele of Pharaoh Merneptah from the late 13th century B.C.E. lists Israel along with a number of other conquered nations. An Assyrian relief shows King Jehu of Israel (845-818 B.C.E.) bowing low before Shalmaneser III. The arch of Titus shows the Temple's menorah being carried off by Roman soldiers in 70 C.E. The inscription that accompanies the carving of Jehu bowing before Shalmaneser III includes an error that might indicate imperial disinterest in the details of a distant province. It refers to Jehu as the son of Omri. According to the biblical text, Jehu came to the throne of Israel by wiping out some 70 sons of Omri, and creating his own dynasty.[54]

Some archaeological evidence questions the details of the Bible. With respect to the story of an Israelite invasion and conquest led by Joshua, findings indicate that some of the cities claimed to be destroyed by Joshua were not settled during this period. Archaeological findings reveal greater prosperity during the period of kings Omri and Ahab in Israel (who are vilified in the *Books of Kings*) than during the glorified reign of Solomon.[55] Findings about the period of Judges seem more in keeping with the biblical record. They lend weight to biblical descriptions of small villages, subsistence agriculture, a lack of sharp differences between more- and less-wealthy Israelites, and the practice of fertility rites.[56]

The Bible and other ancient sources provide little information as to what actually happened as a result of government decisions. Then as now, the realities of implementation could differ greatly from policymakers' proclamations. A British scholar has examined the effects of decrees by Hezekiah and Josiah (kings in Judah during the period 725 to 609) to centralize the rituals of sacrifice in Jerusalem. They did not succeed in eliminating contrary religious practices in the Jewish communities of Samaria and Egypt.[57] It is not known where else the decrees might have been ignored in a manner that did not leave a historical trace.

One scholar concludes that the Persian emperor Cyrus could not have written the words attributed to him in the *Book of Ezra* (i.e., recognizing the supremacy of Yahweh as a reason for allowing the Jewish exiles to return home), because this would have contradicted other statements made by the same ruler with respect to other gods.[58] This scholar may be accurate. The *Book of Ezra* had a Jewish message to convey that may have justified some distortion in describing the emperor's decree. Yet Cyrus also had his purposes. The Persian emperor rebuilt a number of religious sites throughout his empire and declared that he was doing so at the command of the gods associated with them. Perhaps this was Cyrus' way of assuring tranquillity in a population composed of numerous ethnic groups and their gods.[59] Like modern leaders, Cyrus may have intended to send different messages to different people.

The Bible offers competing versions of the same events. *Samuel* and *Chronicles* have contrasting reports as to whether it was David who killed Goliath.[60] *Kings* and *Chronicles* differ as to whether Solomon gave or received parts of the Galilee in a deal with Hiram of Tyre. The chronologies offered in *Exodus* through *Kings* exceed by far the 480 years said in *I Kings 6* to have transpired between the Exodus and Solomon's construction of the Temple.[61] The 13th chapter in the *First Book of Samuel* seems to state that Saul was one year old when he became king. This statement has been viewed as a simple error in transcription that somehow became fixed in the text. Yet some deny that anything in the Holy Book could be a mistake. The Jewish commentator Rashi read the passage as referring to events during the first year of Saul's kingship.[62] A standard explanation for incomprehensible biblical materials offered by religious commentators is that they are a sign of God's inscrutability.[63]

THE APPEALS AND PROBLEMS OF THE BIBLE'S LITERARY DEVICES

The character of the Hebrew Bible stands in the way of systematic analysis. It troubles any who would assess the Holy Book's treatment of God or other heroes as well as biblical equivalents of such modern political ideas as leadership, authority, regime, constitution, or justice. The Bible makes its points with a variety of episodes that show no concern for doctrinal clarity.[64] H. Mark Roelofs contrasts Hebrew existentialism with Greek rationalism and Roman legalism.[65] He describes a lack of what Greek- and Roman-oriented academics would describe as systematic discussions of abstract concepts or the institutions of political regimes.

Political events portrayed in the Bible reveal different and shifting goals, tactics, and moral values without an explicit ordering of priorities. The biblical text jumps back and forth between episodes that are out of sequence. It mixes stories of the Israelites wandering in the wilderness between long sections that proclaim God's law. Similar provisions of the law appear in several places with differences in their formulation. Many of the laws said to be proclaimed during the Exodus seem more suited for a situation of settled agriculture. Scholars work to reconstruct the biblical materials in order to make sense chronologically or thematically. There are many missing details. Some read into what is missing from the Bible from what is known about other ancient societies. The text invites hypothetical extrapolations. The more complete a record that a scholar can produce with interpolations or extrapolations, the less will be its conformity with the Bible, without assuring historical accuracy.[66]

Problems of interpreting the Bible are made even more difficult by the efforts of some ancient authors to obscure the meaning of their work in order to protect themselves and their listeners from retribution. The *Book of Daniel* is said to employ a setting in Persia three or four centuries before the Book's composition in order to write about contemporary conditions.[67] Chapter 6 in *Daniel* tells about intrigues among the advisors of the king to concoct a situation in which Daniel will be killed on account of following Judaic rituals. The story ends by showing the weakness of worldly politicians against the influence of God.[68]

This story seems to be making a point about a foreign government like that of Antiochus IV Epiphanes. Those who purveyed the tale of Daniel might have suffered at the hands of the regime if the story had been written with contemporary details. (Commentators on the New Testament make a similar point about the parables of Jesus: that he provided his lessons by means of veiled stories in order to foil the efforts of Jewish or Roman authorities to accuse him of fomenting rebellion.[69])

Some stories of the Hebrew Bible are not overtly masked but written in an ironic style. They carry a meaning that is either greater or lesser than the explicit words. They add to the literary quality of the Bible without making it easier to understand. In the story of David and Bathsheba, for example, the point is made that the king known as a brave warrior was home in the palace while Uriah and other soldiers were off in battle. It then tells that the king's beautiful neighbor was bathing on her roof in sight of the king's residence. What are we to believe about the king's bravery or the intentions of Bathsheba? In an episode set several decades later, we see a complete picture of Bathsheba's cunning when she plotted to put her son Solomon on the throne in place of his older half-brother Adonijah.[70]

Another trait of the Bible that complicates modern understanding is its tendency to hyperbole. Perhaps the intention was to give an impression of greatness for the Lord's power, the totality of defeats suffered by his enemies, or the extent of the Israelites' losses when he punished them. Whatever the reason, a number of extreme descriptions contradict other biblical materials or fly in the face of credibility.

The reports that appear in the *Book of Joshua* for the total conquest of the Promised Land by the Israelites is one example. Elsewhere in *Joshua* and *Judges* it is said that the conquest was partial.[71] The army of Judah is described as slaying 500,000 warriors from Israel, at a time when it is estimated that the total population of the northern kingdom did not exceed 800,000.[72] Also to be counted as hyperbole are extreme threats or commands attributed to the Lord. The injunction to eliminate all traces of the Amalekites, to the last man, woman, child, camel, and ass[73] may be viewed as a surge of nationalist emotion by a writer who worked a millennium after the purported event instead of a serious plan of genocide. In the words of one modern commentator, this type of language no more stands in need of a political explanation than the bombast of "Onward, Christian Soldiers."[74]

The devices of myth, allegory, and metaphor help to convey the messages of the Bible. Some modern readers take these literally, i.e., those of fundamental faith who interpret the Holy Book as conveying what really happened in history. They illustrate Napoleon's comment that history is fable agreed upon.[75] Others view the fantastic tales of the Bible as stories for children or as literary devices to convey the impression of great and wonderful acts. A modern analyst writes that in the ancient audiences, the more sophisticated who listened to oral renditions of biblical stories were able to tell the difference between a historical record and a literary device.[76] This may have been the case, but it does not help a modern reader to sort a biblical image from the historical record.[77]

Symbolism is another literary device that adds to the layers of meaning in the Bible. The imagination of inspired readers knows no bounds. One example is circumcision as the sign of Israel's covenant with God. A modern commentator sees a symbol that he uses to justify his own view that the concept of the chosen people is not exclusive or racist. Circumcision means that Gentiles can join the community and become Jews and then pass on their Jewishness to their succeeding generations.

> Abraham is the father of any person who seeks to emulate his way of life and to practice its values, norms, and beliefs. . . . The ritual of circumcision performed on the organ of procreation may symbolize Judaism's rejection of racism as the ground of covenantal consciousness. Jewish parents are not only related to their children biologically, but must also participate with them in the large covenantal normative family of Israel.[78]

According to a Christian theologian: "The structure and style of Scripture . . . (is) so unsystematic and various, and a style so figurative and indirect, that no one would presume at first sight to say what is in it and what is not."[79]

What is written about biblical interpretations attributed to the apostle Paul can apply to many other readings by Jews and Christians. "The . . . exegesis . . . have an air of freedom. We cannot be sure that if Paul had interpreted the same passage twice he would have interpreted it in the same way."[80]

It is common to assert that Christians have been more imaginative than Jews in seeing allegories in the Hebrew Bible or being less bound to the original text. In part this reflects a Christian attitude compounded of the view that the Hebrew Bible is the Old Testament that prepares the way for Jesus Christ and of the failure of the Hebrew Bible to acknowledge that status.

A prominent contention by Christians is that the suffering servant in the *Book of Isaiah* predicts the life of Jesus. The text of Chapters 52-53 tells of a man to whom the power of the Lord was revealed, who was despised and wounded for our iniquities. (A Christian translation that he was "pierced"[81] fits the story of the Crucifixion but is not supported by the Hebrew word "mokeh" that appears in the text of Isaiah.) Traditional Jewish commentators view the suffering servant as a symbol for the Israelite nation or as Isaiah's view of himself.[82]

The *Book of Isaiah* is an archetype of biblical obscurity. It is a collection of what may be the work of two, three, or more authors.[83] Different sections seem to have been written as early as the middle of the eighth century B.C.E. while Israel was under pressure from Assyria and as late as the latter part of the sixth century B.C.E. when Judean exiles had returned from Babylon. Some traditional Jewish commentators concede the multiple authorship of *Isaiah*, saying that an Isaiah school continued the perspective of the prophet over several generations. Others insist that the whole book was the work of the prophet himself, who forecast the Babylonian exile and the return of Judeans that was to occur more than 100 years after his death. These commentators have to deal with the Jewish perspective that the prophets spoke to their generations and not concerned with predicting the distant future. (In the context of *Isaiah*, in particular, Jews who assert that the prophet predicted the distant future risk providing some legitimacy to Christians who find a prediction of Christ's coming in that book.) Some traditional Jews try to deal with this problem by claiming that Isaiah did not reveal the latter part of his prophecy to the public but provided it to disciples who were to publicize it when it proved to be accurate.[84] In contrast is the irreverent style of a modern commentator who refers to the Book of Isaiah as a "garbage can of prophecy" on account of its numerous authors and themes.[85]

Religious Jews have been creative in finding their own hidden meanings in the holy text. The *Song of Songs* has been viewed as an expression of God's love for his people and not an expression of carnal desire as its text suggests. Jews have found mystical meanings in the number of letters or words in the Bible or individual passages as well as in interpretations derived from the numerical equivalence of each

Hebrew letter (*gematria*). About Philo, an Alexandrine Jew at the beginning of the common era, a modern commentator writes: "So skillful was his manipulation of the allegorical method of interpretation that (he) could surely have extracted a statement of Plato's Theory of Ideas from a railway timetable!"[86] A leading Jewish scholar was referring to the lack of precision in the ancient documents and the invitation they offer for interpretations of great variety when he wrote that "the only possible interpretation of Torah and Talmud is mystical interpretation."[87]

BIBLICAL COMMENTARY AND SCHOLARSHIP

Embellishing the stories of the Hebrew Bible is an ancient craft, practiced by all major religious groups that trace their heritage to it. Christians and Moslems have read their own religious messages in Jewish history and changed some of the details when they wrote their holy books. Perhaps the first Christians to misquote the Hebrew Bible were those who composed the New Testament.[88] Writings not clearly Jewish or Christian but considered heretical in both traditions built ever more bizarre details onto the themes of the Hebrew Bible and the New Testament. Quarreling church fathers of the second century said of one group: "Every day everyone of them invents something new, and none of them is considered perfect unless he is productive in this way."[89]

Christian sects have published edited versions of the Psalms and Prophets that include creative translations of the original Hebrew that remove all reference to their Judaic context and add references to Jesus.[90] The Mormons have an inspired translation of the *Book of Genesis* as revealed to Joseph Smith that begins with a conversation between God and Moses about Jesus.[91] Moslems agree with the Jews that God revealed his word to Moses but contend that the Hebrew Bible does not record the word accurately. According to one story in the Koran, it was Ishmael (rather than Isaac) who was offered for sacrifice by Abraham. In the Moslem source, Abraham and Ishmael are said to have built the Kabah in Mecca. This has twentieth century political relevance with respect to Judaic claims of a biblical heritage.[92]

Ancient rabbis wrote a great deal about the Hebrew Bible, including stories that may have been passed orally for many generations.[93] The Talmuds are prominent sources of rabbinical work. They assembled and commented on rabbinical oral and written materials accumulated until that time and serve along with the Bible as touchstones of subsequent rabbinical commentaries. A *Jerusalem* or *Palestinian Talmud* was produced in the 5th century C.E., and a longer *Babylonian Talmud* appeared a century or so later.[94] The rabbis embellished the stories of the Bible in their writings, while they claimed to be working within the context of an oral Torah that was handed down whole to Moses along with the written Torah.[95] Jacob Neusner writes that the rabbis "picked and chose as they wished" from Israel's literary heritage.[96]

Ephraim E. Urbach was a prominent Jewish scholar who emphasized the great variety in the rabbis' perspectives on the Hebrew Bible. He also described a trait that confounds any one not familiar with the rabbis' work. They occasionally let "personal overtones and the desire to annoy one's opponents" enter their debates.[97] Urbach is critical of numerous scholars who have tried to create an image of general patterns that are denied by counter examples in rabbinical writing. A reader may wonder if Urbach is just as guilty of the scholarly fault that refuses to consider patterns that run counter to individual exceptions as others may be guilty of unfounded generalization.[98]

Stuart A. Cohen is a political scientist who has studied the writings of the early rabbis. He goes a long way toward accepting that their biblical commentaries reflect what was remembered about politics during the biblical period. However, he is candid in admitting that the Bible and the rabbis are difficult witnesses of history. He refers to biblical references to politics as "oblique" and as "evidence far too sparse to permit viable . . . summaries of political theory and practice."[99] The title that Cohen gives to one chapter summarizes a modern perspective on the history of the biblical period: "History as Propaganda: The Rabbinic Version."

Feminists have been troubled and creative in reading the Bible. While it is common to accuse the Bible of being misogynist,[100] it is also possible to find biblical materials that elevate women. One scholar finds that the wives of the patriarchs are portrayed as wiser than their husbands. Rebecca, in particular, is singled out for knowing the needs of her people more accurately than Isaac and arranging the ruse by which Isaac bestowed his blessing on Jacob rather than

Esau.[101] Also in favor of the power exercised by women in the Bible but not necessarily as a point of praise is the language concerned with Jezebel who was primarily responsible for leading her husband, King Ahab, to depart from the Lord.[102]

Some claims about the sexual messages of the Bible are strained, as when a scholar must defend a position on the basis of what the Bible *does not* include:

> Few (women) appear in the Old Testament, but, when they do, the fact that their female sex is apparently considered unremarkable suggests that their contribution, even in leadership roles, was not infrequent. . . . The legal dependence of women, despite the restrictive inequalities it inevitably imposed, is not, however, to be confused with personal oppression. The Old Testament does not play down the initiative and resourcefulness of women.[103]

Harold Bloom relies on the strength of the female characters in the Torah to conclude that an author of a major strata of the Hebrew Bible was a woman. This is the author of the J text, named after the use of the name *Jehovah* for the Lord. Bloom is a literary critic, and is not bound by the analytic demands associated with more systematic disciplines. He is honest in describing his work, and makes no claim that he has any strong evidence for the proposition. "Even if imagining an author and calling her J is an arbitrary and personal fiction, something like that imagining is necessary if we are to be stirred out of our numbness."[104] Bloom does not go so far as Andrew M. Greeley (Catholic priest, sociologist, and novelist), who is fanciful in referring to God as "she." Bloom concludes that God of the Hebrew Bible is not a sexual being and has no gender.[105]

Meir Shalev is an Israeli writer of historical novels and other works who offers a sharply-worded view of Mordechai and Esther as unprincipled climbers in the Persian court. Shalev also demonstrates the age-old practice of imagination in filling the lacunae of biblical text. He sees the characters' names as signs of assimilation (Mordechai derived from the god Marduk and Esther from the goddess Ashtoreth). Shalev counters the traditional interpretation of *Esther* 3:2-4 that Mordechai would not bow to the prime minister Haman because of his pride as a Jew and the prohibition to bow before anyone but the Lord.

Shalev suggests that Mordechai purposely risked his people's safety by provoking Haman to anti-Jewish actions, with the intention of exploiting Esther's position in the harem to climb over Haman in a court struggle.[106]

The appeal of the Bible appears in the range of modern academics who have applied the concepts of their disciplines in seeking to understand it. Scholars come from the fields of Bible studies, history, Hebrew, linguistics, theology, literary criticism, anthropology, archaeology, sociology, psychology, and political science. Some biblical scholars approach their task with a well-honed critical view of the materials and their own hypotheses. They seek to resolve the smallest details about the Bible's meaning by assembling numerous kinds of evidence: historical records and artifacts from archaeological sites, the examination of word usage and other clues to the period when a particular biblical passage was written. However, even their works are marked by numerous instances when they must speculate because evidence is obscure or incomplete.[107] A contrary view is that it is impossible to be certain as to the intentions of the Bible's authors. Consistent with this is research that pursues not so much what the Bible expresses, as how interpretations of its meaning have changed from one post-biblical period to another and according to the cultures of those who study it.[108]

George E. Mendenhall is a leading figure in the field of research concerned with the emergence of Israelites in Canaan. He rejects the biblical story of a single mass invasion led by Joshua. For him, it is more likely that a number of separate groups came together, most probably during a period of widespread unrest caused by events of uncertain origin. Some of these people may have been peasants or poor city dwellers rebelling against or fleeing from decaying regimes. Some may have wandered in as semi-nomadic migrants from east of the Jordan. Some may have been former slaves who came off the desert.[109]

Mendenhall describes the early Israelite history as a religion that created a people and not a people who created a religion. By this he means that the people crystallized around a religion and later created the stories of *Genesis* through *Joshua* in order to provide a mythic structure to their history. He sees the story of the 12 tribes descended from the sons of Jacob as a myth designed to cement together peoples who came from different roots. In his view there were probably more than 12 ethnic groups. He suggests that Abraham and Isaac might have been the names of tribes absorbed earlier. A war between Israelite tribes described in the *Book of Judges* adds to Mendenhall's view. He sees in the story of the Ephraimites' speech peculiarity an indication of pre-existing language differences among the peoples who became Israelites. Ephraimites would reveal their identity when asked to say the word "shibboleth." From their mouths it came out "sibboleth."[110]

Ambiguities in the Bible are interpreted in contrasting ways by modern writers, each imposing his own twentieth century conception of what is likely to have happened. Some of these differences depend upon which translations of the Bible have been used. Aaron Wildavsky wrote that Joseph's dealings in food and land strengthened pharaoh's autocratic control in a way similar to Stalin's collectivization.[111] This may reflect a translation like the *Revised Standard Version*, which reads "The land became Pharaoh's; and as for the people, he made slaves of them from one end of Egypt to the other." The Hebrew text differs in subtle ways from this rendition. It does not describe involuntary enslavement. Instead, when the people had already sold their animals and exhausted their money, they asked why they should die, and offered their land for sale and themselves as slaves for pharaoh. The biblical text indicates that Joseph bought the land and the people for pharaoh, and transferred people to the cities. For the Egyptians who remained on the land, the rent due to Pharaoh was one-fifth of the produce.[112]

Thomas Mann embellished the same story in a way to describe Joseph as a humane populist, who provided food for the hungry poor, and did not take from them an unreasonable portion of their produce or their right to pass on land tenure to their offspring.[113] In fact, both Wildavsky and Mann added considerably to the sparse text of *Genesis*.[114] Mann's work is longer by 1,100 pages or so than the biblical episodes that supply his inspiration. He enhances the themes of Joseph's arrogance, his ambivalence with respect to Potiphar's wife, the Hebrews' primitive life style compared to Egyptian sophistication, Joseph's assimilation, and his style as an administrator.

While Wildavsky was creative in seeing forced collectivization in the work of Joseph, Daniel J. Elazar takes another direction with respect to later periods described in the Hebrew Bible. He perceives constitutionalism, a polity of equals, confederacy, and a federal republic where other scholars see monarchy and theocracy and question if various laws pertaining to the rights of the poor were enforced.[115]

Elazar also makes unusual claims about the reliability and the dating of the biblical text. In claiming that the Book of Joshua was compiled in the eleventh century B.C.E., Elazar sets himself apart from numerous modern scholars and from traditional rabbis who attribute Joshua's compilation to a later period. Some attribute the *Book of Joshua* to the prophet Jeremiah (i.e., sixth century, B.C.E.).[116] Elazar's assertion of the Bible's concern with honesty in maintaining the historic record, which he illustrates with reference to the battle of Ai, overlooks the concern in the archaeological literature that Ai was not settled during the time it was described in the *Book of Joshua* as being destroyed by the Israelites.[117] His claim that the first chapter of the *Book of Joshua* "outlines the precise form of national political organization" does not square with a simple reading of the text.

Stuart A. Cohen takes a position similar to Elazar's perception of biblical constitutionalism when he writes that the polities of the ancient Israelites exhibited a form of separation between the powers associated with the prophets, priesthood, and monarchy. However, Cohen is less sanguine than Elazar with respect to the evidence for political institutions that appears in the Bible and the early rabbinical writings.

> Characteristically elliptical where such matters are concerned, they seem deliberately to eschew discussions of political theory and to prefer cameo portraits of political behavior. . . . (E)arly rabbinic writings constitute altogether slippery chronicles of their own times; as sources for the writing of political history, they are especially recalcitrant.[118]

A book written by teachers of theology and Greek and titled, *Power, Politics, and the Making of the Bible* invents explicit motives for characters that have no apparent basis in the biblical text. It overlays a simplistic view of perpetual exploitation on the details of biblical episodes, and ignores the spiritual components of ancient regimes. The quality of its writing also falls short of the Bible's.

> . . . biblical terms . . . like "kingdom" sometimes might better be translated "ruling class" or the like. . . .Hosea the prophet represented Yahweh as a father shamed by the realization that his wife, the rich city-dwellers of Israel, was the mother of children, their clients, fathered not by him but by the evil genius of agribusiness.[119]

Michael Walzer demonstrates the diverse messages that can be perceived in the Hebrew Bible. He shows how the themes of Exodus have been adapted by a variety of political movements in different historical periods. He identifies two contrasting themes with significance for modern Israel. On the one hand is what Walzer calls Exodus Zionism. Like Moses' approach to weaning the Israelites from slavery over the course of 40 years, Exodus Zionism copes slowly with the complications of building a new Jewish society amidst a population that includes many non-Jews as well as Jews of different perspectives. On the other hand is what Walzer calls Messianic Zionism. The followers of this school are in a hurry. They want to "force the end" by rash and violent moves. Walzer's implication is that the Lord or some other force is likely to thwart those in a hurry, as the Lord punished those who rebelled against Moses.[120]

Biblical scholarship is a feisty corner of the ivory tower. Some of the warfare reminds a bystander of biblical curses and denunciations of heresy. Norman K. Gottwald appears to be a follower of George E. Mendenhall by virtue of similarities in their treatment of the initial settlement of Israelites. However, Mendenhall feels that Gottwald went to extremes.

> . . . What Gottwald has actually produced is a modern version of the ancient myth-making mentality. Utilizing both the terminology and the driving ideas of a nineteenth century political ideology (i.e. Marxism), he proceeds blithely to read into biblical history whatever is called for in the program of that nineteenth century ideology. . . . Gottwald's work should have been dedicated to George Orwell, whose picture of political bureaucrats rewriting history to make it fit a political party line is remarkably apt . . .[121]

Gottwald does seem to have wandered too far toward the fault of historicism or seeing in history the support for a perspective in modern politics. He began one extensive volume that deals ostensibly with ancient history by making a poetic dedication that links praise for the ancient Israelites with the peasants of Vietnam. He concluded the book with support for ". . . social struggle where people are attempting a breakthrough toward a freer and fuller life based on equality and communal self-possession."[122]

One critic of biblical scholarship emphasizes the focus on isolated details, at the expense of understanding the larger themes:

> The habit of developing far-reaching theories from a novel exegesis of an isolated passage, usually an obscure one at that, and of reaching large conclusions literally from jots and tittles, is deeply ingrained in biblical scholarship.[123]

Another critic writes that there is too much theory chasing too little data and a hope that modern theory will make up for what is absent in the ancient texts.[124] One skeptic writes that "the Bible . . . throws a lot of light on the commentaries."[125] The author of *Ecclesiastes* may have been thinking about commentaries on existing holy books when he wrote: ". . . of making books there is no end; and much study is a weariness of the flesh."[126]

* * *

Best left out of a discussion of politics in the Bible are the many legends about biblical characters. Some have an ancient lineage, while others were invented or refined in medieval or modern times. Many are charming for the way they exaggerate the grandeur of biblical figures or add to the tradition of biblical wisdom. Among these gems from Jewish tradition are:[127]

- When the Lord resolved upon the creation of the world, he took counsel with the Torah. Thus he taught all worldly kings to consult with advisers before undertaking actions.[128]
- God's original plan was to institute rule according to the principle of strict justice. Only when he saw that justice by itself would undermine the world did he associate mercy with justice and made them rule jointly.[129]

- Korah, one of the rebels against Moses, was so wealthy that he required 300 white mules to carry the keys to his treasures.[130]
- God brought David to his sins with Bathsheba and her husband Uriah so that he might say to others, "Go to David and learn how to repent."[131]
- One of the numerous lessons of wisdom that Solomon purveyed was, "Never tell a secret to a woman."[132]
- King Ahab ruled the whole world; 252 kingdoms acknowledged his dominion; he also put on the gates of his capital the inscription, "Ahab denies the God of Israel."[133]

A twentieth century Orthodox rabbi who writes about biblical characters is admittedly eclectic in his scholarship. He describes his material as

> drawn from traditional Jewish sources. In most cases, these sources are not listed, since the material is culled from many levels and types of the rich treasury of Jewish literature; and, in the nature of things, much more is alluded to than is explicitly written.[134]

A reader can only hope that such a writer does not slip into the free use of imagination or legends of doubtful ancestry.

NOTES

[1] See, for example, Morton Smith, *Palestinian Parties and Politics That Shaped the Old Testament* (London: SCM Press, 1987); John Bright, *Covenant and Promise: The Prophetic Understanding of the Future in Pre-Exilic Israel* (Philadelphia: The Westminster Press, 1976); Joseph Blenkinsopp, *A History of Prophecy in Israel: From the Settlement in the Land to the Hellenistic Period* (Philadelphia: The Westminster Press, 1983); Northrop Frye, *The Great Code: The Bible and Literature* (San Diego: Harcourt Brace Jovanovich, 1983); Richard Elliott Friedman, *Who Wrote the Bible?* (New York: Harper and Row, 1987); and Giovanni Garbini, *History and Ideology in Ancient Israel* (New York: Crossroad Publishing Company, 1988).

[2] See the introductions in the multi-volume *The Bible with Commentaries* (Jerusalem: Mossad Harav Kook, from 1971), Hebrew.

[3] Meir Sternberg, *The Poetics of Biblical Narrative: Ideological Literature and the Drama of Reading* (Bloomington: Indiana University Press, 1987), pp. 64, 67.

[4] This book employs the Jewish notation of B.C.E. (Before the Common Era) and C.E. (Common Era), equivalent to the Christian B.C. and A.D.

[5] For an introduction to some of the arguments relevant to whether certain books should or should not be included in the biblical canon, see John H. Hayes, *An Introduction to Old Testament Study* (Nashville: Abingdon Press, 1979), Chapter 1.

[6] Gedalyahu Alon, "The Patriarchate of Rabban Johanan Ben Zakkai," in Alon, *Jews, Judaism and the Classical World* (Jerusalem: The Magnes Press, 1977), p. 314.

[7] On the exclusion of the Books of Maccabees and other parts of the apocrypha, see Michael Grant, *The Jews in the Roman World* (New York: Dorset Press, 1984), Part I.

[8] Michael Fishbane, "Sin and Judgement in the Prophecies of Ezekiel," in James Luther Mays and Paul J. Achtemeier, eds., *Interpreting the Prophets* (Philadelphia: Fortress Press, 1987), pp. 170-87.

[9] Marcia Falk, *The Song of Songs: A New Translation and Interpretation* (San Francisco: Harper, 1990).

[10] Bernhard W. Anderson, *The Living World of the Old Testament* (Essex, England: Longman, 1988), pp. 608-610.

[11] Adin Steinsaltz, *Biblical Images: Men and Women of the Book* (New York: Basic Books, 1984), Chapter 25.

[12] David Hartman, *A Living Covenant: The Innovative Spirit in Traditional Judaism* (New York: Free Press, 1985), p. 218.

[13] Howard F. Vos, *Ezra, Nehemiah, and Esther* (Grand Rapids, Michigan: Zondervan Publishing House, 1987), Part III.

[14] Terence E. Fretheim, *Deuteronomic History* (Nashville: Abingdon Press, 1983).

[15] *I Kings*, 11:4. See Paul D. Hanson, *The People Called: The Growth of Community in the Bible* (San Francisco: Harper & Row, 1986), p. 123.

[16] Max I. Dimont, *Jews, God and History* (New York: Signet Books, 1964), Chapter 3. This interpretation also finds an echo in a traditional Jewish commentary. See Yehuda Kil, *The Book of Kings* (Jerusalem: Mossad Harav Kook, 1981), Volume I, p. 142, Hebrew. Rabbi Steinsaltz is responsible for the application of "Make love, not war" to Solomon's actions. See his p. 157.

[17] David Noel Freedman, *The Unity of the Hebrew Bible* (Ann Arbor: University of Michigan Press, 1991).

[18] Friedman.

[19] Garbini.

[20] Kathleen M. O'Connor, *The Confessions of Jeremiah: Their Interpretation and Role in Chapters 1-25* (Atlanta: Scholars Press, 1988), "Conclusions."

[21] John Van Seters, *Abraham in History and Tradition* (New Haven: Yale University Press, 1975).

[22] George E. Mendenhall, "The Nature and Purpose of the Abraham Narratives," in Patrick D. Miller, Jr., Paul D. Hanson, and S. Dean McBride, eds., *Ancient Israelite Religion* (Philadelphia: Fortress Press, 1987), pp. 337-56.

[23] On the weakness of Israel and its implication for the character of the Bible, see Susan Niditch, *Underdogs and Tricksters: A Prelude to Biblical Folklore* (San Francisco: Harper & Row, 1987).

[24] This section relies on the author's *Ancient and Modern Israel: An Exploration of Political Parallels* (Albany: State University of New York Press, 1991).

[25] Yohanan Aharoni, *The Land of the Bible: A Historical Geography* (Philadelphia: Westminster Press, 1979), p. 6.

[26] Elias J. Bickerman, *The Jews in the Greek Age* (Cambridge: Harvard University Press, 1988), p. 20.

[27] Numbers 13:17-29. Biblical quotations come from a variety of editions and occasionally include the author's own translations.

[28] See, for example, A. Leo Oppenheim, *Ancient Mesopotamia: Portrait of a Dead Civilization* (Chicago: University of Chicago Press, 1977).

[29] Nahum M. Sarna, *Exploring Exodus: The Heritage of Biblical Israel* (New York: Schocken Books, 1987), Chapter III.

[30] Aharoni, p. ix.

[31] For some examples of recent thinking about political geography, see Alan D. Burnett and Peter J. Taylor, eds., *Political Studies from Spatial Perspectives: Anglo-American Essays on Political Geography* (New York: John Wiley & Sons, 1981).

[32] David Biale, *Power and Powerlessness in Jewish History* (New York: Schocken Books, 1987).

[33] Paul D. Hanson, *The People Called: The Growth of Community in the Bible* (New York: Harper and Row, 1986).

[34] Joseph Blenkinsopp, *Gibeon and Israel: The Role of Gibeon and the Gibeonites in the Political and Religious History of Early Israel* (Cambridge: Cambridge University Press 1972), p. 20.

[35] Baruch Halpern, *The Emergence of Israel in Canaan* (Chico, Cal.: Scholars Press, 1983), p. 239.

[36] Thomas L. Thompson and Dorothy Irvin, "The Joseph and Moses Narratives," in John H. Hayes and J. Maxwell Miller, eds., *Israelite and Judaean History* (London: SCM Press Ltd., 1977), pp. 149-212.

[37] Siegfried Herrmann, *Israel in Egypt* (London: SCM Press, Ltd., 1973).

[38] Baruch Halpern, *The First Historians: The Hebrew Bible and History* (San Francisco: Harper & Row, 1988), pp. 5, 61.

[39] Joel Rosenberg, *King and Kin: Political Allegory in the Hebrew Bible* (Bloomington: Indiana University Press, 1986), p. 102. For a skeptical view of the history that can be found in the Bible, see Northrop Frye, *The Great Code: The Bible and Literature* (San Diego: Harcourt Brace Jovanovich, 1983), p. 42.

[40] H. Butterfield, quoted in Yehuda Kil, *The Book of Chronicles* (Jerusalem: Mossad Harav Kook, 1986), p. 19. Hebrew.

[41] A. Leo Oppenheim, *Ancient Mesopotamia: A Portrait of a Dead Civilization* (Chicago: University of Chicago Press, 1977), p. 153.

[42] Paul D. Hanson, *Old Testament Apocalyptic* (Nashville: Abingdon Press, 1987), p. 36.

[43] James W. Flanagan *David's Social Drama: A Hologram of Israel's Early Iron Age* (Sheffield, England: Almond Press, 1988), p. 42; Randall C. Bailey, *David in Love and War: The Pursuit of Power in 2 Samuel 10-12* (Sheffield, England: JSOT Press, 1990), p. 130.

[44] Gabrini, Chapter 13.

[45] See, for example, Tryggve N.D. Mettinger, *Solomonic State Officials: A Study of the Civil Government Officials of the Israelite Monarchy* (Lund: CWK Gleerup, 1971).

[46] Flanagan, p.36.

[47] Robert Alter, *The Art of Biblical Narrative*(New York: Basic Books, 1981), Chapter 2.

[48] Gerhard von Rad, *God at Work in Israel*, translated by John H. Marks (Nashville, Tennessee: Abingdon, 1980), Chapter 1.

[49] William G. Dever and W. Malcolm Clark, "The Patriarchal Traditions," in John H. Hayes and J. Maxwell Miller, eds., *Israelite and Judaean History* (London: SCM Press Ltd., 1977), pp. 70-148.

[50] Archaeologist N. Glick, quoted in Kil, *Chronicles*, p. 21.

[51] John Bright, *A History of Israel* (London: SCM Press Ltd., 1980), p. 75.

[52] Ephraim Stern, "The Bible and Israeli Archaeology," in Leo G. Perdue, Lawrence E. Toombs, and Gary Lance Johnson, eds., *Archaeology and Biblical Interpretation* (Atlanta: John Knox Press, 1987), pp. 31-40.

[53] J. Maxwell Miller and John H. Hayes, *A History of Ancient Israel and Judah* (Philadelphia: The Westminster Press, 1986), p. 190.

[54] II Kings 9, 10.

[55] Keith W. Whitelam, "The Former Prophets," in Stephen Bigger, ed., *Creating the Old Testament: The Emergence of the Hebrew Bible* (Oxford: Basil Blackwell, 1989), pp. 151-68. See also Miller and Hayes, *A History of Ancient Israel and Judah*, pp. 189-90.

[56] Joseph A. Callaway, "Ai(et-tell): Problem Site for Biblical Archaeologists," in Perdue et al., pp. 87-99.

[57] Peter R. Ackroyd, *Israel Under Babylon and Persia* (Oxford: Oxford University Press, 1970), p. 37. For a report of archaeological findings interpreted to show that the reforms were at least partially successful, see Blenkinsopp, p. 143.

[58] Solomon Zeitlin, *The Rise and Fall of the Judean State,* Vol I: 332-37 (Philadelphia: Jewish Publication Society of America, 1962), p. 2.

[59] Chaim Potok, *Wanderings: History of the Jews* (New York: Fawcett Crest, 1978), pp. 213-14. See also Vos, Chapter 1.

[60] Steven A. Moss, "Who Killed Goliath?" *The Jewish Bible Quarterly* XVIII, 1, Fall 1989, pp. 37-40.

[61] Miller and Hayes, p. 87.

[62] Yehuda Kil, *The Book of Samuel* (Jerusalem: Mossad Harav Kook, 1981), p. 112. (Hebrew).

[63] John L. McKenzie, S.J., *The Two-Edged Sword: An Interpretation of the Old Testament*, (Garden City, N.Y.: Image Books, 1966), p. 104.

[64] Martin Buber, "The Man of Today and the Jewish Bible" and "The Faith of Judaism" in his *Israel and the World: Essays in a Time of Crisis*. (New York: Schocken Books: 1963); Gershom Scholem, *Sabbatei Sevi: The Mystical Messiah*, Translated by R. J. Zwi Werblowsky. (Princeton: Princeton University Press, 1973), p. 117.

[65] H. Mark Roelofs, "Hebraic-Biblical Political Thinking," *Polity* XX, 4 (Summer 1988), 572-97; and Roelofs, "Liberation Theology: The Recovery of Biblical Radicalism," *American Political Science Review* 82, 2, June 1988, pp. 549-66.

[66] Albrecht Alt, "The Settlement of the Israelites in Palestine," in his *Essays on Old Testament History and Religion*, translated by R. A. Wilson (Garden City, N.Y.: Doubleday & Company, 1967).

[67] Paul D. Hanson, *Old Testament Apocalyptic* (Nashville: Abingdon Press, 1987).

[68] John Goldingay, "The Stories in Daniel: A Narrative Politics," *Journal for the Study of the Old Testament* 37, February 1987, pp. 99-116.

[69] Hugh J. Schonfield, *The Passover Plot* (London: Corgi Books, 1967), p. 74. Schonfield's book is not innocent of serious scholarship even while its main argument ought to be viewed as fanciful speculation.

[70] Edwin M. Good, *Irony in the Old Testament* (Philadelphia: The Westminster Press, 1965).

[71] *Joshua* 23:9-13. *Judges* 2:20-21. See Fretheim, p. 88; and J. Maxwell Miller, "The Israelite Occupation of Canaan" in Hayes and Miller, p. 213-84.

[72] E. W. Heaton, *The Hebrew Kingdoms* (Oxford: Oxford University Press, 1968), p. 21.

[73] *I Samuel* 15:3.

[74] Heaton, p. 217.

[75] Barbara W. Tuchman, *Bible and Sword: England and Palestine from the Bronze Age to Balfour* (New York: Ballantine Books, 1956), p. 3.

[76] Halpern, *The First Historians*, Chapter 11.

[77] For an example of a sophisticated modern scholar who wrestles with the problems of interpreting metaphors employed in biblical and other ancient Jewish literature, see George W. E. Nickelsburg, *Jewish Literature between the Bible and the Mishnah* (Philadelphia: Fortress Press, 1981), p. 64.

[78] Hartman, p. 32.

[79] John Henry Cardinal Newman as quoted in Aaron Wildavsky, *The Nursing Father: Moses as a Political Leader* (University: University of Alabama Press, 1984), p. 11.

[80] Robert M. Grant with David Tracy, *A Short History of the Interpretation of the Bible* (Philadelphia: Fortress Press, 1984), p. 28.

[81] *The New English Bible* (New York: Oxford University Press, 1970), Isaiah, 53:5.

[82] Amos Hacham, *The Book of Isaiah* (Jerusalem: Mossad Harav Kook, 1984), pp. 567 ff. (Hebrew).

[83] For a view that the book was composed by Isaiah and his students or listeners, see Amos Chacham, *The Book of Isaiah* (Jerusalem: Mossad Harav Kook, 1984).

[84] Amos Hacham, *The Book of Isaiah* (Jerusalem: Mossad Harav Kook, 1984), Hebrew, pp. 13-17.

[85] Good, Chapter 5.

[86] Ronald Williamson, *Jews in the Hellenistic World: Philo* (Cambridge: Cambridge University Press, 1989), p. 146.

[87] Gershom Scholem, *Sabbatei Sevi: The Mystical Messiah*, Translated by R. J. Zwi Werblowsky (Princeton: Princeton University Press, 1973), p. 117. Jonathan Z. Smith makes a similar point when he writes that a preacher's interpretation of sacred text resembles a pagan witch doctor divining meaning from the arrangement of sacred objects. See his *Imagining Religion: From Babylon to Jonestown* (Chicago: University of Chicago Press, 1982), p. 51.

[88] Herman C. Waetjen, *A Reordering of Power: A Sociopolitical Reading of Mark's Gospel* (Minneapolis: Fortress Press, 1989), p. 20.

[89] John Dart, *The Jesus of Heresy and History: The Discovery and Meaning of the Nag Hammadi Gnostic Library* (San Francisco: Harper and Row, 1988), p. 102.

[90] Robert Davidson, *The Courage to Doubt: Exploring An Old Testament Theme* (London: SCM Press, 1983), p 13; Roger Tomes, "The Psalms," in Stephen Bigger, ed., *Creating the Old Testament: The Emergence of the Hebrew Bible* (Oxford: Basil Blackwell, 1989), pp. 251-67; James A. Sanders, "Isaiah in Luke," in James Luther Mays and Paul J. Achtemeier, eds., *Interpreting the Prophets* (Philadelphia: Fortress Press, 1987), pp. 75-85; Thomas M. Raitt, "Jeremiah in the

Lectionary," in Mays and Achtenmeier, pp. 143-56. Passages about the suffering servant in the Book of Isaiah, for example, offered answers for Christians concerned to explain the Jews' rejection of Jesus.

[91] Book of Moses, *The Pearl of Great Price* (Salt Lake City: The Church of Jesus Christ of Latter-Day Saints, 1982).

[92] Stephen Bigger, "A Muslim Perspective" and "Moses," in Bigger, ed., pp. 43-37, 117-34.

[93] For example, *The Fathers According to Rabbi Nathan*, translated by Judah Goldin (New Haven: Yale University Press, 1955).

[94] Barry W. Holtz, ed., *Back to the Sources: Reading the Classic Jewish Texts* (New York: Summit Books, 1984).

[95] Stuart A. Cohen, *The Three Crowns: Structures of Communal Politics in Early Rabbinic Jewry* (Cambridge: Cambridge University Press, 1990). See also Leo Baeck, *Judaism and Christianity* (New York: Atheneum, 1970), p. 59; and D. S. Russell, *From Early Judaism to Early Church* (London: SCM Press, Ltd., 1986), Chapter III.

[96] Jacob Neusner, *Judaism and Scripture: The Evidence of Leviticus Rabbah* (Chicago: University of Chicago Press, 1986), Preface.

[97] Ephraim E. Urbach, *The Sages: Their Concepts and Beliefs* (Cambridge, Massachusetts: Harvard University Press, 1979). p. 620.

[98] For one attempt to find parallels to modern conceptions of human rights in ancient Jewish law, see Haim H. Cohn, *Human Rights in Jewish Law* (New York: KTAV Publishing House, 1984).

[99] Cohen, *The Three Crowns*, p. 17.

[100] Phyllis Trible, *Texts of Terror: Literary-Feminist Readings of Biblical Narratives* (Philadelphia: Fortress Press, 1984). For a description of the status of women during the Roman period, see Joachim Jere-

mias, *Jerusalem in the Time of Jesus: An Investigation into Economic and Social Conditions during the New Testament Period* (London: SCM Press Ltd., 1969), Chapter XVIII.

[101] Adin Steinsaltz, *Biblical Images: Men and Women of the Book* (New York: Basic Books, 1984), Chapters 3, 5.

[102] *1 Kings* 21:26.

[103] Grace I. Emmerson, "Women in Ancient Israel" in R. E. Clements, ed., *The World of Ancient Israel: Sociological, Anthropological and Political Perspectives* (Cambridge: Cambridge University Press, 1989), pp. 371-94.

[104] Harold Bloom,*The Book of J* (New York: Vintage Books, 1990), p. 35.

[105] Bloom, p. 292.

[106] Meir Shalev, *The Bible Now* (Jerusalem: Schocken, 1985), pp. 93-98 (Hebrew).

[107] See, for example, Tryggve N.D. Mettinger, *Solomonic State Officials: A Study of the Civil Government Officials of the Israelite Monarchy* (Lund: CWK Gleerup, 1971); and Joseph Blenkinsopp *Gibeon and Israel: The Role of Gibeon and the Gibeonites in the Political and Religious History of Early Israel* (Cambridge: Cambridge University Press 1972).

[108]Stephen Prickett, *Words and The Word: Language, Poetics, and Biblical Interpretation* (Cambridge: Cambridge University Press, 1986).

[109] George E. Mendenhall, *The Tenth Generation: The Origins of the Biblical Tradition* (Baltimore: Johns Hopkins University Press, 1973); and George E. Mendenhall, "Ancient Israel's Hyphenated History," in David Noel Freedman and David Frank Graf, eds., *Palestine in Tran-*

sition: The Emergence of Ancient Israel (Sheffield, England: The Almond Press, 1983).

[110] *Judges* 12:5-6.

[111] Aaron Wildavsky, "What Is Permissible So That This People May Survive? Joseph the Administrator," *PS: Political Science and Politics* XXII, 4 December 1989, pp. 779-88.

[112] *Genesis* 47:19-24.

[113] Thomas Mann, *Joseph and His Brothers* (London: Penguin Books, 1978), especially pp. 1165-71.

[114] *Genesis* 47:13-26.

[115] Daniel J. Elazar and Stuart A. Cohen, *The Jewish Polity: Jewish Political Organization from Biblical Times to the Present* (Bloomington: Indiana University Press, 1985), pp. 6, 11, 20; and Daniel J. Elazar, "The Book of Joshua as a Political Classic," *Jewish Political Studies Review*, Vol 1, No. 1-2, 1989, pp. 93-150.

[116] Yehuda Kil, *The Book of Joshua* (Jerusalem: Mossad Harav Kook, 1970), p. 34 (Hebrew).

[117] Keith W. Whitelam, "The Former Prophets," in Bigger, ed., pp. 151-68. For the biblical story, see Joshua 7-8.

[118] Stuart A. Cohen, *The Three Crowns: Structures of Communal Politics in Early Rabbinic Jewry* (Cambridge: Cambridge University Press, 1990), pp. 1, 3.

[119] Robert B. Coote and Mary P. Coote, *Power, Politics, and the Making of the Bible: An Introduction* (Minneapolis: Fortress Press, 1990), pp. 35, 50.

[120] Michael Walzer, *Exodus and Revolution* (New York: Basic Books, 1985), Conclusion. Walzer does not specify what is rash and violent in modern history, except for some extreme examples like the Stern Gang's use of violence against the British occupiers of Palestine prior to Israel's independence.

[121] George E. Mendenhall, "Ancient Israel's Hyphenated History," in Freedman and Graf, pp. 91-92. For another example of sharp criticism among biblical scholars, see Robert Alter, *The World of Biblical Literature* (New York: Basic Books, 1992), Chapter 7.

[122] Norman K. Gottwald, *The Tribes of Yahweh: A Sociology of the Religion of Liberated Israel, 1250-1050 BCE* (Maryknoll, New York: Orbis Books, 1979), p. 701.

[123] Yehezkel Kaufmann, *The Religion of Israel: From Its Beginnings to the Babylonian Exile,* translated and abridged by Moshe Greenberg (Chicago: University of Chicago Press, 1960), p. 3.

[124] Robert P. Carroll, "Prophecy and Society," in Clements, pp. 203-25.

[125] Bernhard W. Anderson, *The Living World of the Old Testament* (Essex, England: Longman, 1988), p. xvi.

[126] *Ecclesiastes* 12:12.

[127] For some of the raw material, see Louis Ginzberg, *The Legends of the Jews* (Philadelphia: The Jewish Publication Society of America, 1911; for an abridged version, see Ginzberg, *Legends of the Jews* (New York: Simon and Schuster, 1956).

[128] Ginzberg (1956), p. 1.

[129] Ginzberg (1956), p. 2.

[130] Ginzberg (1956), p. 439.

[131] Ginzberg (1956), p. 546.

[132] Ginzberg (1956), p. 557.

[133] Ginzberg (1956), p. 581.

[134] Steinsaltz, p. xv.

Part II
God and Others

The Hebrew Bible does not convey its messages with general principles or points of doctrine but by stories, poems, historical records, legal enactments, hymns of praise, declarations of doctrine, expressions of advice, and assorted essays. Some of its episodes are literary classics that convey in sparse language difficult problems, heroic behavior, and tragic failure.

Chapters 3-7 examine politically relevant features of major biblical figures. They illustrate the Bible's diversity of politically relevant perspectives, its concern to limit secular authority, its reverence for severe criticism of elites, its expressions of pragmatism and even irreverence. They also show the provocative characterizations that provide the Bible's political vitality and appeal. Three of the characters to be considered are among the most prominent humans in the Bible: Moses who shaped the Israelite nation and who served as God's principal prophet and author of the Torah; David who began a dynasty that was the subject of a separate covenant with God and lasted for 400 years; and Jeremiah, the most overtly political of the prophets after Moses and Samuel, who dealt with a fatal threat to the Judean regime and saw beyond its destruction to the continued relationship between God and his people. Moses, David, and Jeremiah are also among the most fully portrayed characters of the Hebrew Bible, whose attractions and blemishes add much to its literary value and spiritual richness.

The Books of *Job* and *Ecclesiastes* are provocative outliers to what are commonly viewed as the major biblical themes of piety and submission. In truth, the materials associated with Moses, David, and Jeremiah as well as other biblical characters, also belie the simple reverence that many readers see in Scriptures. Yet the challenges are starkest in *Job* and *Ecclesiastes*. The statements of faith that also appear in those books seem weak in relation to the doubts expressed. A treatment of *Job* and *Ecclesiastes* is essential for any study that would emphasize the multifaceted character of the Hebrew Bible and the complexity of its messages.

God is the central character of the Hebrew Bible. He is creator, lawgiver, supreme judge, and implementor of reward and punishment. He is said to be omniscient and omnipotent. He is the one God in a monotheistic pantheon with room for no others. Yet even this symbol of unity and strength shows its diversity and is beset with political difficulties. There are episodes that portray God as limited, or limiting himself, and showing less wisdom or justice than the humans said to serve him.

Chapter 3
Moses: The Prophet Who Was Closest to God

Moses was the greatest of the leaders that God chose for the Israelites. Not only is he credited with composing the Torah according to God's instructions, but the Torah ends with a hero's epitaph: "There has not yet risen a prophet like Moses, who God knew face to face."[1] Moses was a revolutionary who freed slaves, founder of the Israelite nation, principal lawgiver whose legislation has remained at the heart of his people's culture for three millennia, an administrator, a story-teller, a student of God's way, and a politician who strove to find a path among the demands of God, Pharaoh, the Israelites.[2] Except for God, there is no biblical character with more material linked with him than Moses. His story stretches from the beginning of the *Book of Exodus* through the *Book of Deuteronomy.* We read of numerous encounters of Moses with God, his confrontations with Pharaoh, and his wandering of 40 years with the Israelites.

Viewed with the skepticism that is appropriate for political analysis, Moses was too good. While there were numerous murmurings against him and some attempts at rebellion or desertion, Moses enjoyed an incredible record of success despite a situation that was chronically difficult. We read of no revolt that really seemed to threaten him nor even a successful desertion from his wandering band of underfed, thirsty, and impatient Israelites. His story reads as if it were contrived or edited years after the events portrayed and polished to create a legendary leader and lawgiver who could serve as a symbol for subsequent generations.

The starkest realism in the Moses episodes is concerned less with him than with the people he was leading. The chosen people were a miserable and unsatisfied mob that seemed ready to follow those who would provide more food, a greater variety of fruits and vegetables, and a quick change from slavery to freedom. The people tired of the Almighty and tried to replace him with an artifact of gold! A disturbing bit of realism appears in the description of the finery that the Israelites took from the Egyptians when they departed. The episode reminds a modern reader of the excesses of the *nouveau riche*: behaviors that are understandable under the circumstances but nonetheless embarrassing to observers. Were Philip Roth the author of all this, pious critics would intensify their accusations that he is a self-hating Jew.

Moses' story raises and leaves unresolved a number of questions with political relevance: How far could an Israelite go in challenging God or Moses or disobeying their rules? Was there an equivalence of punishment for sins of greater and lesser seriousness? Why, for example, did Aaron get away with the manufacture of the golden calf, while Korah and others suffered dramatic deaths on challenging Moses' leadership? These questions touch the issue of authoritarianism in the polity of the desert. They also seek clarity as to the points at which the authoritarian regime was softened and the nature of its patronage. Was Aaron spared because he was Moses' brother, while Korah died because he represented the claims of a rival family?

Insofar as Moses' story is more intimately involved with God than the portrayals of other biblical regimes, it also raises questions about the ultimate symbol of authority. If God was omnipotent and just, why did Moses have to fabricate the request to Pharaoh that the slaves be allowed to leave temporarily in order to pray in the desert?

Moses' stories are set in the dim, mythic past of the Israelites. Except for the Bible, there is no evidence of his existence. The Book of Exodus, in which the bulk of his story appears, is one of the most complex and controversial in terms of what appear to be oral and written layers that were created, added to, and altered, perhaps over the course of 1,000 years until the period of return from the Babylonian exile. Scholars quarrel about who wrote what, when, and for what purpose.[3]

There is no scholarly consensus about the reality of Moses. For one scholar, the greatness of the roles played by Moses establishes the likelihood of his historical reality.

> The events of exodus and Sinai require a great personality behind them. And a faith as unique as Israel's demands a founder as surely as does Christianity, or Islam, for that matter. To deny that role to Moses would force us to posit another person of the same name.[4]

Another scholar has trouble accepting that one man could have been the leading figure in the variety of great events assigned to Moses. To him, it is more likely that Moses is a composite, legendary figure credited with the exodus from Egypt, the wandering in the wilderness, the receipt of law at Sinai, and the conquest of Transjordan.[5]

MOSES' STORY

Moses' story begins with a baby born in a time of distress for the Hebrews in Egypt. The Book of Exodus describes how his mother abandoned him in order to evade the Pharaoh's decree that newborn Hebrew males be killed. He was discovered by a daughter of Pharaoh and raised in the royal household.[6] By one commentary, the education of an Egyptian court youth prepared him for leading a people whose subjugation would make it unlikely they could produce their own leaders.[7]

Except for his adoption by a princess, the Bible provides no details about Moses' childhood and youth. When he was grown, he somehow identified the Hebrew slaves as his kinsmen and killed an Egyptian who had struck a slave.[8] This signaled his estrangement from the Egyptian court and the onset of his career as leader of the Hebrews.

Moses learned that his relationship with the Hebrews would not be easy. The day after he intervened in behalf of the slave, a quarrelsome Hebrew began what became a long series of murmurings when he challenged Moses' right to be an officer and judge over them.[9] Pharaoh heard about Moses' activity and ordered him killed. Moses escaped to Midian, where he spent a number of years before receiving God's fateful call from the burning bush.[10]

There is much that is repetitious in the story. Just as the Israelites' criticism of Moses began early and returned time and again, so Moses' expressions of doubt before God began in their first encounter. "Who am I that I should go to Pharaoh and bring the children of Israel out of Egypt?"[11] Also at the beginning of the relationship between God and Moses we see the use of magic in order to solve a problem and demonstrate the superior power of the Israelites' God. In their first lesson, God showed Moses that he could turn his staff into a snake, bring disease and then health to his hand, and turn Nile water into blood.[12]

When Moses protested that he was not skilled at public speaking, God asserted that Moses should rely on him to deal with such problems. The Lord showed his temper when Moses continued to doubt his own capacity and that of God to help him. God ended the encounter by instructing Moses to go before Pharaoh with Aaron and to remember to bring his staff in order to perform magic.[13]

Was Moses being overly modest in questioning God's assignment for him, daring in challenging the Almighty, or concerned to obtain from the Lord additional help for his difficult mission? Commentators have speculated for centuries about such issues. Traditional Jews have sought textual clues to minimize Moses' challenge of the Lord,[14] but the biblical text renders the issue unresolvable.

At the onset of their mission, Moses and Aaron seem to have been successful in convincing the slaves that they were messengers who spoke with God's backing. As might be expected, the Pharaoh himself was less gullible. "Who is the Lord that I should listen to his voice to send out the people of Israel. I do not know the Lord and I will not send out the people."[15] Instead of freedom, the Pharaoh responded with vengeance against the Hebrews. They would no longer have straw supplied for making bricks. They would have to find their own straw, without their daily quota of bricks being reduced. The Israelite overseers then complained that Moses and Aaron had made conditions more difficult.[16]

Within the confrontation between Moses and Pharaoh there appears another issue that has troubled commentators. Moses did not ask for freedom but only for a holiday so the slaves could go to the wilderness for a religious feast.[17] Should this be condemned as the kind of lie the Lord's emissary should not tell? or accepted as the dissembling appropriate to a leader of slaves who wants them free? God made no secret of his plans among the Israelites: he told Moses to encourage the Israelites by saying that God would release them from slavery and deliver them to the land that he promised their forefathers.[18]

God told Moses that he would harden Pharaoh's heart, so that he would not let the Israelites go. God usually said that he would do this in order to demonstrate his greater power for the benefit of the

Egyptians.[19] Occasionally, however, it appears that the demonstration was meant to convince the Israelites that their God was powerful and a fitting object of loyalty.

The issue is not without its problems. If God is all powerful, why did not he simply change Pharaoh's heart in order to facilitate the liberation of the slaves and lighten the damage that must be done to the Egyptians? If God was responsible for hardening the Pharaoh's heart, then what was Pharaoh's fault? Was the Pharaoh deprived of free will? There are no convincing answers.

The variety of the questions serves the argument of profound diversities in the biblical text. As will be developed in a later chapter, the Bible portrays a God with several faces, without indicating which is dominant.

Whatever the essential traits of God or Moses, the story proceeded to its well-known conclusion:

- Moses and Aaron demonstrated the superior power of God's magic, first when the snake made out of Aaron's staff swallowed the snakes made out of the staffs of Egyptian magicians.[20]
- Acting according to God's instructions, Moses imposed a series of plagues on Egypt. They escalated in severity from water pollution, frogs, bugs, diseases of cattle and humans, hail, locusts, darkness, and then the death of first-born humans and animals. Some of the plagues struck the Egyptians but not the Israelites.
- On several occasions during the plagues, Pharaoh promised to release the Israelites, and then recanted. He quarreled with Moses over the release of all the Israelites, just the men, or the Israelites plus their flocks. Pharaoh seemed to see through Moses' claim that he wanted only a limited period of freedom in order to worship in the desert.[21]
- After the plague that killed the first born of Egyptians and their flocks, including the Pharaoh's own child, Pharaoh told Moses and Aaron to go to worship their God with all their people and their flocks and asked their God's blessing on him.[22] In order to allow God to perform the extravaganza of parting the water for Israelites and then drowning the Egyptian army, Pharaoh had to recant once again. It was then that he seemed to know for certain that the Israelites had left permanently, not just for a few days to worship in the desert.[23]

- When the Israelites saw the Pharaoh's army, they said that they would rather be slaves in Egypt than die in the desert. The demonstration of God's power over the water persuaded them to be patient for a while.[24] By the end of the next chapter, however, they were complaining again. This time the problem was bitter water. The Lord showed Moses how to sweeten it by throwing in a log.[25]

In one of the last scenes before the departure from Egypt, the text reports that Israelites asked the Egyptians for clothing, jewelry, gold, and silver. God made the Egyptians open-hearted toward them. As a result, the departing slaves were able to despoil the Egyptians.[26]

This story is both helpful and problematic. On the one hand, it explains where the wandering slaves acquired all the finery they are later described as donating for the construction and outfitting of the Tabernacle.[27] On the other hand, it suggests that the Israelites were exploiters as well as exploited. Over the years friendly commentators have described this as God's way of compensating the Israelites at the Egyptians' expense for generations of slave labor. Antagonists have used the story to disparage the Jews and their God.[28] A reader must wrestle with the options left unresolved or conclude that God and the Israelites were beset with difficult conditions that led them to develop complex characteristics that do not sit neatly in simple classifications of morality. The same principle may be applicable to modern Israeli actions in rounding up suspected terrorists and extracting information from them. The procedures do not square with the demands of Amnesty International and some of Israel's own legal commentators, but the pressures faced by Israel are not those of a typical state.

The period in the desert was 40 years of trouble and toil for the Israelites as well as for Moses and God. From the Israelites' perspective, conditions were always worse than they had been in Egypt. They remembered that they had more to eat and a ready supply of drinking water as well as a more varied diet that included meat, bread, fish, vegetables, and fruits.[29] God and Moses worked together in responding to many complaints and provided security against the foreigners who did not want to share their lands with the Israelites.

Some of the peoples' murmurings brought violent responses. The Bible does not specify what led God and Moses to respond one way or the other. However, it appears that demands for a lightening of conditions brought accommodation, while violence came in response to the people's lusting after other gods or efforts to replace Moses as their leader.

The story of the golden calf is prominent among the cases when the Israelites sought foreign gods. It may also have had an element of challenging the leadership of Moses, who had been away for a long time on the mountain where he was receiving the law of God. God warned Moses that the people were up to no good and that he had better return to them.

On account of the idolatry, the Lord wanted to destroy all the Israelites and provide Moses with a new people. Moses dissuaded him from rashness by reminding him of his commitment to Abraham and pointing out that the Egyptians might ridicule God for destroying his people.[30]

The Israelites did not get off lightly. Moses appointed Levites as the Lord's soldiers and had them kill 3,000 of their brothers, friends, and neighbors. And this was only a test of the Levites.[31] The Lord promised that the day would come when he would punish the Israelites further for their sin.[32]

A mystery attached to this story concerns the role of Aaron. The text indicates that he helped the people make the calf,[33] and later offered a fantastic excuse to Moses: "They gave me their gold, I threw it into the fire, and out came this bull calf."[34] Moses concluded that Aaron was guilty of leading the people astray[35] but there is no mention of Aaron's punishment. Aaron Wildavsky concluded that Aaron's escape from punishment reflects a recognition that anti-establishment views deserve representation.[36] For the construction of an idol? Elsewhere it appears that there would be no greater sin. Wildavsky seems to have read too much into the Bible's silence about Aaron's punishment. A more persuasive explanation of Aaron's role is that editors of the Bible were priests who sought to preserve the reputation of the first high priest and their own reputed ancestor.[37]

The revolt of Korah was more clearly a case of seeking to replace the leadership of Moses. Korah was an aristocrat among the Israelites. He was a great-grandson of Levi and thus a descendent of the patriarchs. His standing as a priest may have added to the basis of his challenge to Moses' leadership. The 250 men who followed Korah had rank and good standing in the community. They accused Moses and Aaron for taking too much authority. "Every member of the community is holy and the Lord is among them all. Why do you set yourselves up above the assembly of the Lord?"[38] Dathan and Abiram were rebels along with Korah or participants in another revolt that is reported along with Korah's.[39] Perhaps the status of Dathan and Abiram as Reubenites explains their revolt. By one view, the tribe of Reuben had a claim of priority by virtue of their ancestor being the first born of Jacob. Dathan and Abiram were summoned by Moses to appear before him. They accused Moses of taking them from a land of milk and honey to let them die in the wilderness. They charged Moses with setting himself above them and asserted that they would not answer his summons.

It is not clear from the text whether Korah and his group wanted a populist democracy or wished to replace the Mosaic autocracy with an oligarchy under Korah. Whatever their motives, the response of Moses and God was quick and severe. The next day the protesters assembled before the Tent of the Lord in what seems to have been a face-off against Moses and Aaron. The Lord appeared and instructed the people to stand aside so the rebels could be destroyed. When Moses sought to calm God, he was met with a direct order: stand back from the rebels' dwellings! Moses then told the people that if the rebels died a natural death, it would be a sign that the Lord had not made Moses their leader. Right on cue, the earth split and swallowed Korah, his followers, and all their possessions. Next day, when other Israelites protested about the punishment of the rebels, God sent a plague that killed 14,700 protesters.[40]

Another episode of rebellion began when Moses sent spies to investigate the Promised Land. They returned to report that it was, indeed, a rich place. However, it was populated by fearsome people who would be impossible to conquer. The people cried out in dismay and spoke of choosing someone who would lead them back to Egypt. Moses and Aaron flung themselves on the ground in front of the Israelites. Two supporters of Moses and Aaron, Joshua and Caleb, rent their clothes, and pleaded with the community that their attack on the Land would have the support of God. The people responded by preparing to stone their leaders. This brought a cry of dismay and anger from God: "How much longer will this people treat me with contempt? How much longer will they refuse to trust me in spite of all the signs I have shown them?"[41] As in the earlier episode of the golden calf, God first said that he would do away with the people. Moses again spoke to God's concern for his reputation: what will the Egyptians say?

> If you put them all to death at one blow, the nations who have heard these tales of thee will say, "The Lord could not bring this people into the land which he promised them by oath; and so he destroyed them in the wilderness."[42]

At this point, God expressed further dismay. "Ten times they have challenged me and not obeyed my voice."[43] Yet he acceded to Moses' appeal. Instead of doing away with the people, God decided that the present generation would be denied the privilege of entering the Promised Land except for Joshua and Caleb who had defended his position. The spies who returned from their mission to turn the people against conquest would die immediately.

Another revolt broke out among Israelites who could not endure the Lord's decree that they would not reach the Promised Land. They set off to begin their own conquest. Moses warned them not to undertake another action against God's decisions, but they persisted in a reckless fashion. They went without God's help and were slain by the Amalekites and Canaanites.[44]

There is one episode when Moses seemed willing to share power with other Israelites. It is used by commentators who argue that the Israelites recognized the problems of authoritarianism and sought to achieve a shared leadership or even a separation of powers. Moses himself speaks about the advantages of shared wisdom. Yet the wording is ambiguous. The story might indicate that Moses was willing to share wisdom and some symbols of authority or have access to good advice but not to share the essence of power.

We are told that the Lord took some of the prophetic spirit from Moses and conferred it on 70 elders, who began to prophesy. Then two other men also felt the spirit of the Lord, and they began to prophesy. This led Joshua to warn Moses about the men who acted like prophets and urged Moses to stop them. Yet Moses responded with what might have been a statement in behalf of sharing wisdom or power: "Are you jealous on my account? I wish that all the Lord's people were prophets and that the Lord would confer his spirit on them all."[45] The difficulty involves the meaning of prophecy. Modern scholars have identified a list of traits shown by biblical prophets.[46]

The list is not simple. "Anyone who describes the ideas and effects of the prophetic movement in Israel cannot draw on a broad scholarly consensus."[47] Prophetic traits include:

- assertions to be speaking for God;
- ethical instruction, usually directed against current behavior seen to violate God's laws;
- behaving ecstatically, raving about messages from God, seeing visions, interpreting dreams, and performing miracles;
- serving as God's intermediary in the selection and anointing of leaders and the removal of unsatisfactory leaders; and
- prediction of apocalyptic disasters that will represent God's punishment of his wayward people.

By some interpretations (i.e., the translation of the *New English Bible*), the kind of prophecy at issue in this episode was that of falling into an ecstacy. Perhaps Moses would allow others to praise God in a fit of enthusiasm, provided that they did not also claim to be speaking in the Lord's name and acting as leaders of the people.

There are intermediate episodes between those when God and Moses complied with the peoples' complaints and demands for better conditions, and those when they punished the people severely for rebelling or threatening to revolt. On several occasions, God and/or Moses expressed their impatience with the continuing complaints of the Israelites. There were also episodes of limited punishment. When some Israelites violated the prohibition against collecting food on the Sabbath, they found no food, and the Lord chastised Moses on account of their behavior.[48]

More severe was the response to Israelites who collected more than a fair portion of meat. Then the Lord expressed his anger by directing a deadly plague at the greedy.[49]

No commentator should claim with certainty to sort out and explain these cases of complaint and rebellion. Characteristically, the Bible itself rests with its different stories. It does not explicate general principles as to which murmurings brought positive responses from God and Moses and which brought punishment.

Other challenges that commentators cannot solve without quarrel are those cases when Moses himself seemed to remain within God's tolerance of his behavior and those cases when he overstepped the bounds. Scholars quarrel as to whether Moses did anything without the Lord's direction. Some admit that certain episodes do not clearly indicate that the Lord instructed Moses but insist that Moses did nothing that was not consistent with God's directions.[50]

Especially confusing is an episode recounted in the *Book of Numbers* when the people complain about a lack of water. Moses is commanded to take a staff, speak to the rock, and it will yield water. Then in what may have been a moment of impatience in the presence of a restive crowd, Moses said, "Listen to me, you rebels. Must we get water out of this rock for you?"[51] Then he struck the rock with the staff and water poured forth. Because of this we are told that the Lord condemned Moses and Aaron to die before the Israelites would reach the Promised Land.[52] It appears that Moses and Aaron are to be punished for striking the rock rather than merely speaking to it. This seems to be a mighty punishment for a trivial act. In a previous incident the Lord explicitly told Moses to strike the rock with his staff in order to bring forth water.[53] Was Moses to be punished severely only for confusing the many instructions that he received from God?

Religious commentators have struggled to make bad look good. One view is that Moses' crucial sin was the choice of words spoken to the restless crowd. He asked if "we" (Aaron and himself) are to get water out of the rock. God might have been angered when Moses seemed to take the credit for producing water for Aaron and himself when the credit properly belonged to the Almighty! Another view is that Moses had to be kept out of the Promised Land along with the generation of the slaves in order to demonstrate the equal treatment of the leader and his people by God. Yet another interpretation is that the Lord may have been concerned to produce water by words only, which would have been a more forceful demonstration of his power than bringing it forth by striking the rock with a staff.[54]

An additional explanation is that Moses had to be punished for something, if only to demonstrate that he was not equivalent in perfection to God. Stories of leaders who are occasionally unreliable or immoral (e.g., Abraham, Moses, David, and Solomon) teach the lesson that no person, but only God is a proper object of veneration.[55] Commentators emphasize that the Bible does not depict Moses as divine. Thus, Judaism's primary prophet is kept a rank below the Christians' Jesus, and the God of the Jews is preserved as purely monotheistic.[56]

Much of the textual material that deals ostensibly with Moses' career concerns cultic and legal issues. We read that the Lord ordered Moses to proclaim the laws and order the construction of a Tabernacle and the onset of ritual observations. However, many of the details seem more appropriate for later periods in Israelite history. The instructions for building the Tabernacle and supplying its equipment strain the credibility of someone reading about escaped slaves, even those who preceded their flight by despoiling the Egyptians of gold and other valuables. The Book of Exodus describes contributions of gold, silver, copper, bronze, fine linen, goats hair, tanned skins of rams, seals, porpoises, or badgers, oils, incense, fragrances, dyes, various precious stones, and woods, all of which would be worked by engravers, carvers, weavers, embroiders, and practitioners of other crafts.[57] The proclamation of laws and ritual observances (e.g., those dealing with settled agriculture) seem to have been written into the wilderness story by subsequent generations, perhaps in an effort to gain greater legitimacy for later practices by linking them to God and Moses.

The end of Moses' story repeats a number of the themes that seemed to follow him from the beginning. Moses expressed his dismay yet again at the Israelites' impatience and lack of discipline and predicted that they would be disobedient after his death.[58] God, too, behaved as he did at the beginning of the story. As described by a poem attributed to Moses, God was preoccupied with his image in the eyes of other nations:

> I had resolved to strike down (the Israelites) and to destroy all memory of them, but I feared that I should be provoked by their foes, that their enemies would take the credit and say, "It was not the Lord, it was we who raised the hand that did this."[59]

God remained scornful of idolatry. "Where are your gods . . . Let them rise to help you! Let them give you shelter! See now that . . . there is no god beside me."[60] In the last words in the Book of Deuteronomy and the Torah that are attributed directly to God, the Almighty was concerned to remind Moses of his sin and his punishment of dying before the people reached the Promised Land.

> . . . because both of you were unfaithful to me at the waters . . . when you did not uphold my holiness

among the Israelites. You shall see the land from a distance but you may not enter the land I am giving to the Israelites.[61]

Just as it is appropriate to put ourselves in the position of the wandering Israelites in order to understand the pressures on them and the reasons of their numerous murmurings, so it seems appropriate to put ourselves in the position of the egocentric God. His self-appointed task was the unenviable one of leading a group of slaves through a desert environment and encounters with hostile tribes, on the verge of entering a land even more thickly settled by foreigners not likely to welcome them. A secular reader can look with skepticism on the claims that God is omnipotent and omniscient and view him as a tragic figure beset with an impossible task and inevitable frustration.

An earlier theme that is not repeated toward the end of the story is Moses' reluctance to accept God's mission as the Israelites' leader. Perhaps he had become a hardened autocrat, thoroughly dismayed by his people's lack of discipline and the deficiencies of various figures who sought to oust him as leader.

MOSES AS POLITICAL LEADER

Moses receives more attention than any other biblical figure except God. Yet for all the detail, his character has a unidimensionality or flatness that contrasts with other prominent characters. The comparison is especially striking with David, who is treated in the following chapter. David is more human and less uniformly pious than Moses. David's sins are juicier and more believable than the one sin of striking the rock that is attributed to Moses. David's problems of leadership are more fully described. Revolts against David came closer to ousting him and required prolonged military campaigns. The problems of Moses were no less severe than David's, and probably more severe, yet he was never troubled by a revolt that God could not solve by a quick miracle.

Aaron Wildavsky described a Moses who learned leadership through a series of failures and moved along with his people through conditions of slavery to anarchy, equity, and finally to hierarchy.[62] Wildavsky recognizes that there was much slippage and that Moses had trouble learning. Moses had to force slaves to be free and punish wrongdoers. Yet he could not punish all of them and still retain a people to lead. For Wildavsky, Moses was a nursing father who taught his children and allowed them to make mistakes while they created history on their own. Wildavsky describes Moses was a master politician who could adopt a hierarchical form of leadership without enslaving the people to himself.[63]

Wildavsky's analysis is provocative in applying the concepts of political science to Moses' leadership, but he finds too much pattern in the biblical episodes. There is no doubt that the first condition that Moses encountered was slavery. However, there is no apparent progression through what Wildavsky described as the later states of anarchy, equity, and hierarchy. It seems more accurate to read the text as describing a condition of perpetual autocracy, with God and Moses as the autocrats, having to deal with more or less continuous demands by the people and occasionally by individuals who saw themselves as potential leaders. While Korah's revolt is a major element in what Wildavsky describes as the stage of equity (with Korah as an agent of equity), it reads better as a competing aristocrat's demand to replace the present leader or perhaps to replace Moses with an oligarchy of himself and his followers. While Wildavsky places Korah in the third stage of equity, the incident is reported after Moses seems well along in his development of what Wildavsky calls the fourth stage of hierarchy. Korah appears in the 16th chapter of *Numbers*. In the 18th chapter of the earlier book of *Exodus,* Moses is already responding positively to the advice of Jethro to appoint subordinates who will help in dealing with the many details of leadership, in what seems like the beginning of a hierarchy.

Moses is too good to have been true. Everything he did is meant to carry out the word of God and to achieve what is good for his people. Perhaps he came to covet power or a monopoly of his status as God's principal prophet. However, there are no episodes in which he desires personal possessions or someone else's wife.

Somewhat like Jeremiah, Moses whined in response to God's demands on him and once asked that God kill him rather than force him to endure the burdens of office.[64] Jeremiah was responsible for the term *jeremiad*, and he set a standard of self-woe, anxiety, and doubt that Moses does not match. Moses' tasks were more difficult, yet his complaints were milder than those of Jeremiah. Moses' stories lack the edge of despair that are apparent in Jeremiah's complaints: that the Lord's call has caused popular ridicule, a lack of support, an inability to bring the people to the condition demanded by God, loneliness, and persecution by political elites.[65]

Moses succeeded in keeping the Israelites together through all those years in the desert and brought them to the borders of the Promise Land before dying. He accommodated the imminent end of his career unselfishly and identified Joshua as his successor without the threat of a *coup* or the onset of senility like that at the end of David's career. In order to assure that Joshua would begin his reign with an aura of legitimacy, Moses anointed him in front of the whole nation.[66] Moses is a character who is more perfect than human, who seems to have been created or at least polished years after he is said to have lived by writers concerned to produce an ideal founder for the nation.

The glorification of Moses continued beyond the composition of the Torah. The prophet Isaiah compared the Lord's opening of the sea before the Israelites to the salvation that will come at a later time.[67] Jeremiah quoted the Lord as recalling the youthful love of Israel for him in the wilderness, seeming to overlook the chronic complaints linked to the exodus.[68] Jeremiah employed Moses' record as an intermediary with God as a standard for describing how terrible the contemporary Israelites were behaving: "The Lord said to me, Even if Moses and Samuel stood before me, I would not be moved to pity this people."[69]

Moses' leadership of the Israelites occurs prior to the establishment of a kingdom. He leads a people but not a state. Yet already his story includes a number of themes that are repeated in the Bible's treatment of later figures. If Moses' story was created or edited in retrospect, these themes may have been inserted by writers conveying messages to their contemporaries. The regime of the desert was authoritarian, with Moses and the Almighty as the authorities. Yet there were several features of the regime to soften its autocratic character. Moses dares to question God on an occasion when the Almighty decreed mass punishment, similar to Abraham's questioning in a similar story about the sinners of Sodom and Gomorrah. Moses permits some sharing of the designation as prophet ("I wish that all the Lord's people were prophets"[70]). Moses also convened the people to explain the benefits and expectations that came from God. There are some signs of a concern for popular approval of leaders' actions, although there are no detailed indications of legitimacy provided to mass initiatives or opposition to God and Moses.

The regime of God and Moses was weak, and the leaders had to cope with pressing limitations. The Almighty had to deceive the Egyptians about the slaves' intentions ("Let my people go, that they may hold a feast unto me in the wilderness").[71] Both God and Moses lamented the murmurings against them but carried on with people who were difficult to lead. They kept the Israelites in the desert long enough for a new generation to grow up that could conquer the Promised Land. As portrayed in the *Book of Judges*, however, that conquest was only partial. From the desert until the end of the biblical period, the regimes of the Hebrews, Israelites, or Jews were portrayed as weak in power and spirit. They fell out of favor with the Lord as often as they came back to favor. It was only for the brief period of David and Solomon that the portrayal is one of power and grandeur. And even that was grand and powerful only by comparison with other ministates of the region or by comparison to past and future in Israelite history.

It is conventional among rabbis to esteem Moses. They refer to him as "Moses our rabbi" and describe themselves as his spiritual descendants. In rabbinical tradition, Moses received the oral Torah as well as the written Torah from God in Sinai. This is yet another effort to make Moses' words and deeds consistent with God's instructions. The doctrine of the oral Torah is said to include all proper interpretations of the language in the written Torah. Hence, whatever Moses did that is not clearly preceded by an instruction from God in the written Torah can be said to reflect Moses' knowledge of the oral Torah. Following the Mosaic model, it is the task of each rabbi to comprehend the written Torah and its interpretations as guided by his teachers (i.e., the oral Torah) and to add commentaries to the oral Torah that reflect his own understanding of them.

The biblical Moses is too good even for some rabbis. They relate stories to supplement the biblical text that show Moses to be a more human and quarrelsome figure, who struggled with God as his death approached. In some of these tales, Moses accepts his death only when he is convinced that everlasting life would be even less desirable.[72] Perhaps we should view these tales as affirming a Jewish tendency to political realism that is lacking in biblical episodes about Moses. As will be shown in the next chapter, there is no lack of realism in the biblical stories about David.

It is not necessary for realists to touch up the biblical stories of the Israelites or those of Korah, Dathan, Abiram, Aaron, and others who would cater to mass yearnings for instant gratification or a golden god. The fickleness of the chosen people is a trait that appears earlier and continues later in the biblical stories but is especially prominent in the stories of Moses. There may be no more important political lesson in the Moses story than the challenges to one who would lead a difficult population in an impossible situation. The story of Moses solves the problem with a figure of legendary proportions. Later biblical stories portray leaders who fail yet nonetheless win a measure of praise.

* * *

The Bible portrays Moses as the greatest human and God's most cherished emissary but not the equal of God. Moses is mythic in his perfection and his lack of faults.[73] If there was a Moses, he lived long before his story was written and edited into the form that has reached us. That may explain the flat, mythic nature of his character. A secular conclusion is that God was an extension of Moses and not the reverse as portrayed in the Bible. That is, Moses created the story of God to legitimize Moses' leadership of the Hebrews. Or that both God and Moses were created by a later generation of elites in need of legitimacy for their laws and rituals. Any of these notions may be true, but they do not obliterate the story that has survived for at least two and one-half millennia as a classic of literature and a focus of profound belief.

NOTES

[1] *Deuteronomy* 34:10-12. That the Torah supposedly written by Moses ends with an account of his death and burial is one of the mysteries that the Bible has left for its readers to ponder.

[2] Aaron Wildavsky, *The Nursing Father: Moses as a Political Leader* (University, Alabama: University of Alabama Press, 1984), p. 201.

[3] Among the motives that commentators speculate lay behind the Moses stories are: to provide national myths with an emphasis on a great leader and Israelite unity for a period when the people were weakened and tempted to assimilate to dominant gentile surroundings; to provide legitimacy for legislation dealing with conditions of settled agricultural or urban communities by linking them with stories of Moses who transmitted the laws of God to the people; or to rewrite cultic history and traditions in order to favor one group of priests, those who claimed descendence from Aaron, as opposed to those descended from Moses or other Levites. See, for example, Bernard W. Anderson, *The Living World of the Old Testament* (London: Longman, 1988); Richard Elliott Friedman, *Who Wrote the Bible?* (New York: Harper and Row, 1987).

[4] John Bright, *A History of Israel*, 1972 edition, p. 124, quoted by George W. Coats, *Moses: Heroic Man, Man of God* (Sheffield, England: Sheffield Academic Press, 1988), p. 11. See also Nahum M. Sarna, *Understanding Genesis: The Heritage of Biblical Israel* (New York: Schocken Books, 1966), especially Chapter IV; and Sarna, *Exploring Exodus: The Heritage of Biblical Israel* (New York: Schocken Books, 1987).

[5] Martin Noth, *A History of Pentateuchal Traditions,* translated by Bernhard W. Anderson (Englewood Cliffs, N.J.: Prentice Hall, 1972), cited by Coats, "Introduction."

[6] *Exodus* 2:1-10.

[7] Nehama Leibowitz *Studies in Shemot (Exodus).* Translated and adapted by Aryeh Newman (Jerusalem: The World Zionist Organization, 1981), p. 40.

[8] *Exodus* 2:11-12.

[9] *Exodus* 2:14.

[10] *Exodus* 2:16-3:6.

[11] *Exodus* 3:11.

[12] *Exodus* 4:1-9.

[13] *Exodus* 4:10-17.

[14] See Leibowitz, p. 77.

[15] *Exodus* 5:2.

[16] *Exodus* 5:21.

[17] *Exodus* 5:1.

[18] *Exodus* 6:2-8.

[19] *Exodus* 7:3-6.

[20] *Exodus* 7:12-13.

[21] *Exodus* 10:24-29.

[22] *Exodus* 12:31.

[23] *Exodus* 14:5-6.

[24] *Exodus* 14:11-18; 31.

[25] *Exodus* 15:25.

[26] *Exodus* 12:35-36.

[27] *Exodus* 35.

[28] Leibowitz, pp. 185-86.

[29] *Exodus* 16:2-8; *Numbers* 11:5.

[30] *Exodus* 32:10-14.

[31] *Exodus* 32:26-29.

[32] *Exodus* 32:34-35.

[33] *Exodus* 32:1-5.

[34] *Exodus* 32:24.

[35] *Exodus* 32:25.

[36] Wildavsky, p. 111.

[37] Friedman, p. 72.

[38] *Numbers* 16:3.

[39] Harry M. Orlinsky, *Essays in Biblical Culture and Bible Translation* (New York: KTAV Publishing House, Inc., 1974), p. 31.

[40] *Numbers* 16:1-50.

[41] *Numbers* 14:11.

[42] *Numbers* 14:16.

[43]*Numbers* 14:22.

[44] *Numbers* 14:1-45.

[45] *Numbers* 11:24-30.

[46] For example, Abraham J. Heschel, *The Prophets* (New York: Harper & Row, 1962); Eric William Heaton, *The Old Testament Prophets* (London: Darton, Longman and Todd, 1977); John Barton, *Oracles of God: Perceptions of Ancient Prophecy in Israel after the Exile* (London: Darton, Longman and Todd, 1986). For a comparison of biblical prophets to pagan shamans, see Thomas W. Overholt, *Prophecy in Cross-Cultural Perspective: A Sourcebook for Biblical Researchers* (Atlanta: Scholars Press, 1986). For a commentary on prophecy by a Mormon intellectual, see Hugh Nibley, *The World and the Prophets* (Salt Lake City: Deseret Book Company, 1987).

[47] Klaus Koch, *The Prophets: The Assyrian Period* (Philadelphia: Fortress Press, 1983), p. vii.

[48] *Exodus* 16:27-30.

[49] *Numbers* 11:32-34.

[50] Nehama Leibowitz, *Studies in Bamidbar (Numbers),* translated and adapted by Aryeh Newman (Jerusalem: The World Zionist Organization, 1980), pp. 225-29.

[51] *Numbers* 20:10.

[52] *Numbers* 20:8-13.

[53] *Exodus* 17:6.

[54] Leibowitz, *Studies in Bamidbar*, pp. 241-46.

[55] See, for example, Andrew M. Greeley, *Myths of Religion* (New York: Warner Books, 1989), Part II, Chapter 3; and Elias J. Bickerman, *The Jews in the Greek Age* (Cambridge: Harvard University Press, 1988), p. 205.

[56] David Daiches, *Moses: The Man and His Vision* (New York: Praeger, 1975), "Epilogue."

[57] *Exodus* 35. The list of items varies with the translation.

[58] *Deuteronomy* 31:29.

[59] *Deuteronomy* 32:26-27.

[60] *Deuteronomy* 32:38-39.

[61] *Deuteronomy* 32:51-52.

[62] Wildavsky, especially pp. 19-25, 206.

[63] Wildavsky, p. 206.

[64] *Numbers* 11:11-15.

[65] *Jeremiah* 20:7-8;14-18.

[66] *Numbers* 27:15-22.

[67] *Isaiah* 43:16-17.

[68] *Jeremiah* 2:2-3.

[69] *Jeremiah* 15:1.

[70] *Numbers* 11:24-30.

[71] *Exodus* 5:1.

[72] Burton L. Visotzky, *Reading the Book: Making the Bible a Timeless Text* (New York: Anchor Books, 1991), Chapter 8.

[73] It should be recalled that some scholars assert that Moses was less mythic and unidimensional than characters in the ancient legends of non-Israelites. See Robert Alter, *The Art of Biblical Narrative* (New York: Basic Books, 1981). Perhaps it is fairest to say that while Moses was less mythic in the simplicity and purity of his character than figures in other ancient stories, he was more mythic than David and other biblical figures.

Chapter 4
David: The Pious and Sinful King

For those concerned with the politics that appears in the Hebrew Bible, David is an obvious subject for inquiry. He is the Bible's most sharply defined political figure. More than other characters, the Bible details his youth, his development and decline as a person and political actor. He is a complex figure, who experiences conflicting pressures, wrestles with temptation and failure, and expresses norms of political and religious significance. His story is crucial to the development of the Israelite monarchy. The Davidic dynasty ruled for over 400 years until it was ended by the Babylonian conquest and has served until now as a symbol of glory and hope in Judaism and Christianity. There is no indication that the Israelites conceived of distinct concepts like "religion" and "state," or "faith" and "politics." For moderns, however, David's life displays tensions at the intersections of the behaviors and norms associated with those terms.

Throughout the material about David there appears a recognition of difficult political realities, an acceptance of behavior that does not match ideals, and the need to balance good against bad. He is credited with developing the institutions of the Israelite state to a greater degree than his predecessor Saul. He also extended the boundaries of what he controlled to those resembling modern Israel, with extensions beyond to the east and north. His kingdom was short lived in Jewish history, if it existed at all beyond the descriptions in the Bible. Even if those boundaries accurately depicted history, they were not extensive or long lasting in comparison with other ancient empires. In his novel about David, Joseph Heller includes this parody of immodesty: "I had taken a kingdom the size of Vermont and created an empire as large as the state of Maine!"[1]

David's story shows the willingness of the Bible's authors and editors to elevate a juicy character, warts and all, to among the greatest of Judaic heroes. The seamy side of David shows that the Israelites could bestow their esteem on imperfect humans and not only on idealized figures like Moses. His immoral personal behavior was matched by his doubtful public activities. As a young man, he was even willing to take the field against Israelites while under the tutelage of a Philistine king.

David's character shows more clearly than Moses the problems of governing. David was tested and ultimately worn down by the problems of seizing power, maintaining control, managing subordinates, using resources wisely, and then passing on authority to the next generation.

The biblical material concerned with David is hardly less problematic than that about Moses. A number of questions are raised and left without resolution: Did Saul deserve to lose the favor of the Lord when his sins seem to have been less serious than those of David? What was the problem with the census that brought disaster on the people yet seems to have been instigated by God?

David's encounter with Goliath is portrayed in full detail but is curiously not linked with surrounding episodes. King Saul did not recognize the young hero as the musician who had served him earlier. Other biblical portrayals of Goliath's death credit the feat to Elhanan, son of Jair.[2] Perhaps the story was invented centuries after it was said to have occurred in order to enhance David's reputation as God's anointed king.[3] Readers familiar with American myths may compare it to the story of young George Washington admitting to his father that he chopped down the cherry tree, saying, "I cannot tell a lie." A number of scholars express doubt that David authored the psalms attributed to him.[4] Others find more indications of myth than history in all that is concerned with David.[5]

These problems require a skeptical perspective upon the Bible's portrayal of David. What follows is not a record of historical reality but a description of how a leading political figure was portrayed by those who wrote, compiled, and edited what became the final version of the Hebrew Bible. More than for other revered figures, they portrayed David's ugliness as well his beauty. The message, according to the rabbis, is that humans are flawed. Believers who must repent from their sins can learn how to do so from David. Only God is above reproach. As we shall see in Chapter 7, however, even God can be problematic. In the Bible as in politics, there is much to exercise an observer's capacity to judge nuances. Those looking for the obvious and the simple see only part of what exists.

A BIBLICAL BIOGRAPHY

David first appears as a boy, then as a man who strove for personal power, assembled a kingdom out of warring tribes, and extended the kingdom to its historical limits. Then he declined through phases of personal weakness, indecision, and perhaps senility. The image that emerges is a complex individual, whose contrasting traits appeared in different episodes or competed with one another at the same time.

The young David was gentle, innocent, pure of heart, trusting of God, and a precocious fighter. He soothed the moody Saul by playing the lyre. He is said to have challenged Goliath with these words: "You have come against me with sword and spear and dagger, but I have come against you in the name of the Lord of Hosts, the God of the army of Israel which you have defied . . ."[6] Other episodes give rise to the conclusions that David was also a "bloodthirsty oversexed bandit,"[7] a skilled leader and cunning politician, or a man of "courage and generosity," whose traits resembled those of God who brought the lowly slaves out of Egypt and concerned himself with the poor and the weak.[8]

The 16th and 17th chapters of the *Book of First Samuel* offer three different introductions to David's story. They each have a mythic quality and do not refer to one another. They suggest separate sources that were put together long after the time when they were supposed to have occurred, without being edited into a smooth narrative. One focuses on the prophet Samuel and reads like the tale of Cinderella. It tells how Samuel was led to anoint as future king the youngest of Jesse's sons, a simple shepherd who had not been among the sons that Jesse invited to meet with the prophet.[9] The second story tells about the dark moods of King Saul and an attendant who knows of David, "cunning in playing, a mighty valiant man, and a man of war . . . and the Lord is with him."[10] The third story is David's encounter with Goliath. Although it comes after the story of David playing the lyre for

Saul, neither the King nor his commander-in-chief recognize the young hero.[11]

Before David went out to face Goliath there was an interview with the king in which the lad sounded like a boasting peasant: "I am my father's shepherd; when a lion or bear comes and carries off a sheep I go after it and attack it and rescue the victim from its jaws. Then if it turns on me, I seize it by the beard and batter it to death."[12] David seemed to be overly blessed with good looks and an appealing manner. He entered Saul's household, established a close relationship with the king's son Jonathan, succeeded in his military assignments, and was promoted to a position of command. The people's response was too positive. Saul became uneasy when Israelite women sang of Saul killing his thousands and of David killing tens of thousands.[13]

David continued his ascent despite Saul's jealousy. Like the poor boy in a fairy tale, David won a princess for having served the king. In this case, however, the gift was part of a plot to kill David. The bride price was 100 Philistine foreskins. Presumably, the original owners of the foreskins would not willingly have them taken.

When David bettered his assignment and delivered 200 Philistine foreskins, he received Michal as his bride. But the couple did not live happily ever after. David was assured of the king's enmity,[14] and Michal became a nagging wife who ended her days ignored in David's harem.

The Bible depicts Saul's sanity as continuing to deteriorate. At one point Saul accused his advisors of misleading him about David's movements: ". . . do you expect the son of Jesse to give you all fields and vineyards, or make you all officers . . .Is that why you have all conspired against me?"[15] Saul accused a priest of aiding David and would not accept the priest's defense that it was appropriate for him to help a royal office holder and the king's son-in-law. The king ordered that 85 priests be killed, along with all the women, children, babies, and animals of their village.[16] Saul and David alternately pursued and fled from one another across several chapters of *First Samuel*. There is one farcical scene of the king urinating within sight of the concealed David[17] and another of David stealing some of the sleeping king's equipment in order to prove that he could have killed him.[18] David was steadfast in refusing to kill Saul because he had been anointed as the Lord's king. Saul repeatedly recognized David's loyalty, embraced him, swore that he would do him no harm, and then began to pursue him again.[19] David concluded early on that he must escape from the mad king.[20] Saul heard conclusively from the ghost of Samuel what he suspected for some time: that God had chosen David as king in his place.[21]

David was not only a chivalrous innocent who spent his time in flight and forewent opportunities to harm his king. He gathered around him "every one that was in distress, and every one that was in debt, and everyone that was discontented . . ."[22] David's force is numbered at one point as 400, and at another as 600.[23] Their activity seems to have focused on self-defense and material support. It was coping at its most basic, allowing David to accumulate power while out of favor at court until he became king of a realm larger than Saul's.

The episode of Nabal depicts David operating a protection racket. He and his men collected resources from farmers whom they protected from marauders, with themselves among the potential marauders. Nabal's wife Abigail pleaded with David not to take revenge on her husband for refusing to pay for protection. By the end of the story, Nabal was dead and Abigail was David's wife.[24] The story reinforces the image of Saul's weakness and his inability to protect the countryside from David and his ilk.

Other episodes that cast doubt on David concern his relations with the Philistines. He allied himself with Achish, the son of a Philistine king, and received for his services the town of Ziklag.[25] Achish asked David to join him in a campaign against the Israelites. As would be expected from a vassal who had been awarded a town for his support, David agreed.[26] Before the battle could be joined, other Philistine commanders refused to fight alongside an Israelite.[27] David protested his loyalty to Achish: "What have I done . . . that I should not come and fight against the enemies of my lord the king?"[28] Achish listened to his Philistine colleagues and sent David back to Ziklag.[29] It may have helped David when he aspired to be an Israelite king that he had not been allowed to join the Philistines' campaign against his own people.

David was more clearly true to Israelite traditions in his campaigns against the Amalekites. He pursued and destroyed one band that had raided Ziklag and took booty and prisoners, including David's own wives.[30] At other times he seems to have attacked Amalekites simply as targets of opportunity: "he left no one alive, man or woman; he took flocks and herds, asses and camels, and clothes too . . ."[31] In light of the Amalekites' role as Israelite enemies since the time of the exodus, David may have been "waving the bloody flag" in order to strengthen his bonds with Israelites who were justly suspicious of his affinity with the Philistines.[32]

One Amalekite who suffered from David was the man who reported that he had happened upon the mortally wounded Saul and had administered the *coup de grace* at the king's request. The Amalekite had to be killed, according to David, because he admitted killing the Lord's anointed.[33]

Saul's death provided David with an opportunity to regularize his situation. He was declared king over the people of Judah, with Hebron as his headquarters.[34] According to a modern commentator, this could have occurred only with the consent of his Philistine overlords.[35] In the north, Saul's commander Abner made Saul's son Ishbosheth king of Israel. The initiative assigned to Abner rather than Ishbosheth is one sign provided by the Bible that Saul's son was dependent and otherwise ineffective. Another was his name. It is a composite of "ish" (man) and "bosheth" (shame). There began a war between David and the house of Saul, which resulted in David's victory and the extension of his reign over the northern tribes of Israel. At one point Ishbosheth is said to have remained king of Israel for two years.[36] Elsewhere it is said that the war was long drawn out, with David growing steadily stronger while the house of Saul grew steadily weaker.[37] The end came with a falling out between Ishbosheth and his commander Abner. Abner offered to bring all of Israel with him to David. The weak Ishbosheth returned Michal to David, taking her from the man who Saul had made her husband.[38]

Abner's fate provided an early signal of David's weakness. Although Ishbosheth's turn-coat commander had been given a safe conduct by David, David's commander Joab killed him in revenge for Abner having killed Joab's brother during the war. David protested his own innocence in the killing and cursed Joab. Yet the only punishment that he imposed on Joab was an order that he attend Abner's funeral.[39]

Ishbosheth was killed by two of his officers who sought to curry favor with David and were killed by David for their efforts.[40]

The elders of Israel made David their king; he captured Jerusalem from the Jebusites and began a rule over the united kingdom that was to last for 33 years.[41]

The Bible describes David's court as more elaborate and institutionalized than Saul's although less opulent than Solomon's. While at Hebron, before uniting the two kingdoms of Judah and Israel, David contracted what seems to have been a dynastic marriage with the daughter of the king of Geshur, an area to the northeast of the Sea of Galilee.[42] After the conquest of Jerusalem, Hiram of Tyre sent materials and workmen to help in the construction of a palace.[43] David had officers in charge of stores, labor, vine-dressers, wine-cellars, olives and sycamore figs, oil, herds, camels, asses, and flocks. There were counselors, tutors for the king's children, the army commander, and an officer entitled the king's friend.[44] There were also priests and Levites (said to number 38,000) with cultic responsibilities.[45] *I Chronicles* mentions the king's possessions with no indication that the author was sensitive to a distinction between the king's personal property and that of the state or monarchy.

A story that is placed early in his career provides insight into David's sensitivity to the needs of his men and his attractions as a leader. He sided with his reserve and support troops against the fighting troops who opposed sharing booty with their colleagues.[46] David also appeared as a righteous man and a skillful commander in an episode that appears in *II Samuel* and again in *I Chronicles*. It began when he expressed a craving for a drink of water from the well at the gate of Bethlehem, then controlled by the Philistines. When three of his men stole through the enemy lines and obtained the water, David refused to drink it: "God forbid that I should do such a thing! Can I drink the blood of these men who risked their lives for it?"[47]

David combined political and military skills. He continued as a fighter or as an organizer of war after he created the united kingdom. One historian concludes that Israel's wars of conquest began and ended under David, with later Israelite wars being defensive, usually to resist expansionist policies of the great powers.[48]

What is known about the Promised Land at the time of David serves to diminish the biblical portrayal of power and glory. The country was poor and marginal, without the agricultural wealth, the large populations, or the elaborate royal courts associated with Egypt or

Mesopotamia.[49] The Israelite settlement in the land may have been facilitated by a general destruction that began as early as 1500 B.C.E. The empires of Egypt to the south and the Hittites to the north seem to have been weakened by an invasion of outsiders. Mesopotamia was also in a period of dormancy that may have lasted through the reigns of David and Solomon. In these conditions, there may have occurred something like the expansion of Israelite power that the Bible attributes to David's sagacity.[50]

The Bible reports that David alternately threatened, conquered, or made deals with the Ammonites, Moabites, Edomites, and Aramaeans as well as the Philistines.[51] One commentator notes that David knew how to deal firmly with adversaries during war but generously with those who accommodated him.[52] His treatment of Moabite prisoners of war must be entered on the firm side of the ledger. He made them lie on the ground and used a cord to measure off the size of two groups to be killed and one group to be spared.[53]

One of David's conquests was provoked by the Ammonites' insult to his ambassadors.

> Hanun took David's servants, and shaved off the one half of their beards, and cut off their garments in the middle, even to their buttocks, and sent them away.[54]

David's conquests extended from the Aramaeans at the Great Bend of the Euphrates[55] in the northeast to the Philistines in the southwest.[56]

David struggled at home with members of his own family and rebellions against his regime. According to the Bible, his problems were God's punishment for the sin of taking Uriah's wife as his own.[57]

His wife Michal was one source of problems. When Saul sought to trap David at home, Michal warned David and helped him escape. But then she lied to Saul that David had threatened to kill her if she did not help him.[58] We do not know if she resisted Saul's decision to take her from David and marry her to Palti (or Paltiel) during the period when David was an outlaw.[59] We do read that Michal was something of a shrew. When she rejoined David after Saul's death, she ridiculed him for dancing ecstatically while the Ark was brought to Jerusalem, allowing his cloak to open and expose his private parts and thereby disgracing himself in front of servant girls. (Joseph Heller's novel, *God Knows*, makes the point that biblical heroes did not have underwear.)[60] The Bible says explicitly that Michal was to live out her life without bearing a child.[61] It hints that David punished Michal for her criticism of him by keeping her unloved in his harem and paying more attention to servant girls than to her.[62]

The decadence of the royal family appeared most clearly in the sordid story of Amnon and Tamar. Amnon raped his half-sister and then abandoned her. David expressed anger but did not punish Amnon.[63] (The *New English Bible* includes a passage that David "would not hurt Amnon because he was his eldest son and he loved him," but there is no basis for this in the Hebrew.) Absalom revenged his sister's disgrace by murdering his half-brother Amnon. There followed several years of scheming among family members and court officials, first about how the king should be informed of Amnon's death, then the banishment of Absalom, his return to the court, and a reconciliation with his father the king.[64]

David also failed to discipline a wayward son when Absalom suborned the people's loyalty at the gates of Jerusalem.[65] When Absalom mounted an open rebellion and declared himself king in Hebron, David again failed to act decisively. He initially fled and accepted curses from a bitter member of Saul's family without making a response.[66] When he did organize his forces, David ordered his commanders to "deal gently for my sake" with Absalom.[67]

In what to a modern reader seems like a comic insert, Absalom's advisors pressed him to clarify the act of rebellion by having intercourse with the concubines that David left to look after the palace: "They set up a tent for Absalom on the roof, and he lay with his father's concubines in the sight of all Israel."[68] No mention is made of the Absalom's vigor or the concubines' sentiments. Upon David's return, he put the women under guard and treated them as sullied property: . . . "he maintained them but did not have intercourse with them. They were kept in confinement to the day of their death, widowed in the prime of life."[69]

Absalom's revolt was more than the rebellion of an ambitious son. Absalom had remnants of Saul's family with him as well as other leading families and substantial popular support.[70] The support of a Saulist contingent (most likely based in the north, like Saul's kingdom) and passages such as "the men of Israel had transferred their allegiance to Absalom"[71] suggest that his rebellion drew its support from the northern kingdom of Israel. Absalom himself was from Judah, and some passages suggest that David had support in the north.[72] However, other material adds to the conclusion that it was a civil war based partly on the enmity between different regions. Absalom's mother had been a princess of Geshur, a kingdom on the northeastern border of Israel. After Absalom had been killed, it is written that one of David's messages won all the hearts in Judah, but Israel is not mentioned.[73] On another occasion, it is written that "All the people of Judah escorted the king over the river, and so did half the people of Israel."[74] A historian sees these as clues that David reacted to the rebellion by strengthening his position in Judah at the expense of further alienating the northern region.[75]

If the north-south split in the Absalom's rebellion is only speculative, the regional element in the subsequent revolt of Sheba is more certain. It began with the proclamation: "What share have we in David? We have no lot in the son of Jesse. Away to your homes, O Israel."[76] The next lines report that, "The men of Israel all left David . . . but the men of Judah stood by their king . . ."[77]

Personal Decline

The Bible asserts that David's decline began with his adultery and the killing of Bathsheba's husband. As noted above, that was not the first episode where he was morally suspect. The line of doubtful behavior can be traced backward at least to the episodes with Nabal and David's vassalage to the Philistine Achish. The war with Ish-bosheth includes Joab's disregard of David's order to protect Abner and David's failure to punish Joab. In the early details of the Bathsheba story, even before the adultery and killing, it is apparent that the once brave warrior was at home in the palace while Joab, Uriah, and other troops were fighting in Ammon. With all this, there was no immediate sign of personal weakness after David's famous sin. His empire continued to grow, and the problems of Amnon and Tamar, Absalom, and Sheba were years in the future.

Several episodes suggest a gradual decline. Even before the rebellions of Absalom and Sheba, Joab chastised his king for failing to lead his troops in battle: "You had better muster the rest of the army yourself, lay siege to the city and take it, lest I take it and name it after myself."[78] David's flight during Absalom's rebellion indicates less than heroic behavior as did his acceptance of a curse from a member of Saul's family. The king organized a defense but acceded to the troops' call that he not endanger himself by taking part in battle.[79] When David mourned Absalom's death, he received a stinging rebuke by the general who killed Absalom against David's explicit orders.

> You have put to shame this day all your servants, who have saved you and your sons and daughters, your wives and your concubines. You love those who hate you and hate those that love you. . . Now go at once and give your servants some encouragement; if you refuse, I swear by the Lord that not a man will stay with you tonight, and that would be a worse disaster than any you have suffered since your earliest days.

The Bible indicates that David responded to this dressing down with quiet compliance.[80]

Perhaps to put Joab in his place and to obtain the support of those who sided with Absalom, David chose Absalom's general Amasa as the commander of his army. Then David did not punish Joab when he killed Amasa during the rebellion of Sheba.[81] In a later campaign, David was taken prisoner by the Philistines and had to be rescued by his troops. His officers then swore that David should never again go to war with them.[82]

There is a curious episode concerned with a census that also reveals David's weakness. The story does not refer to the king's age, but appears in the last chapter of *II Samuel*, just prior to the opening chapter of *I Kings* where David is described as a very old man. The story is introduced with a statement that the Israelites felt the Lord's anger when God incited David against them and instructed him to count the population. It is not said why the census ordered by God would be bad. Joab resisted the king's instructions to carry out the census but was overruled. Later David recognized that he did wrong and that it was necessary to be punished by God. The story indicates that 70,000 people died of a pestilence that the Lord sent by way of punishment for a census that God himself had initiated.

Commentators have wrestled with this story over the centuries. They have sought to explain the condemnation of David's census, while censuses taken during the period in the wilderness were trouble free.[83] One hypotheses is that David's census was to be taken in preparation for apportioning taxes, work levies, or military recruitment involved with conquests or plans to build the Temple. Popular opposition to the levies, not the advice of Nathan against building the Temple, may have been the factor that dissuaded David from going forward with the Temple.[84] The census during the exodus was meant to determine the size of each tribe in order to apportion among them the Promised Land. A connection with the divine gift of the land rather than impositions of taxes or compulsory work may explain the different responses to the two censuses.[85]

David's weakness declined to its lowest point in his final days. According to the story in *I Kings*, there was both a messy transition to Solomon's reign, and a vignette suggests that the once virile David was senile and impotent. His failure to discipline his family and prepare an orderly transition may have been endemic in a royal setting of many wives and sons, a lack of strong dynastic tradition, and murderous intrigues among the princes and their supporters. While David was still alive, his oldest surviving son Adonijah allied himself with Joab and took steps to have himself proclaimed king. A counter-plot of Nathan the prophet and Bathsheba stopped Adonijah and put Bathsheba's son Solomon on the throne. A modern scholar calls this "*a coup d' etat* organized by Solomon and his supporters at court."[86]

The procedure that David is said to have followed in crowning his son suggests an old man's insensitivity to tensions in his regime and may have contributed to the regional problems that eventually split the kingdom. David had acquired his own reign over Judah and Israel in stages, with at least the nominal consent of elites in both regions. However, he ordered that Solomon be mounted on the royal mule and anointed by the priest Zadok and the prophet Nathan. David proclaimed that Solomon was king over both Israel and Judah without asking the consent of either.[87]

Adonijah expected the worse. He ran to the altar and grasped its horns in the posture of a man seeking the refuge of the holy place. Solomon promised him protection and ordered him to come home.[88]

While this was happening, David was described as a very old man who was always cold. The solution was to employ the beautiful virgin Abishag to keep him warm. However, the biblical text says that

David "knew her not."[89] It appears that the man who once behaved like an "oversexed bandit" could no longer function.

There is some confusion in the Bible over David's last words. A saintly version appears in *II Samuel*, where David praises the justice, glory, and reliability of God.[90] In contrast is a settling of accounts by a bitter old man in *I Kings*. David is described as advising Solomon to do away with two problems that David had been unable or unwilling to solve: his general Joab (let not his hoar head go down to the grave in peace) and the member of Saul's family whose curses he was forced to endure while fleeing from Absalom (his hoar head bring thou down to the grave with blood).[91] After David's death, Solomon and Adonijah had a disagreement about who would inherit Abishag, and the new king ordered that his half-brother be killed.[92]

DAVID'S THEMES

David's appearance at a crucial stage of Israelite history as well as the multifaceted and extreme nature of his character invite attention to a number of themes having political relevance. They concern David's success or failure in creating political institutions that could withstand the strains of Israelite tribal and regional loyalties and the treatment of David in history. Was David a political genius or a manipulator who failed to build lasting institutions? Was he a man of faith, an opportunist, or a combination of those traits who is portrayed both as an individual of mythic proportions and as a human who struggled, sometimes clumsily, with serious problems? As in the case of other questions asked about the Bible's treatment of diverse and even contrasting political themes, the most honest answer is "all of the above."

David as Builder of a State

A simple view of David's record as a state builder can be either positive or negative. His descendants ruled in Jerusalem for over 400 years, from the onset of his reign in the eleventh century B.C.E. until the destruction by the Babylonians in 586 B.C.E. Yet Judah and Israel remained united only for some 70-80 years until the death of Solomon. The division of the united kingdom severely weakened the

Israelites in a situation where their land was chronically set upon by larger empires. Israel and Judah alternately fought and allied with one another until the northern kingdom disappeared under an Assyrian onslaught during the 720s B.C.E.

It is common to explain the division of the kingdoms as due to the proximate causes of harsh taxation and forced labor undertaken to construct the Temple and other public works during Solomon's reign. The regional character of the revolt is linked to tribal and regional loyalties, deeply seated in Israelite history, that were only partly overcome during the periods of Joshua, Judges, Saul, David, and Solomon. The roots of regional loyalties may have been in the physical divisions of the land with its mountains, deserts, valleys, foothills, and coastal plains that separated the inhabitants and produced tensions among them.

> . . .geographical features tend to separate the land into smaller districts and serve as stumbling blocks to unification . . . Palestine, in spite of its limited area, is divided into many smaller districts which differ radically from one another. . . . This situation was never conducive to national or political unity.[93]

The *Book of Judges* describes a condition where the Israelite tribes occasionally united against outsiders but also fought one another. In one case, the tribe of Benjamin was almost eliminated by other tribes acting in concert.[94] The reign of Saul represented a step toward a united polity. However, his support was mainly in the north. In one episode the Bible notes that 300,000 came to support Saul from Israel and only 30,000 from Judah.[95] At another time only 10,000 from among 200,000 foot soldiers came from Judah.[96] Modern scholars disagree about the extent of Saul's kingdom. By one view, the area he controlled reached from about 10 kilometers south of modern Arad to near Metullah in the north and across the Jordan almost to Amman. It did not reach the Mediterranean Coast and did not include areas around Jerusalem and Beit Shean.[97] According to another view, Saul did not control the Judean area south of Jerusalem.[98]

The biblical record provides only clues as to what David contributed or failed to contribute to national integration. The rebellions of Absalom and Sheba point to regional tensions that festered among the Israelites. Biblical reports of censuses taken by David and Solomon at different times indicate a sizable non-Israelite population within the Promised Land.[99] There is no clear indication that the non-Israelite population was a source of problems during David's reign. Before he became king, David showed an opportunistic sense for how to deal with non-Israelites. He accepted a position of vassalage under the Philistines and he married non-Israelites, but he was violent toward the Amalekites.

Scholars write about the personalized nature of the united kingdom and the failure of David or Solomon to institutionalize it in a way that it could benefit from the continuing support of Israelites from all tribes and regions.[100] Perhaps the Bible's silence on the subject should be taken as the lack of a regional policy. If so, the insensitivity to the issue was a legacy that Solomon exacerbated with high taxes and work levies. At the start of Rehoboam's reign (i.e., David's grandson) the king revealed overt insensitivity to regional concerns. When asked to lighten the burdens on the north, Rehoboam responded that he would make the northerners' yoke heavier than it was in his father's reign.[101] Then the north rebelled, and the kingdom split.

David's Character

David was one of the most complex figures in a Bible whose specialty is stories that reveal the problems in being consistently just, righteous, or humane. Alongside of episodes that portray a man of intense faith are those that reveal opportunism. Again we should recall that we are not examining the historical David. He is hidden. We are examining the David created by the compilers of the Bible. David's complexity suggests that the compilers gave credence to persons who were torn. Like other biblical heroes, David could not maintain at all times the values that the Bible espoused.

There are numerous indications of David's faith. He is credited with a song of thanksgiving upon being delivered from the threat of Saul. It begins "The Lord is my rock, my fortress, and my deliverer."[102] In what are called David's last words, he said, "The God of Israel has spoken, the Rock of Israel has said to me; when one rules justly over men, ruling in the fear of God, he dawns on them like the morning light . . ."[103] David is reported to have consulted God as to whether he should attack the marauding Philistines and whether Saul would continue to pursue him.[104] God spoke to David on several occasions, sometimes giving him detailed instructions as to the plan of battle. ("Do not attack now but wheel round and take them in the rear opposite the aspens.")[105]

David sought to serve the Lord by bringing the Ark of the Tabernacles to Jerusalem and later by building a Temple. During the transfer of the Ark, the Lord struck down Uzzah when he touched the Ark in an effort to keep it from falling. David was confused as to God's action and halted the procession out of fear that the Ark's presence would bring harm to his city.[106]

The story of David's role in building the Temple is a complicated one with different versions. The prophet Nathan first endorsed David's proposal to build a Temple but then received another message from God. The messages differ, depending on their biblical source. In *II Samuel* God is presented as modest, and satisfied to be identified with a tent and tabernacle: "Did I ever ask any of the judges whom I appointed shepherds of my people Israel why they had not built me a house of cedar?"[107] In *I Chronicles* Nathan's explanation concerns David's military record.

> . . . the word of the Lord came to me, saying: thou hast shed blood abundantly, and hast made great wars; thou shalt not build a house unto my name, because thou has shed much blood upon the earth in my sight.[108]

A commentator infers that David was dissuaded from building the Temple when there was popular opposition to a census that he took prior to recruiting forced labor. By this interpretation, the opposition to the Temple was an early expression of the Israelites' opposition to taxation and work levies, which led eventually to rebellion and division of the kingdom.[109]

The author of *I Chronicles* indicates that David went much further toward actually constructing the Temple than did the author of *II Samuel*. The writer of *Chronicles* says that David presented Solomon with detailed plans,[110] solicited contributions,[111] and assembled material to be used in the building.[112]

ADJUSTING THE RECORD

It is the argument of this chapter that David's character was the most fully human, problematic, political, and believable of biblical figures. For some of the later biblical writers, he seems to be have been too human. The problematic features of David's biography that appear in *Samuel* and *Kings* benefited from the attention of the chronicler. *I Chronicles* repeats much of what appears in the earlier historical books but with excisions, additions, and changes in detail that seem intended to put a better face on David. It leaves out the young David's offer to fight against the Israelites alongside the Philistines. Bathsheba does not appear in *Chronicles*, neither as the cause of adultery and killing nor one who schemes for the selection of Solomon as David's successor. The succession story in *Chronicles* is a smooth one, without a plot by Adojinah or mention of a young virgin who must warm an aged David.

The David of *Chronicles* is more God-fearing than the David of earlier books. As the story of David's defeat of the Philistines at Baal-perazim is told in *II Samuel*, it ends with David and his men carrying off the idols left behind by the Philistines.[113] As the story is told in *Chronicles*, David orders that the idols be burned.[114] *Chronicles* tells a more complete story of cultic rituals accompanying the journey of the Ark to Jerusalem.[115] *Chronicles* details David's plan for the Temple to be built by Solomon as well as the daily rituals that were said to be performed during David's reign.[116]

Chronicles also changes the origin of David's problematic census. As the story is told in *II Samuel*, it is God who incites David to count Israel and Judah.[117] In *Chronicles*, it is Satan who causes David to count the people.[118]

The chronicler's repair of David's image was nothing compared to what has been done for him by post-biblical Jewish legends:

> Even after David became king he sat at the feet of his teachers, Ira the Jairite and Mephibosheth. To the latter he always submitted his decisions on religious questions, to make sure that they were in accordance with law. Whatever leisure time his royal duties afforded him, he spent in study and prayer. He contented himself with sixty breaths of sleep. At

> midnight the strings of his harp, which were made of the gut of the ram sacrificed by Abraham on Mount Moriah, began to vibrate. The sound they emitted awakened David, and he would arise at once to devote himself to the study of the Torah. . . .
>
> By nature David was not disposed to commit such evil-doing as his relation to Bathsheba involved. God himself brought him to his crime, that he might say to other sinners: "Go to David and learn how to repent." . . . as for the death of Uriah, it cannot be laid entirely at David's door, for Uriah had incurred the death penalty by his refusal to take his ease in his own house, according to the king's bidding.[119]

* * *

The stories of David's rise to power in the *Book of First Samuel* read like fairy tales written retrospectively. First he is the male version of Cinderella: the littlest brother kept in the fields by his father and brothers but finally discovered as God's anointed. Another episode has David boasting to Saul of killing lions with his bare hands and then dispatching the Philistine giant who no experienced soldier had dared fight. When David is offered a princess in exchange for 100 Philistine foreskins, he responds by delivering 200 foreskins.

Saul has to fall for David to rise further. The Bible offers two explanations, with the first being trivial in the extreme and the second only slightly more weighty. The first story involves Saul's failure to wait further for the tardy Samuel and performing a pre-battle sacrifice that had been the prophet's responsibility. Would God have preferred the king to wait on procedural formalities and risk the loss of an important military opportunity? The second story involves Saul's failure to destroy all of the captured Amalekites and their property as instructed in an order said to be from God. Elsewhere God reveals himself to be pragmatic as when he sent the Israelites on a long way to the Promised Land around the settlements of the powerful Philistines and when he backed down from his initial decision to destroy all the Israelites at the scene of the golden calf. Could not the pragmatic God have allowed Saul to bend the rules in order to acquire good implements and flocks for his marginal people?

The story of God's anointment of David provides an acceptably pious explanation for the elevation of an opportunistic fighter who had lived on the margins between Israelite and Philistine regimes. The reality of the young David may have been closer to a bandit chief than a saint, but such an emphasis would not do for the founder of a dynasty that lasted for 400 years and whose seed was to provide a messiah.

The Bible describes David's monarchy as the first *institutionalized* regime of the Israelites. The king was not simply a mobile leader of troops like Saul but had a court made up of officers with specialized responsibilities. There was a capital city, troublesome census, tax collection (perhaps related to the problematic elements of the census), extensive construction, territorial expansion, and international relations. This first king of the Davidic dynasty was not a faceless autocrat but thoroughly human with both positive and negative sides to his character. He was solicitous towards his subordinates, hesitant to kill the king he perceived as anointed by God, ambivalent toward signs of rebellion, and accepted sharp criticism from his subordinate Joab and the prophet Nathan. These are signs of a leader who was reluctant to exercise absolute power. David's lusting for Bathsheba and his killing of Uriah are the other sides of an ancient Oriental despot, who could have what he wanted when he sought to override the restraints of God's law.

NOTES

[1] Joseph Heller, *God Knows* (New York: Dell Publishing Company, 1984), p. 256.

[2] *II Samuel* 21:19; *I Chronicles* 20:5.

[3] Steven A. Moss, "Who Killed Goliath?" *The Jewish Bible Quarterly* XVIII, 1, Fall 1989, pp. 37-40.

[4] Robert Davidson, *The Courage To Doubt: Exploring an Old Testament Theme* (London: SCM Press, 1983), Chapter 10.

[5] James W. Flanagan, *David's Social Drama: A Hologram of Israel's Early Iron Age* (Sheffield, England: Almond Press, 1988), p. 42; and Randall C. Bailey, *David in Love and War: The Pursuit of Power in 2 Samuel 10-12* (Sheffield, England: JSOT Press, 1990), p. 130.

[6] *I Samuel* 17.

[7] Walter Brueggemann, *David's Truth: In Israel's Imagination and Memory* (Philadelphia: Fortress Press, 1985), pp. 15-16.

[8] Paul D. Hanson, *The People Called: The Growth of Community in the Bible* (New York: Harper and Row, 1986), p. 101.

[9] *I Samuel* 16:12. On the parallels between biblical stories and folklore, including the Cinderella story, see Susan Nidith, *Underdogs and Tricksters: A Prelude to Biblical Folklore* (San Francisco: Harper & Row, 1987).

[10] *I Samuel* 16:18.

[11] See especially *I Samuel* 17:55-58.

[12] *I Samuel* 17:34-35.

[13] *I Samuel* 18:1-8.

[14] *I Samuel* 18:21-29.

[15] *I Samuel* 22.

[16] *I Samuel* 22:9-20.

[17] *I Samuel* 24:4.

[18] *I Samuel* 26:12.

[19] *I Samuel* 24:16-21; 26:21.

[20] *I Samuel* 27:1.

[21] *I Samuel* 28:18.

[22] *I Samuel* 22:2.

[23] *I Samuel* 22:2; 23:13.

[24] *I Samuel* 25:2-44.

[25] *I Samuel* 27:6.

[26] *I Samuel* 28:1-2.

[27] *I Samuel* 29:1-5.

[28] *I Samuel* 29:8.

[29] *I Samuel* 29:10-11.

[30] *I Samuel* 30:14-21.

[31] *I Samuel* 27:7-9.

[32] Tadmor, p. 95.

[33] *II Samuel* 1:16.

[34] *II Samuel* 2:4.

[35] John Bright, *A History of Israel* (London: SCM Press Ltd., 1980), p. 196.

[36] *II Samuel* 2:10.

[37] *II Samuel* 3:1.

[38] *II Samuel* 3:12-21.

[39] *II Samuel* 3:26-33.

[40] *II Samuel* 4:5-12.

[41] *II Samuel* 5:1-5.

[42] *II Samuel* 3:3.

[43] *II Samuel* 5:11.

[44] *I Chronicles* 27:25-34

[45] *I Chronicles* 23:2-4.

[46] *I Samuel* 30.

[47] *II Samuel* 23:15-17; *I Chronicles* 11:17-19.

[48] Roland de Vaux, *Ancient Israel*(New York: McGraw-Hill, 1961), Volume I, p. 250.

[49] See, for example, A. Leo Oppenheim, *Ancient Mesopotamia: Portrait of a Dead Civilization* (Chicago: University of Chicago Press, 1977).

[50] George E. Mendenhall, *The Tenth Generation: The Origins of the Biblical Tradition* (Baltimore: Johns Hopkins University Press, 1973); John M. Halligan, "The Role of the Peasant in the Amarna Period," in David Noel Freedman and David Frank Graf, eds., *Palestine in Transition: The Emergence of Ancient Israel* (Sheffield, England: The Almond Press, 1983), pp. 15-24; and Keith W. Whitelam, "Israel's Traditions in Origin: Reclaiming the Land," *Journal for the Study of the Old Testament* 44, June 1989, pp. 19-42. For an earlier portrayal of similar themes, see Albrecht Alt *Essays on Old Testament History and Religion*, translated by R. A. Wilson (Garden City, N.Y.: Doubleday & Company, 1967).

[51] Siegfried Herrmann, *A History of Israel in Old Testament Times*(London: SCM Press, Ltd., 1975), p. 160.

[52] Yehuda Kil, *The Book of Chronicles* (Jerusalem: Mossad Harav Kook, 1986), p. 94. (Hebrew).

[53] *II Samuel* 8:2.

[54] *II Samuel* 10:4.

[55] *I Chronicles* 19:16.

[56] *I Chronicles* 20:4.

[57] *II Samuel* 12:10. A slightly different formulation appears in *I Kings* 15:4.

[58] *I Samuel* 19:17.

[59] Michal's husband is called Palti in *I Samuel* 25:44, and Paltiel in *II Samuel* 3:15-16.

[60] Heller; see also Stefan Heym, *The King David Report* (New York: G.P. Putnam's Sons, 1973).

[61] *II Samuel* 6:23.

[62] *II Samuel* 6:22.

[63] *II Samuel* 13:21.

[64] *II Samuel* 13:30-14:33.

[65] *II Samuel* 15:1-6.

[66] *II Samuel* 16:10.

[67] *II Samuel* 18:5.

[68] *II Samuel* 16:22.

[69] *II Samuel* 20:3.

[70] *II Samuel* 16:4.

[71] *II Samuel* 15:13-15.

[72] *II Samuel* 19:9.

[73] *II Samuel* 19:14.

[74] *II Samuel* 19:40.

[75] H. Tadmor, "The Period of the First Temple, the Babylonian Exile and the Restoration," in H. H. Ben-Sasson, *A History of the Jewish People* (Cambridge, Massachusetts: Harvard University Press, 1976), pp. 100-101.

[76] *II Samuel* 20:1.

[77] *II Samuel* 20:2.

[78] *II Samuel* 12:28.

[79] *II Samuel* 2-4.

[80] *II Samuel* 19:5-8.

[81] *II Samuel* 20:10.

[82] *II Samuel* 21:15-17.

[83] Compare, for example, Numbers 26 with *II Samuel* 24.

[84] Carol Meyers, "David as Temple Builder," in Patrick D. Miller, Jr., Paul D. Hanson, and S. Dean McBride, eds., *Ancient Israelite Religion* (Philadelphia: Fortress Press, 1987), pp. 357-76.

[85] Nehama Leibowitz, *Studies in Bamidbar (Numbers)*, translated and adapted by Aryeh Newman (Jerusalem: The World Zionist Organization, 1980), pp. 21-22.

[86] Tryggve N.D. Mettinger, *Solomonic State Officials: A Study of the Civil Government Officials of the Israelite Monarchy* (Lund: CWK Gleerup, 1971), p. 121.

[87] *I Kings* 1:32-40.

[88] *I Kings* 1:49-53.

[89] *I Kings* 1:4.

[90] *II Samuel* 23:1-7.

[91] *I Kings* 2:1-9.

[92] *I Kings* 2:17-25.

[93] Yohanan Aharoni, *The Land of the Bible: A Historical Geography* (Philadelphia: Westminster Press, 1979), pp. 5, 21, 42.

[94] *Judges*, 20, 21.

[95] *I Samuel* 11:8.

[96] *I Samuel* 15:4.

[97] Yohanan Aharoni, *Carta Atlas of the Biblical Period* (Jerusalem: Carta, 1974), Hebrew, Map 90.

[98] A. D. H. Hayes, "The Period of the Judges and the Rise of the Monarchy," in John H. Hayes and J. Maxwell Miller, eds., *Israelite and Judaean History* (London: SCM Press Ltd., 1977), pp. 285-331.

[99] During the time of David, the Book of Second Samuel (24:9) records 800,000 Israelite warriors among the people of Israel, and 500,000 among those of Judah. It is written in Second Chronicles that Solomon used a similar mode of recording and found 153,600 strangers in his kingdom (2:17). This reading of the ancient census assumes a constancy of biblical usage, whereby the "warriors" counted by David would have been Israelite adult males, and the "strangers" counted by Solomon would have been non-Israelite adult males. The proportions derived from these figures, overlooking the unknown time differences between the two censuses, indicate that Israelites were 89 percent of the population.

[100] Herrmann, *A History*, p. 148; and Albrecht Alt, "The Formation of the Israelite State in Palestine" and "The Monarchy in Israel and Judah," in his *Essays on Old Testament History and Religion*.

[101] *I Kings* 12:1-15.

[102] *II Samuel* 22:2.

[103] *II Samuel* 23:3-4.

[104] *I Samuel* 23:2-5; 11-12.

[105] *II Samuel* 5:23.

[106] *II Samuel* 6.

[107] *II Samuel* 7:7.

[108] *I Chronicles* 22:8.

[109] Carol Meyers.

[110] *I Chronicles* 28:11-19.

[111] *I Chronicles* 29:6-8.

[112] *I Chronicles* 29:2-4.

[113] *II Samuel* 5:21.

[114] *I Chronicles* 14:12.

[115] *I Chronicles* 15:25-29.

[116] *I Chronicles* 16:37-42.

[117] *II Samuel* 24:1.

[118] *I Chronicles* 21:1.

[119] Louis Ginzberg, *Legends of the Jews* (New York: Simon and Schuster, 1956), pp. 545-46.

Chapter 5
Jeremiah: A Political Prophet

Along with Moses and Samuel, Jeremiah was among the most political of the prophets. He was also one of the most detailed characters in the Hebrew Bible. He was extreme in both the style and the substance of his prophecy. He threatened kings, priests and competing prophets with the end of their regime and urged capitulation in the face of a foreign army. His career occurred in a geopolitical setting that was among the most ominous in a national history that typically was under pressure. He gave vent to some of the most desperate and plaintive expressions of being trapped in a role that was unwanted. He was beset with intense adversaries on several occasions and hounded almost to death. Yet he also had well-placed supporters. There is no indication that he ever succeeded in changing the behaviors of elites or the people. However, he persisted in his intense public criticism of political leaders despite the national emergency and surpassed what modern democracies have allowed to critics when they have been under stress.

This chapter is directed at identifying the important features of Jeremiah's surroundings and the political significance of his prophecy. Like material considered in previous chapters, that dealing with Jeremiah raises complex issues about the biblical polities and leaves them unresolved. The sharpness of Jeremiah's criticism more clearly than other biblical material legitimizes political dissent about the most basic issues of regime policy, at a time when the regime is threatened by invasion. Yet his style seems guaranteed to fail in the world of politics. The text proclaims his demands with a shrillness that brooks no tolerance of competing prophets. There is no pondering of norms from a perspective of skepticism as shall be apparent in the next chapter's discussion of *Ecclesiastes*.

Jeremiah succeeded in finding supporters even while he failed to affect officials' actions. The questions of who determines policies and what determines political support are there in Jeremiah for a modern reader to ponder as well as the question of how such a misfit in politics could win such a venerated place in the Books of the Lord. A reader of Jeremiah is reminded of modern Israelis who scream their criticisms of one another on such issues as the definition of a Jew, the sale of non-kosher meat, the proper observance of the Sabbath, and what concessions should be made to the Palestinians or other adversaries.

Another provocative issue concerns the prophet's silence about King Josiah. Elsewhere in the Bible, Josiah is described as one of the Israelites' greatest kings. Jeremiah was a contemporary but offers no explicit judgment about Josiah's reign. Should this silence be read along with some passages in *Chronicles* that are critical of Josiah. If so, then Jeremiah offers some lessons in political judgment with respect to Josiah to parallel those in the material on David: even great leaders are not simply to be venerated but to be judged in detail according to their actions.

THE HISTORICAL AND GEOPOLITICAL SETTING

Jeremiah was not only a prophet of the Lord. He was also a man anchored in time and space. Jeremiah's period is less mythic than those of Moses or David. The prophet lived when portions of the Bible were already written, and his own book describes the writing of his prophecies. In contrast with the periods of Moses and David, there are sources from the archives of other regimes which substantiate key points in the biblical record.

Jeremiah's nation was small, poor, weak militarily, and located in a place that was important to the greater powers. During his era it was subject even more than usual to the actions of great powers. Egyptian and Mesopotamian regimes competed for dominance. Assyria had recently collapsed, but Judah had few advantages in the power vacuum that resulted.

> Assyria's crash was not to bring peace to Judah. . . the Babylonians . . . and the Egyptians . . . both had their eye on erstwhile Assyrian holdings west of the Euphrates. And between the upper and nether mill-

stones of their rival ambitions Judah was caught and crushed.[1]

During Jeremiah's youth there had been a spurt of religious revival and a hope for national autonomy and expansion. *Kings* and *Chronicles* praise Josiah's reign (639-609) for religious observances in contrast to previous reigns of Manasseh (696-642) and Amon (641-640) that were marked by the royal propagation of foreign cults. Josiah's period was also a time of national opportunity. As the Assyrian empire weakened and eventually collapsed, Josiah encroached on the population and the territory that had been the northern kingdom of Israel until the Assyrian conquest of 722. Egypt also coveted the spoils of the Assyrian empire. Josiah was killed at Megiddo in what *II Chronicles* describes as an ill-advised military campaign against the Egyptians.[2]

The Egyptians did not rest with putting an end to Josiah's ideas of expansion. They intervened in Jerusalem by unseating Josiah's son, Jehoahaz, who had been chosen to replace Josiah. They removed Jehoahaz to Egypt and chose his brother Jehoiakim as Judah's king. The Egyptians also fined Judah 100 talents of silver and one talent of gold.[3] A commentator reads the biblical text to indicate that Jehoiakim might have been older than Jehoahaz. Insofar as Judean elites had passed over Jehoiakim and chose the younger brother as king when Josiah was killed, it would appear that Jehoiakim was not viewed as the best royal material.[4] Nonetheless, Jehoiakim became Egypt's man on the throne of Judah.

For much of the next ten fateful years, Jehoiakim led a pro-Egypt party in the court of Jerusalem. Jehoiakim departed from his pro-Egyptian posture for a period after Babylon's defeat of Egypt at Carchemish in 605 or perhaps after Babylon's sacking of Ashkelon in 604. Yet he owed his crown to an Egyptian intervention, and Egypt was the closer of the two great powers. A modern scholar concludes that troops could reach Jerusalem from Egypt after a march of 15 days while Babylonian troops were 75 days' distance.[5] Babylon was stronger, however, and intent on holding Judah. Its conquest of Jerusalem in 597 seems to have been provoked by Jehoiakim's withholding of payments, perhaps in response to a Babylonian setback at Egyptian hands in 601.[6]

Jehoiakim's regime was also one of economic pressure. Both the Egyptians and the Babylonians demanded payments. According to Jeremiah, Jehoiakim exploited his own people by forcing them to work on the expansion of his palace without compensation (22:13-14).

Jehoiakim died or was killed at about the time of the conquest in 598 or 597. Babylon took Jehoiakim's successor Jehoiachin (or Jeconiah) to exile and appointed Zedekiah to rule in Judah. Even though the Babylonians chose Zedekiah, he, too, proved unable to resist Egyptian overtures and pro-Egyptian sentiments in his court. Commentators agree in depicting Zedekiah as weak and vacillating. Some explain his problems as reflecting his doubtful status. The exiled Jehoiachin may still have been viewed as king, with Zedekiah only a regent.[7]

Details of Zedekiah's rebellion with respect to Babylon are not known with certainty. However, the Babylonians invaded Judah and imposed a siege on Jerusalem in 588. The Egyptians made a move to help, which caused a lifting of the siege. The Egyptian assistance proved to be only temporary. Babylon destroyed Jerusalem in 586 and ended all semblance of Judean independence.

Jeremiah lived in a monarchical regime whose institutions are not well documented. There is no indication that the kings of Judah were bound by domestic councils in the way of modern constitutional monarchs. On occasion they permitted criticism and allowed disputes among officers of the court. There were precedents of severe criticism from individuals who asserted that they spoke the words of God. However, there are also biblical stories of anti-regime prophets being hounded or killed by the kings of Israel and Judah.

Reflecting its place toward the end of Israelite prophecy, Jeremiah's book shows stylistic traces and the themes of earlier prophets and other episodes in the Hebrew Bible. Jeremiah's self-doubt resembled that of Moses but in a more extreme fashion: Jeremiah cursed himself and God in ways that exceeded Moses' concern for his own fitness. Jeremiah's fruitless quest for one just and honest man in Jerusalem (5:1) recalled the Lord's negotiations with Abraham over the destruction of Sodom.[8] Jeremiah's persistent concern with the activities of the kings and other elites suggests an aspiration to be a king maker or king deposer like Samuel or at least an advisor and chastiser like Nathan. There is criticism of social injustice that recalls Amos. Jeremiah's prominent concern with idolatry and syncretism and his use of harlotry as a metaphor are in the style of Hosea. Jeremiah's promise of a rebuilt Israel and Judah, together with a new and permanent covenant to be written on the hearts of the people, recalls the visions of Isaiah. His bizarre behavior in putting a yoke upon his shoulders reminds a reader of Isaiah's walking naked in public.[9]

There are also passages that resemble sections of books that may have been written later than Jeremiah. His plaintive query "Why do the wicked prosper and traitors live at ease?" (12:1) suggests a central theme in the *Book of Job*. A passage about neighbors who "learn the ways of my people" and "form families among my people" (12:16) rings like the openness to converts in the *Book of Ruth*.

There are problems with *Jeremiah* familiar to biblical scholars. The book illustrates the complaint of Martin Luther that the prophetic books "maintain no kind of order but leap from one matter to another so that a man can neither understand nor endure it."[10] The author(s) or editor(s) seemed oblivious to issues of historical chronology. The text jumps back and forth over a career 40 years in duration with abrupt changes of subject and then a return to previous themes. By one view, there were four separate periods of prophecy, separated by periods when Jeremiah was prevented from expressing himself or otherwise occupied.[11] Scholars of different perspectives agree in finding traces of several hands in the book but disagree as to how many. There are claims of three or five literary strata and an accretion of numerous oral traditions.[12] An obvious problem lies in the book's inclusion of details that may have occurred 17 years after the prophet ceased to express himself (52:31-34). The following chronology of Jeremiah's work and its historical context combines the major historical events of the prophet's era with those points of his prophecy that can be dated by explicit comments in the biblical text. The lack of sequence in the biblical citations included with the chronology documents the non-chronological character of the text.

The *Book of Jeremiah* alludes to historical events that are not fully specified and prophecies that cannot be dated and linked to events. (What is the source of the disaster brought from the north in 4:6? Or the distant land from which come the hordes of invaders in 4:16?) In adjacent passages the God who speaks through Jeremiah cannot seem to decide whether his people's punishment is subject to cancellation if they repent (22:4), or if the verdict is final (22:6).[13] There are statements at odds with Judaic doctrines: that man's ways are not of his own choosing (10:23) and that the Lord has made a woman behave like a man (31:22).[14]

As in the case of other biblical characters, there is an endless but futile search among scholars for the *real* prophet. According to one specialist, "There is a great deal of silliness written about Jeremiah."[15] Academics seek to clarify when was he born, when he began his prophecy, and what portions of the book can be attributed to him, to his scribe Baruch, or to later writers and editors.[16] The prophet's despondent laments about his own inadequacy and the injustice of his suffering on account of God's call to prophecy (i.e., his jeremiads) have led some to call him a man of "small vision and narrow self-centeredness" or marked by psychological disorder. The same passages are also interpreted as the cries of a distressed community expressed through the corporate symbol of the prophet.[17]

A puzzle that has political relevance concerns the prophet's relation with King Josiah. Josiah reigned during the period 639-09 and is credited with initiating a religious revival. Jeremiah 1:2 says that

---

Chronology: Jeremiah's Work and Its Historical Context*

639 B.C.E	Josiah began his reign.
626	Jeremiah received the word of the Lord (1:2).
609-08	Death of Josiah; Jehoahaz II put on throne by Judeans but removed by Egyptians and replaced by Jehoiakim; Jeremiah ordered by God to stand in the Temple court and tell the people that they have a chance to repent, but that God will destroy them if they do not change their ways; as a result the priests, prophets, and the people seized Jeremiah and threatened him with death; Jeremiah was defended by other officers who cited the precedent of Micah who had prophesied Jerusalem's destruction, but was not put to death by King Hezekiah; Uriah put to death by Jehoiakim; Ahikam son of Shaphan used his influence to save Jeremiah (26:1-24).

605 Battle of Carchemish; Jehoiakim became Babylonian vassal; after three years, according to *II Kings* 24:1, he broke with Babylon.

604 Jeremiah reported the Lord's anger; his intention to destroy via the Babylonians but to punish the Babylonians 70 years later (25:1-14).

604-03 Jeremiah dictated scroll to Baruch for reading in the Temple (which Jeremiah was forbidden to enter) concerning the calamity the Lord was planning; on the advice of officers, including Gemariah son of Shaphan, Jeremiah and Baruch went into hiding; King Jehoiakim sent for Jeremiah's scroll, burnt it as it was read to him, and ordered that Jeremiah and Baruch be found (36).

Lord instructs Jeremiah to dictate prophecy of destruction of the whole world (45).

598-97 Death of Jehoiakim; brief reign of King Jehoiachin (Jeconiah); invasion by Babylon, resulting in exile of Jehoiachin, members of his court and others; Zedekiah made king; Jeremiah told the story of the good and bad figs as symbols of the exiles and those who remain in the land (24:1-10).

597 Envoys from Edom, Moab, Ammon, Tyre, and Sidon met with Zedekiah, seemingly to consider acts of resistance to Babylon (27:1-3) Jeremiah put on an ox yoke and reported the Lord's assertion that the nations must submit to Babylon's yoke; confrontation between Hananiah and Jeremiah on the issue of optimistic vs. pessimistic prophecy; Hananiah broke the yoke of wood; Jeremiah replaced it with a yoke of iron and predicted Hananiah's death within a year; Hananiah died within seven months (28).

588-86 During siege of Jerusalem Zedekiah imprisoned Jeremiah for prophesying defeat and capture of the king (32:2-5); Jeremiah bought plot of land at Anathoth as a symbol of his faith in God's promise for the future; prophesied that God will punish Judah for idolatry via Babylon, but will later restore Judah's fortunes (32) as well as those of the previously destroyed Kingdom of Israel; also that David will never lack a successor on the throne (33); Jeremiah predicted Zedekiah will be captured but will die a peaceful death (34:4); Jeremiah expressed criticism of Jerusalem elites who released slaves during an early phase of Babylon's siege and then re-enslaved them when the siege was lifted; despite the lifting of the siege, he prophesied that the Lord will bring back the Babylonians to destroy the city (34:16-22).

During lifting of siege, Jeremiah left Jerusalem to claim his land; he was arrested for going over to Babylonians; he was flogged and imprisoned (37:11-16); Zedekiah intervened to improve conditions of his confinement (37:21).

During the siege, a group of officers reported to the King that Jeremiah was weakening the resolve of the people and the soldiers and must be put to death; King Zedekiah allowed them to do with Jeremiah as they wish; they threw Jeremiah into a muddy pit where he seemed likely to die, but a Cushite eunuch appealed to the King in Jeremiah's behalf; Zedekiah spoke to Jeremiah, promised him protection, heard Jeremiah's warning that he will be captured if he does not surrender; King expressed his fear and ambivalence and warned that his own officers should not hear details of this conversation with Jeremiah (38).

Siege of Jerusalem lasted one year and seven months (39:1); Zedekiah captured, blinded, and taken to Babylon; Jeremiah handed over to Gedaliah, the grandson of Shaphan, who extended to him protection from enemies (39); after a period of time that is not made clear, Gedaliah assassinated (41:2), and Jeremiah taken to Egypt by a group who challenged Jeremiah's prophecies against the migration to Egypt (42:1-43:7)

560 Jehoiachin brought out of prison and lived as pensioner of King of Babylon (52:31-34)

* Periods given for incidents of Jeremiah's prophecy reflect specific occurrences mentioned in the biblical text. Josiah's reign.

---

the prophet received the word of God during the thirteenth year of Josiah's reign. However, none of his prophecies are clearly dated prior to Josiah's death.

Richard Elliott Friedman reasons that Jeremiah was a supporter of Josiah and edited the books of Deuteronomy through Kings in order to highlight the virtues of Josiah's reign.[18] Friedman also proposes that Jeremiah viewed himself as a priest in the Mosaic, as opposed to Aaronic, line and that important issues of biblical interpretation can be explained by viewing textual composition and editing as reflecting a factional dispute between different groups of priests who sought to enhance their own status by casting a favorable light on their ancestors.

Friedman's work is exciting in proposing an integrated, political view of biblical composition. Insofar as it turns on Jeremiah's affinity to Josiah, however, it is problematic. One passage in the *Book of Jeremiah* seems to call on the people not to weep for the dead Josiah but for his son Shallum (Jehoahaz) who was taken away to Egypt (22:10-12). Other passages can be read as the prophet's criticism of Josiah's reform: that it led the people to superficial observances rather than true righteousness and provided a false sense of security which had to be replaced with an awareness of the Lord's threats (6:13; 8:10-11).[19] According to some commentators, Jeremiah's criticism about playing politics with Egypt and Assyria (2:18) were directed against Josiah.[20] A positive comment about Josiah in the *Book of Jeremiah* can be described as condemnation via faint praise. Josiah appears to be the "father" in the following: "Did not thy father eat and drink, and do justice and righteousness? Then it was well with him. He judged the cause of the poor and needy; Then it was well (22:15- 16)." More glowing comments in the *Book of Lamentations* said to be Jeremiah's eulogy for Josiah (4:1,20) are not clearly directed at Josiah and are not clearly the work of Jeremiah.

Numerous scholars have noted the lack of explicit comments in the *Book of Jeremiah* about Josiah's reforms. This may be due to the failure of Josiah's reforms to succeed in their goals of centralizing cultic practice in Jerusalem and ridding the country of idolatry. It may be due to Jeremiah's perception that the reforms led Judean elites to be overly confidant in the protection of the Lord, against his own assertions that they must behave righteously or suffer Jerusalem's destruction. Or Jeremiah's silence about Josiah may reflect the lack of any clear indication that the prophet and the king ever met.[21]

The earliest major incident of Jeremiah's prophecy that is dated by the biblical text occurred in 610-609 after Josiah's death. Jeremiah preached in the Temple court that the people had a chance to repent but that God would destroy them if they did not change their ways (26:1-6). It may have been then that Jeremiah idealized the relationship between Israelites and God during the Exodus and the period in the wilderness, overlooking incidents of complaint and rebellion: "I remember the unfailing devotion of your youth, the love of your bridal days, when you followed me in the wilderness" (2:2).

PRINCIPAL LINES OF JEREMIAH'S PROPHECY

Commentaries on religious doctrine would call attention to Jeremiah's concern with idolatry, lewdness, harlotry, adultery, astrology, and human sacrifice. It is appropriate for a political analysis to focus on his persistent efforts to influence the kings and other elites, his quarrels with competing prophets and other court figures, his extreme actions in advocating opposition to the regime and its policies, to the point of being viewed by various commentators as a traitor, collaborator, and fifth columnist,[22] his lack of success in influencing policy, and his refusal to be silenced by those who were intent on ending his career.

A prominent theme of Jeremiah's political prophecy is his criticism of the court's policy to favor a commitment to Egypt rather than Babylon. Jeremiah perceived that Babylon was the coming power and that Judah had better align itself with the winner. Jeremiah also cursed Jehoiakim and his court for violating the laws of God with pagan observance. While there is no indication that Egypt promoted syncretism in Judah, there is also no indication that Josiah's cultic reforms were successful.[23] Thus, it might have been easy for Jehoiakim to revert to the customary tolerance of Judean kings for foreign cults and even to join in the observances.

Jeremiah called shame on King Jehoiakim and prophesied the destruction of his court for social injustice, the shedding of innocent blood, and cruel acts of tyranny (22:13-17). It was Jehoiakim who cut up the scroll containing Jeremiah's prophecy of Judah's destruction, fed the pieces into the fire, and ordered that Jeremiah and Baruch be arrested (36:21-26). The king had already killed Uriah for uttering similar prophecies, so Jeremiah and his scribe had been advised to go into hiding.

Jeremiah's prophecies against the regime of Zedekiah were no less harsh. However, that king was at least ambivalent toward Jeremiah. He alternately acquiesced in the demands of courtiers to silence Jeremiah and called the prophet to the palace in order to speak with him directly and lighten the terms of his confinement. On no occasion did Zedekiah accept the demands for policy changes that Jeremiah said would save him and his regime.

A political analyst might question Jeremiah's severe criticism of prophets who said that Jerusalem was secure or who urged a foreign policy accommodating Egypt rather than Babylon. There is no indication other than Jeremiah's accusations that other prophets were insincere in claiming to report the Lord's word or that they were entirely off the mark in their assessment of Judah's international options. Their prophecies were inherently more attractive than Jeremiah's in promising God's protection; they were in keeping with the tradition that Jerusalem was inviolable, and they were suitable with respect to one geopolitical reality: Egyptian forces were closer to Jerusalem than those of Babylon.

Jeremiah might have reached his pro-Babylonian position on account of a deep-seated antagonism toward Egypt as the country that earlier had enslaved God's people. Or he might have reacted against the regime that killed King Josiah and then put the abominable Jehoiakim on Judah's throne. As a prophet of the Lord, Jeremiah might have seen himself as inspired to see the course of foreign policy most likely to save God's people and their holy city. He was correct in perceiving Babylon as the ascendant power that would destroy the Judean regime if Judah did not honor its obligations as a vassal. Perhaps his claim of hearing from the Lord was employed to legitimate his assessment of Babylon's greater power and greater inclination to use that power in Judah.

Modern commentators assert that Jeremiah was no political scientist but a prophet who proclaimed what he perceived as God's plan.[24] The prophet might seem to deserve praise for a savvy assessment of international politics. Yet we should recall that the details of the prophet's demands with respect to foreign policy that we read in the *Book of Jeremiah* were all compiled and edited after the fact, when Babylon had already demonstrated its intentions and capacity and Egypt its weakness or lack of resolve. We do not know what the prophet actually thought or said before the destruction of Jerusalem.

A number of episodes and expressions point to the extreme fashion of Jeremiah's prophecy. He proclaimed that not a single honest and just man could be found in Jerusalem and that each generation was more evil than the last (7:25-27). Destruction will be complete and ugly.

> (The Lord said that I). . . will make Jerusalem heaps, a lair of jackals . . . the cities of Judah a desolation, without an inhabitant (9:10) . . . (Jerusalem will be) an astonishment, and a hissing; every one that passeth thereby shall be astonished and hiss because of all the plagues thereof . . . (the city's residents will) eat the flesh of their sons . . (19:8-9) . . . (the Lord) will give all Judah into the hand of the king of Babylon, and he shall carry them captive to Babylon, and shall slay them with the sword. . . all the treasures of the kings of Judah . . .(they) shall . . . carry them to Babylon (20:4-5).

Jeremiah was also extreme in promising redemption after disaster.

> I will make a new covenant . . .I will set my law within them and write it on their hearts . . . No longer need they teach one another to know the Lord; all of them, high and low alike, shall know me . . . I will forgive their wrongdoing and remember their sin no more (31:31-34).

Jeremiah confronted the emissaries of foreign kings dressed in an ox's yoke to symbolize his prophecy that they and Judah must accept the rule of Babylon. On one occasion Jeremiah was said to be a madman posing as a prophet of the Lord (29:26-27). During the final siege of Jerusalem he was charged with weakening the resolve of the soldiers and the people by urging their surrender (38:2-4). He continued in his bizarre performances even after he failed to avert the destruction of Judah and was taken to Egypt. He claimed to be instructed by the Lord to erect barricades at the entrance to the Pharaoh's palace (it is not said that he succeeded in this action) and to proclaim the destruction of Egypt and the temples of its gods (44:8-13).

The prophet seems to have been a chronic disputant, impelled to conflict regardless of his adversaries' postures, their motives, or the reasoning by which they reached their postures. There is no indication that he ever responded to the assertions of others or that he accommodated criticism or advice. He preached rather than argued. He proclaimed his own positions and cursed opponents. Perhaps his claim of being a prophet and hearing the words of the Lord saved him from the need to converse, discuss, and adjust in the manner of ordinary mortals. He expressed doubts about his capacity to carry the Lord's word and to stand up to his adversaries but not about the substance of what he presented as the Lord's message.

Jeremiah did not mention prominent prophets whose periods overlapped with his (Zephaniah, Nahum, Habakkuk, and Ezekiel),[25] and he had no praise for Uriah, who was killed by Jehoiakim for uttering prophecies similar to his own (26:20-24). More than other prophets, Jeremiah railed against competitors for falsely claiming to speak the word of the Lord. He grouped other prophets together with priests and scribes as liars, frauds, adulterers, and hypocrites. Jeremiah's special wrath seemed directed at those prophets who promised the Lord's protection for Jerusalem or urged adherence to Egypt against Babylon. Jeremiah predicted Hananiah's death within one year and may have enjoyed the news that Hananiah died within seven months (28:16-17). About the prophets Ahab and Zedekiah, Jeremiah condemned their names to be used as curses by the Judeans after their deaths at the hands of the Babylonians (29:21-23).

The traumatic events of Jeremiah's youth might have contributed to his style. The Assyrian empire had been dealt a heavy blow after having been a dominant regional power for centuries. The reign of Josiah held out the promise of religious revival and national resurgence and then failed to achieve both aspirations. Jehoiakim was put on the throne by Egypt, then badgered between Egypt and Babylon externally and between Judean elites who supported alignment with one or the other internally . Paganism competed with God's law. It was not a time that invited moderation. Jeremiah was not simply a participant in policy disputes but a sharp-tongued and bizarre protagonist who claimed to be speaking for the Almighty.

Jeremiah was also extreme in the vengeance that he proclaimed on Babylon. The country that was said to be doing God's will by destroying Jerusalem and Judah would itself be destroyed for its deeds. While Israel would be punished but not made an end of (46:28), Babylon would be destroyed with no survivors (50:17,26-27). Babylon must fall for the sake of Israel's having fallen (51:49). The severity of punishment decreed for Babylon appears out of keeping both in the context of Jeremiah's earlier support for the Babylonian camp in the court of Jerusalem and his assertion that the destruction of Jerusalem was a mission given to Babylon by God.

Jeremiah seemed to fail at every one of his efforts to intervene with policymakers or the people. Judah continued unto its destruction in its idolatry and other sins and its refusal to accept a vassal's status under Babylon. The prophet was extreme in his self-doubts. He cursed his birth (20:14-18), accused God of having forsaken him and causing that he be reproached, outwitted, and mocked (20:7-8).

Time and again Jeremiah managed to survive the efforts of the mob or the political elite to silence him. There were periods when he was forbidden to prophesy in public. On some of these occasions, he evaded the restrictions by sending Baruch to read his messages. King Jehoiakim sought to arrest Jeremiah, but a group of officers had anticipated the king's anger and urged Jeremiah and Baruch to hide (36:19).

The prophet was in and out of trouble several times during Zedekiah's reign. Once he was arrested as a traitor when he tried to leave the city and was flogged and imprisoned (37:11-16). When Jeremiah was accused of weakening the resolve of the soldiers, the king first acceded to the wishes of officers who seemed intent on killing the prophet but later responded to the request of another official that Jeremiah be saved. The vacillating king then sought the counsel of Jeremiah but asked the prophet not to reveal the details of their conversation. The king told Jeremiah that the silence was to save the prophet, but the king may have feared for his own life against the possibility of a *coup d'etat* (38:14-28).

This episode is one of those in the Bible that expresses ambivalence with respect to the role of prophets in relation to the political elite. The prophet spoke out against a major policy (paying tribute to Egypt rather than Babylon) and even urged soldiers to abandon their positions at a time of crisis. The prophet did not succeed in changing the policy of the king, but the king offered him protection against those who wanted him killed as a traitor. It recalls the story in *I Kings* about a confrontation between Ahab and the prophet Micaiah.

Micaiah is a minor character in the Hebrew Bible. He appears in one episode of *Kings* that is repeated in *Chronicles*.[26] The story begins when Jehoshaphat, the king of Judah, visits Ahab king of Israel in order to consider a joint military expedition. The kings consult 400 court employed prophets who respond as synchophants: "Go up; for the Lord shall deliver it into the hand of the king."[27]

Jehoshaphat was not satisfied, and he asked Ahab if there was not another prophet they might consult. Ahab responded in a way to indicate that there was another prophet but not one who was endeared to the court: "There is yet one man, Micaiah the son of Imlah, by whom we may inquire of the Lord: but I hate him; for he doth not prophesy good concerning me, but evil."[28] Micaiah was no fool. His first response to the kings was similar to that of the court prophets. But when pressed by Ahab, he offered a prophecy of disaster: "I saw all Israel scattered upon the hills, as sheep that have not a shepherd: and the Lord said, These have no master: let them return every man to his house in peace."[29] Micaiah went on to say that the Lord had sent an evil spirit to deceive the other prophets who had supported the king's war plans.

At this point the episode resembles that involving Jeremiah and Zedekiah. King Ahab does not take the advice of the distasteful prophet, but neither does he liquidate him. Rather, he orders that Micaiah be put in prison and fed on bread and water "until I come in peace."[30] The prophet's final words were defiant. "If thou return at all in peace, the Lord hath not spoken by me."[31] We read no more about Micaiah, but Ahab is killed in the battle.

On the one hand, the stories of Micaiah and Jeremiah show the problems in standing up to the political elite. On the other hand, they show the protected status of individuals considered to be prophets of the Lord. In regimes that existed long before the modern developments of freedom of speech and other civil rights, these prophets escaped with their lives.

Jeremiah was not alone in opposing the Egyptian option. The family of Shaphan seemed to be at the core of a pro-Babylonian party and supported the prophet. Shaphan had been a ranking aide of Josiah and was instrumental in his religious revival.[32] Shaphan's son Ahikam used his influence to save Jeremiah on one of the occasions when the prophet was threatened; he was among a group of court officers who argued that Jeremiah should not be punished because the prophet Micah had not been punished by King Hezekiah despite having prophesied the destruction of Jerusalem (26:17-24). On another occasion, Shaphan's son Gemariah was among those who advised Jeremiah and Baruch to hide from Jehoiakim (36:12-19). Another son of Shaphan, Elasah, conveyed a letter from Jeremiah to the exiles in Babylon, which urged them to build houses and seek the welfare of their place (29:3-7). Shaphan's grandson, Ahikam's son Gedaliah, was appointed by the Babylonians to take charge of Judah after the conquest of 586 (40:50) and to protect Jeremiah (39:14). Gedaliah was killed by a member of the Davidic family. Then Jeremiah failed to persuade a group of Judeans to stay in the land and not to go to Egypt. This was the prophet's last in a long line of failures to convince people who were set on a contrary course. There seemed to be no one who could save the prophet from his antagonists, and he was taken to Egypt along with Baruch.

JEREMIAH'S POLITICAL LEGACY

There are implications of lasting political value in the *Book of Jeremiah*. As in other biblical material of political significance, however, those in Jeremiah must be inferred on the basis of limited evidence. The text is detailed and time bound and is not explicit in offering general points of political theory.

Jeremiah's career and prophecy reflected Judah's strategic location between empires and a chronic weakness that derived from its poor economy and small population. Unlike modern Israel, Judah had no technological advantages over its neighbors, and it did not enjoy the support of a distant, greater empire. We can only speculate about the subsequent evolution of history if Jeremiah, Jehoiakim, or Zedekiah could have threatened Babylon with nuclear weapons.

The prophet stood firmly against a dominant party in a foreign policy dispute. It appears that most of the relevant elites supported the idea of relying on Egypt. Jeremiah said this would be fatal and urged complying with the demands of Babylon. Events proved Jeremiah to be correct. We can admire Jeremiah for standing against what was prevailing wisdom and politically correct. However, a reader with a preference for persuasion over declaration would prefer more reasoned arguments and fewer curses.

The *Book of Jeremiah* also portrays features of an ancient regime that a modern democrat might admire. Even though democracy or limited government was not institutionalized in terms familiar to us, some Judean elites allowed criticism in the most severe terms under the most trying conditions. Jeremiah's success in getting away with direct criticism of the regime's policy compares well with the record of modern democracies toward dissidents during World Wars I and II and the Cold War.

However, the explanation of the prophet's freedom limits the applicability of his case to modern polities. Jeremiah's claim to be speaking for the Lord provided his protection. The theocratic element in the Judean state and precedents established by earlier prophets provided a basis of authority superior to the kings that could protect a critic who was perceived as a prophet of the Lord.[33]

A modern democrat concerned with free speech is left with several problems that the *Book of Jeremiah* does not solve. In a secular regime, an appeal to God's truth cannot substitute for reasoned argument about public policy. Jeremiah's shrill style would seem to limit rather than facilitate discourse about political controversies. Like Jeremiah, a modern critic must reckon with a severe personal cost for expressing opinions that run counter to popular and elite views. Under conditions of national emergency, a secular advocate of capitulation is likely to be even more defenseless than a recognized prophet of the Lord in ancient Judah.

After the selection of David, God's name is used more often in the Hebrew Bible to ennoble critics of the Israelites' regimes than their kings. The prophets Nathan, Elijah, Amos, Hosea, and Jeremiah are portrayed as speaking the word of God as they chastised or cursed God's people and the figures who were ruling them.

Why was Korah designated a rebel against Moses and not the equivalent of Elijah who prophesied against Ahab and Jezebel? Why did Micaiah and Uriah receive only brief but positive treatments in the *Books of Kings* and *Jeremiah* but did not become the subjects of more thorough reports? Scholars who probe the mysteries of prophecy have no convincing answers. The explanation may be no more complicated than that the prophets who were most successful in history had good luck in directing criticism against regimes that acquired a lasting reputation for waywardness and attracting dedicated disciples who recorded their message in ways that succeeding generations found to be inspired.

NOTES

[1] John Bright, *Jeremiah: The Anchor Bible* (Garden City, N.Y.: Doubleday & Company, 1965), p. xlvi.

[2] *II Chronicles* 35:20-25.

[3] *II Kings* 23:33.

[4] Bright, *Jeremiah*, pp. xcvi-xcvii.

[5] Professor Israel Ephal, "Lamentations," Israel Television, July 30, 1990 (9th of Av).

[6] Bright, *Jeremiah*, p. xlix.

[7] Bright, *Jeremiah*, p. l.

[8] *Genesis* 18:23-33.

[9] *Isaiah* 20:2.

[10] Quoted in Klaus Koch *The Prophets: The Assyrian Period* (Philadelphia: Fortress Press, 1983), p. 165. For a book that is both tantalizing and frustrating in identifying numerous problems of interpretation relevant to Jeremiah and his period, and leaving the reader without hope of a clear resolution of the problems, see Peter R. Ackroyd, *Exile and Restoration: A Study of Hebrew Thought of the Sixth Century BC* (London: SCM Press, Ltd., 1968).

[11] Klaus Koch *The Prophets: The Babylonian and Persian Periods* (Philadelphia: Fortress Press, 1984), pp. 16-17.

[12] Koch, *The Prophets: The Babylonian and Persian Periods*, p. 15; Menachem Bola, Commentator, *The Book of Jeremiah* (Jerusalem: Mossad Harav Kook, 1983), Hebrew, p. 43; and Kathleen M. O'Con-

nor, *The Confessions of Jeremiah: Their Interpretation and Role in Chapters 1-25* (Atlanta: Scholars Press, 1988), pp. 149-54.

[13] See Jeremiah Unterman, *From Repentance to Redemption: Jeremiah's Thought in Transition* (Sheffield: JSOT Press, 1987).

[14] The New English Bible offers an extreme but not entirely untenable translation from the Hebrew in rendering this passage: the Lord has . . . a woman turned into a man.

[15] Walter Brueggemann, "The Book of Jeremiah: Portrait of the Prophet," James Luther Mays and Paul J. Achtemeier, eds., *Interpreting the Prophets* (Philadelphia: Fortress Press, 1987), 113-29.

[16] See, for example, James L. Crenshaw, "A Living Tradition: The Book of Jeremiah in Current Research" in Mays and Achtemeier, pp. 100-12.

[17] O'Connor, "Introduction."

[18] Richard Elliott Friedman, *Who Wrote the Bible?* (New York: Harper & Row, 1987).

[19] John Bright, *A History of Israel* (London: SCM Press Ltd., 1980), p 323.

[20] Bola, p. 27.

[21] Bola, "Introduction." John Bright admits that he is forced to speculate about Jeremiah's view of Josiah and his reforms by virtue of the limited and ambiguous material in Jeremiah's book. However, he finds indications that Jeremiah initially supported the reforms, but came to be disappointed in their results. Bright, *Jeremiah: The Anchor Bible*, pp. lxxxii-lxxxiii.

[22] For these assessments of Jeremiah as they appear in the works of Max Weber and other scholars, see Koch *The Prophets: The Babylonian and Persian Periods*, pp. 60-61.

[23] Bola, "Introduction." See the introduction to Bright's commentary on Jeremiah for a slightly more positive view of the success enjoyed by Josiah's reforms.

[24] Abraham J. Heschel, *The Prophets: An Introduction* (New York: Harper & Row, 1962), p. 138; Brueggemann; and Bright, p. cviii.

[25] Bright, *Jeremiah*, "Introduction."

[26] *I Kings 22* and *II Chronicles 18*.

[27] *I Kings 22:6.*

[28] *I Kings 22:8.*

[29] *I Kings 22:17.*

[30] *I Kings 22:27.*

[31] *I Kings 22:28.*

[32] *II Kings* 22:10-12.

[33] The precedent can also be traced to Moses, who criticized Pharaoh and then allowed himself to be criticized by those who called themselves prophets as told in the episode of Eldad and Medad that appears in *Numbers* 11.

Chapter 6
Job and *Ecclesiastes*: Biblical Outliers

The *Books of Job* and *Ecclesiastes* differ from other portions of the Hebrew Bible that are politically relevant. They deal not with the Israelite people or regime but with the plight of individuals who could be anyone, anywhere. Although not explicitly identified as such, both deal with what may be called problems of the universal person searching for meaning amidst personal chaos or disappointment. Both are classics of ambiguity. These books are also the place to look for indications that the authors and editors of the Bible could tolerate diverse norms that have modern political relevance. And they have other indications that something like *political correctness* prevailed among the same editors.

Neither *Job* nor *Ecclesiastes* escapes the dispute of commentators as to their essential messages. Both *Job* and *Ecclesiastes* can be read as deeply rooted in the biblical norm of faith in the Almighty or as proclaiming the injustice of God and the uncertainty of reward for righteousness and punishment for sin. Neither expresses simple faith like that which appears in Isaiah:[1] "Happy the righteous man! All goes well with him, for such men enjoy the fruit of their actions. . . . Woe betide the wicked! with him all goes ill, for he reaps the reward that he has earned."[2] Or the 37th *Psalm*: "I have been young and am now grown old, and never have I seen a righteous man forsaken."[3]

Both *Job* and *Ecclesiastes* are relevant to a number of political issues. The doubts they raise about the justice and reliability of God question the faith in supreme authority that numerous readers see in the Bible. The skepticism that appears in both books must be taken into consideration by anyone who would argue that the Hebrew Bible counsels blind faith in divine or worldly authority. *Ecclesiastes* is explicit in expressing distrust of government. *Job* suggests that God himself can lack self-confidence, be deceitful, and answer a reasonable complaint with bombast that has nothing to do with the matter at issue. As will be noted below, it is possible to see ridicule of the Almighty in the Bible's description of Job's encounter with him!

Job is ostensibly set in the land of Uz, and *Ecclesiastes* (*Kohelet* in Hebrew, which can be translated as Preacher) claims to be the work of King Solomon. Neither of these assertions are taken seriously by modern secular commentators. Both books appear to be written by Israelites (or Judeans or Jews) although some scholars question this with respect to *Job*. While some conclude that most of each book is the work of one writer, others find evidence of numerous editorial insertions.

Both books are problematic. They do not present their ideas in a straightforward, systematic manner. The essence of *Job* is a series of dialogues set within a story about Job's misfortunes. The speakers talk past one another. The stages of the dialogue do not clearly relate to what has preceded or will follow. *Ecclesiastes* is an essay that includes personal advice resembling the *Book of Proverbs*, as well as observations about God and human life. Both books include allusions whose objects are unclear as well as various assertions that seem to qualify or contradict one another.

THE *BOOK OF JOB*

The Prologue of *Job* is important for the messages that a reader might take from the book. It establishes that Job is a blameless, upright, and God-fearing man and that he is subject to an experiment between God and Satan that tests Job's faith under conditions of severe deprivation. This setting defines the truth of Job's persistent claim that he is innocent of wrongdoing. The Prologue also indicates something about God, whose importance ranges beyond the story of Job. God's omnipotence and omniscience seem compromised by his willingness to test his certainty about Job against the allegation of Satan.[4] The story also provides one of the most striking instances in the Hebrew Bible that can be cited as a case of God's injustice. God allows Job to be subject to the most extreme suffering, including the death of his children, for no reason other than to settle a dispute with Satan. The suffering of the children who die presents its own problem, perhaps even more severe than the suffering of Job.[5]

There were two experiments to test Job's faith. The first involved the loss of Job's children and his possessions and did not shake his faith. It resulted in his affirmation that became part of the Hebrew burial service: " The Lord gives and the Lord takes away; blessed be the name of the Lord."[6] The second experiment touched Job even more directly with bodily suffering. It left him with miserable sores, sitting on a pile of ashes scratching himself with a piece of broken pottery. On the basis of the subsequent dialogues an umpire of the dispute between God and Satan might conclude that this experiment brought Job to question his faith if not to renounce it.

Job found the challenge to his faith more severe by the lack of support from his wife and friends. His wife told him to give up his faith and his life: "Are you still unshaken in your innocence? Curse God and die."[7] The three participants in Job's dialogues provide the biblical demonstration of the epigram: With friends like those, Job did not need enemies. They were the challengers and foils for Job's claims of his innocence and his outbursts against God's injustice.

There are three cycles of speeches and responses involving Job and his protagonists. Each speech is a monologue. They lack the give and take of genuine conversation. The protagonists assert that Job's losses must reflect his faults. They said

- God is just, and oversees a system of reward for good deeds and punishment for bad[8]
- man cannot be more righteous than God[9]
- Job's trouble cannot come from nothing[10]
- Job should rely on God, and ask his mercy[11]
- God cannot be unjust; perhaps the children of Job sinned[12]
- God is just; he is likely to have extracted less punishment from Job than warranted by Job's sins[13]
- God is inscrutable; Job cannot fathom his mystery[14]
- Job is arrogant for claiming to be innocent when his punishments indicate his guilt[15]
- why should God punish Job if he is righteous? Job must have done something[16]

In his statements to the three friends, Job expresses despair and rages at God in a way that belies the traditional assertion that Job is a model of resolute patience.[17] Patience may be an apt label for the Job who responded with a statement of faith to the first testing of God and Satan but not for the Job of the dialogues that followed the second test.

Job demanded to know what he had done to deserve his punishment.[18] He challenged God to say why he had become his target.[19] Job would not be silenced but would speak his mind.[20] He recognized that he could not win an argument against God because God would not answer him.[21] He wished for a neutral referee or a judge who would listen to his case against God in a court.[22] Job suffered because God mocked his innocence.[23] Job asked if God was gaining an advantage from oppressing him.[24]

Job complained not only about the loss of possessions and his health. He also railed against the unanswerable challenges to his integrity. He could not prove his claim of innocence without the assent of God. His friends did not believe him, and he was wretched without the comfort of those close to him.[25]

Job asserted that many wicked men go unpunished.[26] He knew that death is the end of life for both the successful man and the failure.[27] He did not expect a reward after death. He demanded that God punish sinners themselves and not visit their punishment on their sons.[28]

Now and then Job expressed faith in the midst of his rage. God would not let the ignorant (i.e., Job's friends) triumph.[29] In spite of all, Job felt that a righteous man who maintains his course would grow strong again.[30] He knew that a fair judge would defend and vindicate him.[31] He feared God yet refused to silence his criticism of him.[32] He swore by God (not an action to be taken lightly in Israelite culture) that he was innocent, did not lie, and that God had denied him justice.[33]

Chapter 28 is said to be a poem about wisdom. Commentators have described it both as part of Job's speeches and as an insertion made by a later editor that does not mesh with the surrounding text.[34] The chapter fits with the resignation and God-fearing character of Job that is a prominent, if not the sole, theme in the book: "From where comes wisdom . . . that is hidden from the eyes of all living creatures. . . . to man, the fear of God is wisdom and to depart from evil is understanding."[35]

At times Job seemed to overstate his claims and to deserve his friends' charges of arrogance. In one speech he described his days of wealth and honor. Men waited on his opinions as they waited for rain, and he did many good deeds for those who were less fortunate than he.[36] After his losses, he found himself scorned by men whose fathers he would have not have put with the dogs who kept his flocks![37] Perhaps in recognition that he had been led to immodesty, Job admitted his turmoil. He despaired that terror had overwhelmed him and swept away his resolution and his hope for victory.[38] He then expressed his fear of God and begged again that the Almighty answer him. Job would plead in court the whole record of his life in his defense.[39]

Elihu was not initially a participant in the dialogue between Job and the three friends but a young by-stander who warmed to the dispute and criticized all the participants. To Job he reasserted the conventional doctrines of God's justice, the reward of good deeds and the punishment of evil. To the friends he charged that they had not answered Job directly. Elihu asserted that it was the task of God, not man, to rebut Job. Again to Job Elihu concluded that God does no wrong and that God is so great that man cannot know him. Elihu called Job a sinner and rebel for his endless ranting against God.[40]

It was God's turn when Elihu finished. For those who expect a full admission or settling of accounts, the divine performance is disappointing. There was a great wind and much noise, but the words were beside the point. God asserted his status and put man in his lower place. It is God who will ask questions, and man who will answer.[41] The questions attributed to God are tendentious and bombastic: Who are you to speak to me as you do? Where were you when I created the earth? Did you proclaim the rules that govern the heavens? Did you determine the laws of nature? Do you know where the darkness dwells? Do you know when the mountain goats are born? Can you pass a cord through the whale's nose?

On the surface, God's speech is a forthright proclamation of his power. However, a modern reader might wonder if an author meant it to be a ridicule of the Lord, by emphasizing his loud evasion of Job's plight. The ambiguity continues in Job's response. What can the miserable man say in response to the Almighty's questions? "What can I say. . . I already spoke, and will not speak again."[42] Is this a statement of surrender, or Job's assertion that he said his piece and cannot penetrate God's self-righteousness? Saadia Gaon, in his commentary of the tenth century, noted that Job's response to God is ambiguous. Saadia wrote that Job either indicated his acquiescence in God's power or his feeling of being overborne by a God who had the upper hand in a dispute that could not be judged by a neutral arbitrator.[43] A modern scholar calls Job's short speech a "noncommittal response."[44]

Job's final statement is more clearly submissive. He said that God can do all things and that no purpose is beyond him. Job admitted that he spoke about things that he did not understand. In the past he knew of God by report. Now he has seen him with his own eyes. The final words of Job are important but vague enough to have been translated in significantly different ways. The *New English Bible* translates *Job* 42:6 as, "I melt away, I repent in dust and ashes." The translation of the Jewish Publication Society of America[45] adds a significant retraction of Job's earlier criticism of God to its rendition. Its addition has no obvious source in the Hebrew text: "*I abhor my words* (emphasis added), and repent, seeing I am dust and ashes."

An epilogue provides God another opportunity for settling accounts. He criticized one of Job's friends for not speaking out like Job (perhaps this is God's endorsement of free speech) and compensated Job with additional children and material possessions. God did not tell Job that he was the subject of an experiment involving Satan, and he did not bring back to life the children of Job who died in Chapter One as part of God's experiment.

THE *BOOK OF ECCLESIASTES* (THE PREACHER)

The opening lines of the *Book of Ecclesiastes* identify the speaker as the son of David, king in Jerusalem. By Jewish tradition that specifies the author as Solomon. Such a claim may have been crucial in convincing ancient rabbis that the book ought to be included in the biblical canon. Opponents pointed to numerous contradictions and sacrilegious statements in the book. Proponents asserted that none were as wise as Solomon and that adversaries of *Ecclesiastes* simply did not understand the working of Solomon's mind.[46]

A simple reading of *Ecclesiastes* finds expressions of emptiness, futility, meaninglessness, folly, and vanity. The author attaches these labels to the pursuit of wisdom and pleasure. Death is the end of us all, the wise as well as the foolish.[47]

Rabbinical critics of *Ecclesiastes* were correct. The book is an artful compilation of observations, replete with contradictions, and no clear message as to what is more and less important. There is material for the unrepentant cynic as well as the profoundly pious.

Timeliness, relativity, or a dependence of judgment on the situation as opposed to a faith in absolutes can be found among the values offered by *Ecclesiastes*. "Everything has its season . . . a time to be born and a time to die; a time to plant and a time to uproot; a time to kill and a time to heal . . . a time to love and a time to hate; a time for war and a time for peace."[48]

Wisdom is to be preferred to foolishness and is better than money or possessions. However, the pursuit of too much wisdom, or too much of anything, is like chasing the wind. One should not be overly righteous or overly wise. Why make a fool of oneself? It is best to enjoy what can be attained and to live the best life possible.[49]

The Preacher is suspicious of authority. Government is likely to be corrupt."If you witness in some province the oppression of the poor and the denial of right and justice, do not be surprised at what goes on, for every official has a higher one set over him, and the highest keeps watch over them all."[50]

Scholarship is unreliable. By one reading of a difficult passage the Preacher urges his readers not to use a surplus of words.[51] More certain are the oft-quoted lines from the concluding chapter: "the use of books is endless, and much study is wearisome."[52]

God is not to be denied. Those who see piety as the Preacher's major point cannot be ignored. Man has a sense of time past and future but no comprehension of God's work from beginning to end.[53] The "vanity," meaninglessness, or impermanence that the Preacher describes relates most clearly to the things of human existence. Earth, the heavens, and the Lord are everlasting.[54] It will be well with those who fear God and obey his commands.[55] God knows all our secrets and brings everything we do to judgment.[56] Yet God is inscrutable, and one should not be overly righteous. *Ecclesiastes* repeats that death is the end of the just as well as the unjust.[57]

Pragmatism competes with piety in the Preacher's hierarchy of values, with neither obviously more important than the other. To a position-holder he advises against resignation if a ruler expresses anger. Submission makes amends for great mistakes.[58] The prime of life is to be enjoyed, but it will pass and seem in retrospect to be emptiness.[59] At different points the book seems both to express the theme of

Job ("there is a just man that perisheth in his righteousness, and there is a wicked man that prolongeth his life in his wickedness")[60] and to repeat the argument of Job's friends ("Whoso keepeth the commandment shall feel no evil thing").[61] The epilogue is not helpful to the reader who wishes to know just what are the most important values of the Preacher. It says that the speaker turned over many maxims in order to teach, that he chose his words carefully in order to give pleasure, even while he taught the truth. The third verse from the end is the classic remark against too much study. The last two verses urge the reader to fear God and obey his commands.

DECIPHERING THE AMBIGUOUS

Commentators disagree about *Job* and *Ecclesiastes*. Arguments focus on the authorship of the books as well as their principal doctrines. Readers of the Bible in translation have their own problems, insofar as key passages lend themselves to strikingly different renditions.

Conclusions about the origins of *Job* range from the period of the patriarchs (sixteenth century B.C.E. or earlier) to the post-exile fifth century B.C.E.[62] The text provides no explicit claims of authorship. The character of the Hebrew, the portrayal of Job's surroundings, and the portrayal of God lend themselves to different interpretation. There is no explicitly Israelite designation in the book. *Job* is placed in the land of Uz, wherever that is. A number of parallels have been found between Job's story and other ancient literature from the Near East. Some scholars conclude that the book is a foreign insertion into the Hebrew Bible or an Israelite's adaptation of foreign tales.[63] However, the Prologue refers prominently to the Israelite concept of God-fearing as well as to Israelite rites of sacrifice.[64]

Assertions about the origins of *Ecclesiastes* range from the reign of Solomon (c. 965-927 B.C.E.) to the first century C.E. Its language points to a late period in the development of biblical Hebrew, perhaps 700 years after Solomon's death. According to one scholar, its author was familiar with Greek philosophic concepts but did not necessarily know Greek.[65] Another scholar writes that the inclusion of Persian words and the absence of words clearly derived from Greek dates the composition toward the end of the Persian period to the beginning of the Greek period. This same scholar writes that the claim of Solomon's authorship "is like saying . . . that a book about Marxism in modern English idiom and spelling was written by Henry VIII."[66] Another scholar refers to an ancient rabbi who quipped that King Solomon wrote Song of Songs in his youth, Proverbs in mature years, and Ecclesiastes in his senility. This scholar admits what seems to be numerous complexities and even contradictions in the text but thinks that the preacher's "eyes were alert, and his powers of observation undiminished (he) . . . spoke eloquent truth."[67]

Commentators find in the contradictions of *Ecclesiastes* indications of several editings, some of them made to increase the conventional piety of the book in order to pass muster with the rabbis who opposed its inclusion within the canon.[68] However, Robert Gordis is one specialist who is skeptical of the argument that ancient scholars would have bothered to dress up *Ecclesiastes*. It would have been easier to consign the book, like apocryphal and pseudepigraphal writings, to the archives. "The various Hakam (sages) glossators and Hasid (pious) interpolators are merely figments of the scholarly imagination."[69] Gordis sees *Ecclesiastes* as a unified work, most likely of a single author. From clues in the text, he concludes that the writer was a resident of Jerusalem, probably a teacher at one of the wisdom academies for upper-class youth, who was familiar with the striving and the frustrations of the court and economic elites. The Preacher's comments about age and the fate of one's possessions lead Gordis to conclude that he was old when writing the text and was a bachelor or a man without children.

Gordis also emphasizes what is *not* in the text. Its lack of social commentary distinguishes it from the prophets and suggests that the writer led a sheltered life in court circles. The writer's concern was the fate of individuals rather than the collective. He was especially concerned with individuals (probably like himself) who had striven for ideals or personal accomplishment in their younger years and then pondered the frustrations of old age and the emptiness of what lies beyond.[70]

The texts of both *Job* and *Ecclesiastes* support widely different interpretations as to their doctrines. *Job* is the man who suffers without cause; whose steadfastness is tested; who confronts indifference and evil; a pawn between God and Satan; the lonely challenger of divine justice and providence; a man undergoing an Odyssey of faith; frustrated by the futility of ultimate questions; a target of God's unlimited power; an individual in poignant struggle with his God;[71] "a thoughtful religious man (who) will live always on a knife-edge between belief and doubt";[72] a representative of the incomprehensibility of God and the unresolved problems of good and evil;[73] and the scapegoat who is abandoned by those who were once dependent on him, is left to suffer without support, and is assigned the blame for his suffering.[74]

These issues are inherently moral, and by implication political. Insofar as they question the character of God, they also question the propriety of all lesser authorities, including government. By questioning God's justice, they also raise doubts about the attainability of justice in a human arena. *Job*, like *Ecclesiastes*, emphasizes the unreliability of supreme norms and thereby threatens to undermine human authority, the rule of law, and all else that keeps regimes politically solvent.

One rabbinical interpretation deals with the problem of justice by claiming that the *Book of Job* is fiction! God did not test Job by destroying his wealth and killing his children. Rather, it is a story made up to show that the power of Job's faith helped him endure great suffering.[75] A modern rabbi in the liberal stream of Judaism finds support in Job for his view that God is not omnipotent. Bad things do happen to good people for reasons that God does not control. The appeal of God, in this view, derives from all the good that he does contribute to the world and his role as a source of comfort to those who suffer because of factors beyond God's control.[76] Robert Frost depicts a long-belated apology from God to Job and offers a fanciful explanation of God's behavior in the biblical story: the Almighty used the case of Job in order to free himself from the simple reward to the good and the punishment to the bad, and to provide him with the godlike capacity to reward and punish as he wished.[77]

Traditional commentators accept that the *Book of Job* expresses faith in a Lord who at times is inscrutable. For a religious Jew, the book does not have to make sense in modern terms. It is clear from other books that the survival of the individual may be less important to God than the survival of the nation.

In the eyes of some modern readers, the *Book of Job* demonstrates the fickleness and the injustice of authorities who claim that their high positions render it necessary to act in ways that ordinary mortals find unclear or unacceptable.[78] Job is on a journey that is troubled and endless, without assured certainties.[79] For one reader, the greatest injustice is that Job never learns that his suffering resulted from an experiment conducted by God and Satan.[80] A sociologist of religion asserts that all cultures deal in one way or another with the issue of divine injustice (theodicy). There are more and less sophisticated ways of explaining why the good suffer and preparing each individual for death without requiring that each admit that death is a result of sin. The story of Job is an elaborate way of dealing with the issue. The rational explanation of Job's friends cannot solve Job's problem, because there is no rational explanation. In this view, Job's submission to the inexplicable is a statement of faith for an issue with no satisfactory answer.

> . . . every human order is a community in the face of death. Theodicy represents the attempt to make a pact with death. . . the necessity of this attempt will persist as long as men die and have to make sense of the fact.[81]

Religious thinkers in the Jewish and Christian traditions differ in how they interpret Job's view of this life and an afterlife. Jewish commentators concede that Job hints at a redress after death but assert that he generally indicates that the balance must occur in this life. Job states explicitly that man has no hope from the world after his death. ("A man dies, and he disappears.")[82] Christians see Job as an example of the suffering servant found in the *Book of Isaiah* and personified most fully in Christ. For Christians, a redemption and resurrection is available to redress the balance of Job's suffering. That secure future, based upon Christ, is not available to traditional Jewish readers.[83]

The ambiguity of the texts infects its commentators. One writes that the preacher of *Ecclesiastes* was not indignant like Job; he did not thunder like a prophet at injustice but smiled at the wrong and corruption that he perceived to be eternal and inherent in the scheme of things. This same commentator seems to double back on himself when he writes that the Preacher was not cheaply cynical but expressed himself with an intensity that was almost prophetic.[84]

The concept of "God-fearing" appears at several junctures in *Job* and *Ecclesiastes*, as well as elsewhere in the Hebrew Bible. A passage in *Ecclesiastes* reads "that whatsoever God doeth, it shall be for ever; nothing can be added to it, nor any thing taken from it: and God hath so made it, that men should fear before him."[85] The wording above is taken from the translation of the Jewish Publication Society of America. "Fear," however, may be too uni-dimensional, especially in its English connotation. The same Hebrew word is translated as "awe" by the New English Bible and may also be rendered as "faith," "piety," "respect," or "veneration."[86]

Job and *Ecclesiastes* conclude with declarations that God is a rock of certainty in a world where secular values are unreliable.[87] In both books, however, there are enough contrary statements to lead some readers to be skeptical about the Almighty's reliability. The conclusion of *Job* claims to lay the problem at rest but leaves readers with "a feeling of chagrin at the seemingly magnificent irrelevance of much of the content of the divine speeches. . . (by) one who appears to be the Slayer of all."[88] And, "the surprise is that someone expects Job to be comforted to the same degree for the death of his children as the loss of his camels and donkeys."[89]

Another view about the complexities in *Job* contributes directly to the theme of this book. It is that dissonance in *Job* reflects the tensions that existed in Israelite views of themselves and God and the willingness of those who composed and compiled the Bible to admit different perspectives about major issues.[90] The title of a modern commentary (*In Turns of Tempest*) captures both the anguish of Job and the anguish of one who would understand the book: "The marvel of the Book of Job is that it constantly outruns our certainties that we know how to find the truth about it."[91]

Pious commentators on *Ecclesiastes* have their own escape from troublesome text: the Preacher's endorsement of the pleasures to be derived from eating and drinking is an allegory meant to convey the enjoyment of Torah and good deeds.[92]

ARE THEY OUTLIERS WITH RESPECT TO OTHER BIBLICAL TEXTS?

The themes of skepticism, doubt, or uncertainty with respect to ultimate values appear more prominently in the *Books of Job* and

Ecclesiastes than elsewhere in the Hebrew Bible. Yet these writings are not alone in expressing such thoughts. Abraham questioned God's justice in threatening to destroy the entire populations of Sodom and Gomorrah.[93] Moses challenged God's threats to destroy all of the Israelites, first on account of the golden calf,[94] and again because of the response to the fearful report of the spies who came back from the Promised Land.[95] God's experiment with Job recalls his cruel testing of Abraham in leading him to the verge of sacrificing Isaac.[96] Saul is said to have lost God's calling to be the Israelite king for the seemingly trivial fault of performing a pre-battle sacrifice without waiting for the arrival of Samuel. Samuel's withdrawal of God's mandate from Saul leaves many readers wondering about the fickleness of that mandate. Less prominent but equally troubling is the case of Uzzah, who was killed by God for his attempt to keep the Holy Ark from falling on its way to Jerusalem.[97] Later, we read that 70,000 Israelites died of pestilence on account of David's sin in conducting a census; we are told that God incited David to count the people, and we are never told what was wrong with counting them.[98]

The prophet Habakkuk begins a passage by noting that the eyes of God are too pure to look upon evil, but then asks: "why dost thou countenance the treachery of the wicked? Why keep silent when they devour men more righteous than they?"[99] Even the *Psalm*s are not entirely soothing with respect to God's righteousness. *Psalm* 73 expresses doubts similar to those of Job before expressing everlasting faith:

> My feet had almost slipped . . . because the boasts of sinners roused my envy when I saw how they prosper. . . So it was all in vain that I kept my heart pure. . . Though heart and body fail, yet God is my possession for ever.

One commentator calls *Ecclesiastes* "the skeptic par excellence of the Old Testament."[100] Another is even more outspoken in describing *Ecclesiastes* as an outlier:

> *Ecclesiastes* is the strangest book in the Bible . . . it denies some of the things on which the other writers lay the greatest stress, notably that God has revealed himself and his will to man, through his chosen people Israel. In *Ecclesiastes* God . . . is rather the mysterious, inscrutable Being whose existence must be presupposed as that

> which determines the life and fate of man, in a world man cannot change, and where all his effort and values are rendered meaningless.[101]

This commentator calls *Ecclesiastes* a most unusual preacher, "a rationalist, an agnostic, a skeptic, a pessimist, and a fatalist," whose nihilism is a recipe for suicide. Yet he also finds that the sense of pessimism is dispelled by a joy for life and an advocacy of wisdom and moderation. He concludes that "Qoheleth's book is needed in the Bible as a counterweight to smug assurance and unreflective belief."[102]

* * *

The *Books of Job* and *Ecclesiastes* represent the ancients' efforts to deal with challenges to the Lord's omnipotence and justice. It is not clear whether God is meant to win or lose. Both conclude with pious statements of faith. Yet both provide more than enough material to challenge God's reputation.

Not the least of the material to be used against the Almighty is the speech attributed to him in Chapters 38-41 of *Job*. The creator of the universe threatens his own reputation for omniscience by a series of boasts that are entirely beside the point of Job's problem. God does not explain Job's suffering or admit to his inexcusable wager with Satan but shouts a series of tendentious questions.

A God-fearing reader may see these questions as preparing the way for Job's submission and a fitting end to a troublesome story. Or as demonstrating that God need not, perhaps should not, answer human challenges. However, the speeches attributed to God and Job can also be read as conceding Job's earlier claims that the figure known as God is unjust and out of touch with human reality.

The political implications are far reaching: If God is an unreliable Lord, can human rulers be any better or worth any fealty by citizens? This is one of the Bible's most profound episodes that demonstrate the diversity of its norms and invite a reader to ponder the nature of justice and authority.

As with much else in the Bible, there is no final resolution. Job's friends provide one answer to Job's challenge: mere humans cannot possibly comprehend God's motives or question his justice. In other words, what is unknown is beyond challenge. Scholars with a religious commitment make a similar defense of God's punishments of what seem to have been the trivial errors of Moses and Saul: since the punishment was severe, the sins must have been extreme. The incorporeal nature of God and his inscrutability protects him from all criticism.

Jeremiah resembled Job's friends in his explanation of Israelite suffering. The prophet credited God with a major disaster in Israelite history in a way that allows the Almighty to remain as national protector. The Babylonians were God's instruments of punishment. Jeremiah added the appealing prognosis that God was clearing the way for a new beginning and a new covenant that will assure the people's faith and righteousness. Jeremiah is more persuasive than Job's friends. The prophet details the sins of Judah that brought God's punishments. The reader knows from the beginning that Job is innocent of every sin except perhaps for that of hubris and asking God the source of his pain.

The explanation of disaster used by Job's friends and Jeremiah has reappeared time and again in Jewish history, most recently in connection with the Holocaust. Pious commentators say there must be an explanation of the people's suffering in God's punishment for wrongdoing. But what wrongdoing was so great as to justify the Holocaust? The wounds are too raw for the issue to be settled. Numerous rabbis refuse to see God's hand in Europe: "To name the Holocaust punishment for Israel's shortcomings is an absurd obscenity. There can be no default or offense that would merit the penalty of camps of extermination."[103] Some Orthodox rabbis insist on following the model of Job's friends and Jeremiah. They blame the Zionist movement or Reform Judaism for provoking God.[104] Punishment for Zionism or Reform Jewry would not appear to be the work of a just God, insofar as many Zionists and a large proportion of the German Jewish population, including many members of Reform congregations, left Europe in time to escape extermination. Members of anti-Zionist ultra-Orthodox communities in Eastern Europe died in proportionately higher numbers.

One message of *Job* is that the Lord works in mysterious ways and may punish individuals who seem innocent. Another message of *Job* is that things are not that simple. We have seen God's behavior, and it does not encourage trust.

NOTES

[1] Robert Gordis, *Koheleth: The Man and His Work: A Study of Ecclesiastes* (New York: Schocken Books, 1968), p. 123. For a political commentary on *Job*, see William Safire, *The First Dissident: The Book of Job in Today's Politics* (New York: Random House, 1992).

[2] *Isaiah* 3:10-11.

[3] *Psalms* 37:25.

[4] See, in particular, *Job* 2:3.

[5] On the theological problematics inherent in the characters of God and Satan as portrayed in *Job*, see David Penchansky, *The Betrayal of God: Ideological Conflict in Job* (Louisville, Kentucky: Westminster/John Knox Press, 1990).

[6] *Job* 1:21.

[7] *Job* 2:9.

[8] *Job* 4:9.

[9] *Job* 4:17.

[10] *Job* 5:6.

[11] *Job* 5:8.

[12] *Job* 8:3-4.

[13] *Job* 11:6-7.

[14] *Job* 11:6-7.

[15] *Job* 15:4.

[16] *Job* 22:2-9.

[17] As in the *Epistle of James* 5:11.

[18] *Job* 6:24.

[19] *Job* 7:21.

[20] *Job* 7:11.

[21] *Job* 9:2,15-17.

[22] *Job* 9:33.

[23] *Job* 9:22-23.

[24] *Job* 10:2-3.

[25] *Job* 19:6,19.

[26] *Job* 21:19.

[27] *Job* 21:23-25.

[28] *Job* 21:19.

[29] *Job* 17:4.

[30] *Job* 17:9.

[31] *Job* 19:25-29.

[32] *Job* 23:15-17.

[33] *Job* 27:2-5.

[34] Marvin H. Pope, *Job*, The Anchor Bible (Garden City, N.Y.: Doubleday, 1973), pp. xx, xxiv-xxvii.

[35] *Job* 28:20-21,28.

[36] *Job* 29:2-25.

[37] *Job* 30:1.

[38] *Job* 30:15-16.

[39] *Job* 31.

[40] *Job* 32-36.

[41] *Job* 38-41.

[42] *Job* 40:4-5.

[43] Moshe Greenberg, "*Job*," in Robert Alter and Frank Kermode, eds., *The Literary Guide to the Bible* (London: Fontana Press, 1987), pp. 283-304.

[44] Edwin M. Good, *In Turns of Tempest: A Reading of Job* (Stanford, California: Stanford University Press, 1990).

[45] *The Holy Scriptures According to the Masoretic Text* (Philadelphia: The Jewish Publication Society of America, 1955).

[46] Mordecai Zar-Kavod, "Introduction to Kohelet," in *The Five Scrolls* (Jerusalem: Mossad Harav Kook, 1973), p. 26, Hebrew.

[47] *Ecclesiastes* 2:16.

[48] *Ecclesiastes* 3:1-8.

[49] *Ecclesiastes* 2:13; 3:12; 4:6; 7:11-17.

[50] *Ecclesiastes* 5:8. See Robert Davidson, *The Courage to Doubt: Exploring an Old Testament Theme* (London: SCM Press, 1983), pp. 191-192.

[51] *Ecclesiastes* 6:11. The Hebrew of this passage employs a word that can be rendered as *thing* or *word.* The King James translation is, "Seeing there be many things that increase vanity, what is man the better?" The New English Bible translation is, "The more words one uses the greater is the emptiness of it all; and where is the advantage to a man?"

[52] *Ecclesiastes* 12:12.

[53] *Ecclesiastes* 3:11.

[54] *Ecclesiastes* 1:4.

[55] *Ecclesiastes* 8:13.

[56] *Ecclesiastes* 12:13-14.

[57] *Ecclesiastes* 7:16-17; 8:14-17; 9:2-6.

[58] *Ecclesiastes* 10:4.

[59] *Ecclesiastes* 11:9-10.

[60] *Ecclesiastes* 7:15.

[61] *Ecclesiastes* 8:5.

[62] Some of the disputes are summarized by Penchansky in his Appendix.

[63] Pope, "Introduction" and Amos Chacham, "Introduction," in *The Book of Job* (Jerusalem: Mossad Harav Kook, 1984), p. 21, Hebrew.

[64] *Job* 1:1-5.

[65] Gordis, p. 68; see also Salo W. Baron and Joseph L. Blau, *Judaism: Postbiblical and Talmudic Period* (Indianapolis: Bobbs-Merrill, 1954), Introduction.

[66] R. B. Y. Scott, *Proverbs and Ecclesiastes* (Anchor Bible) (New York: Anchor Books, 1965), p. 196.

[67] James L. Crenshaw, *Ecclesiastes: A Commentary* (London: SCM Press Ltd., 1988), p. 54.

[68] Scott, pp. 191-207.

[69] Gordis, p. 73.

[70] Gordis, Chapter X.

[71] Nahum N. Glatzer, ed., *The Dimensions of Job: A Study and Selected Readings* (New York: Schocken Books, 1969), p. 4.

[72] Scott, p. 207.

[73] Harold Bloom, "Introduction," in Bloom, ed., *The Book of Job* (New York: Chelsea House Publishers, 1988), pp. 1-6.

[74] Rene Girard, "'The Trail Trodden by the Wicked': *Job* as Scapegoat," in Harold Bloom ed., *The Book of Job* (New York: Chelsea House Publishers, 1988), 103-34; and Girard, *Job: The Victim of His People*, translated by Yvonne Freccero (Stanford: Stanford University Press, 1987).

[75] Chacham, pp. 18-19.

[76] Harold S. Kushner, *When Bad Things Happen to Good People* (New York: Avon Books, 1981), Chapters 2, 8.

[77] "A Masque of Reason," *Complete Poems of Robert Frost* (New York: Holt, Rinehart and Winston, 1964), especially pp. 589-90.

[78] William Morrow, "Consolation, Rejection, and Repentance in *Job* 42:6," *Journal of Biblical Literature* 105, 2, June 1986, pp. 201-25.

[79] Davidson, Chapter 9.

[80] Meir Shalev, *The Bible Now* (Jerusalem: Schocken, 1988), Hebrew, pp. 105-11.

[81] Peter L. Berger, *The Sacred Canopy: Elements of a Sociological Theory of Religion* (New York: Anchor Books, 1967), p. 80.

[82] Chacham, p. 13. The reference is to *Job* 14:10.

[83] Glatzer, p. 27.

[84] Gordis, pp. 80-81.

[85] *Ecclesiastes* 3:14.

[86] *The Holy Scriptures According to the Masoretic Text* (Philadelphia: The Jewish Publication Society of America, 1955). For a similar choice of the word fear by an expert on the Book of *Ecclesiastes*, see Michael V. Fox, "The Meaning of *Hebel* for Qohelet," *Journal of Biblical Literature*, 105, 3, September 1986, pp. 409-27. In behalf of "piety," see M. G. Easton, *Bible Dictionary* (New York: Crescent Books, 1989), p. 254.

[87] Fox.

[88] Pope, pp. lxxxi-lxxxii.

[89] Shalev, p. 111. For a poignant novel that treats the period of the revolts against the Romans with a *Job*ian theme, see Milton Steinberg, *As a Driven Leaf* (Behrman House, Inc., 1939).

[90] Penchansky.

[91] Good, p. 397.

[92] Gordis, p. 69.

[93] *Genesis* 18:24.

[94] *Exodus* 32.

[95] *Numbers* 14:16.

[96] *Genesis* 22.

[97] *II Samuel* 6:6.

[98] *II Samuel* 24:1-16.

[99] Habakkuk 1:13.

[100] James G. Williams, "Proverbs and *Ecclesiastes*," in Alter and Kermode, pp. 263-82.

[101] Scott, pp. 191-92.

[102] Scott, p. 207.

[103] David W. Weiss, *The Wings of the Dove: Jewish Values, Science, and Halacha* (Washington: Bnei B'rith Books, 1987), pp. 203-04.

[104] Menachem Friedman, "The Hasidim and the Holocaust," *Jerusalem Quarterly* 53, Winter 1990, pp. 86-114.

Chapter 7

The Several Faces of God

God of the Hebrew Bible is a prime, although elusive, candidate for political analysis. No figure more typifies the Bible's reputation for providing firm foundations (Rock of Israel is one of his Hebraic designations), yet no biblical figure surpasses the diversity of characteristics identified with him. This secular political analysis concludes that God is a bundle of contradictions. The authors and compilers of biblical text left no protocols to explain their activities. We can only wonder how they viewed the various episodes concerned with the Almighty.

The Bible's episodes about God reveal numerous traits relevant to political norms. The Lord's omniscience, omnipotence, and transcendence (i.e., otherworldliness) exist alongside traits of a God who struggles with humans who have free will and power. God has authoritarian and autocratic traits, including the well-known jealousy, along with a prominent concern for justice, plus responsiveness, forgiveness, and mercy. On two prominent occasions God engages in dialogue with the leader of his people who seeks to soften his proclamation of severe punishment. God is ethnocentric and geocentric in relation to the chosen people and the Promised Land. Yet he is also universalistic in showing concern for all the world's people, including those described as among the cruelest enemies of his people. God shows the pragmatism of a teacher and tactician. He led his people around obstacles that seemed too strong for their military prowess and postponed his own gratification with a people who proved to be problematic. God is the preeminent focus of reverence but appears to be a tragic figure in episodes where he is indecisive, cannot achieve his purposes, or is bombastic in response to the questions of believers. The weight of the biblical text is on the side of God the almighty and the just. Yet there is at least a bit to instill in his people a skepticism toward all objects of reverence.

WHICH GOD?

Even limiting a political commentary about God to the Hebrew Bible (a primary source of monotheism) provides no answer to the question of which God or which conception of God. A secular reader cannot but ask if we are speaking of God the creator or God the created. Did God create the world and choose the Jews as his people? Or did the Jews devise a concept of God that has served them (and others) well for many years?[1] Is it possible to differentiate the traits of the Almighty from those portrayed by the authors and editors of the Hebrew Bible? These questions are unanswerable as well as unavoidable. A reader of the holy text can go no further than suspicions. The multiple facets of God's nature and the several roles he is seen to have played suggest that he was shaped by biblical authors and editors for their own purposes. In ancient as well as modern times, claims about the intentions of this ultimate authority might advance the human fortunes of policy advocates who identified God's purposes with their own.

The Israelites seemed to change their conception of God from one period to another. Perhaps they learned god concepts from neighboring cultures and adapted them to their own evolving ideas.[2] A close reading of biblical passages that appear to be most ancient in their origins shows an emphasis on God's omnipotence in competition with other deities. They describe a God who demonstrated his power over competing gods and demons. They suggest the legitimacy of other gods but assert that they are less powerful than the God of the Israelites. These early passages do not reveal the highly developed notions of justice and righteousness that appear in portions traced to later periods.

Early Israelite portrayals of God are described as appropriate to wandering pastoralists like the patriarchs: God promised land and lots of progeny to help with the flocks and the baggage. Some biblical passages as well as archaeological findings suggest that the early Israelites conceived of a female consort for their God and worshipped variations of their God from one local shrine to another.[3] Perhaps the numerous names for God that appear in the Bible reflect separate deities that developed around localities, tribes, clans, or families and were absorbed into what became the Israelite conception of the Almighty.[4]

Jewish monotheism might not have been completely established until after the end of the prophetic age.[5] A number of rabbis have pondered a phrase in the first chapter of *Genesis* that uses plural terms: "And God said, let *us* make man in our image."[6] Perhaps this means that God had heavenly helpers.

The prophets claimed that God spoke to them. Yet the test of true or false prophecy is never clearly specified.[7] At the intellectually sophisticated end of the biblical continuum, the *Books of Job* and *Ecclesiastes* express skepticism about the justice of God and other Judaic norms. There are passages in both books that are conventional expressions of faith in God. In the eyes of some scholars, these were added in order to pass muster with the rabbis who decided to accept or reject writings for inclusion in what became the canonized Bible. The *Book of Ecclesiastes* also benefited from the claim that Solomon was its author. Supporters argued that critics of the book were limited in their understanding of Solomon's profound message.[8] This was a version of the device still used by religious commentators who wish to explain away a problematic element of holy scripture. When all other explanations fail, God and his emissaries are deemed to be inscrutable.[9]

Beyond the several versions of God and his activities that can be discerned in the Bible are additional varieties in writings that would add to the Bible. A professor of theology suggests that we overcome the masculine gender apparent in the ancient Hebrew with words for God that are nonsexist.[10] A feminist theologian would improve on both the Hebrew Bible and the New Testament with a version of the trinity, or alternatively a quarternity, in which one figure is feminine.[11] A rabbinical tale is embroidered on the perplexing episode in which Abraham's wife Sarah (then still called Sarai) entered the pharaoh's harem in exchange for sheep and cattle, asses, male and female slaves and camels. The Bible indicates that God struck the pharaoh and his household with grave diseases, which resulted in the return of Sarah to Abraham.[12] The rabbinical legend asserts that guardian angels protected Sarah from Pharaoh and his men until their diseases rendered them impotent and saved her from disgrace.[13] The point is not that such doctrines or stories are illegitimate as conveyed by their advocates, but that they have no obvious basis in the Hebrew Bible.

THE FOCUS OF INQUIRY

Because the Hebrew Bible deals extensively with God and the domestic and international problems of the Israelites, there is a problem of focusing a chapter dealing with the politically relevant aspects of God. Virtually the whole of the Hebrew Bible is fair game. Insofar as the language of the Bible is often ambiguous and lends itself to metaphorical interpretation, there is the additional problem of deciding how to read the material. Even where God's concern for his people's welfare is not explicit, commentators can find political allusions. The problems are conceded in the recent spurt of interest by political scientists in the Hebrew Bible and the politically explicit commentaries offered by scholars in other academic professions.[14]

The episodes chosen for consideration in this chapter are those with a linkage to God and issues of governance. While they cannot claim to be exhaustive, they are extensive in representing the range of biblical materials dealing with God as a political actor. No effort is made to represent the political traits of God that are typical, or especially prominent in the Hebrew Bible, as opposed to those that are exceptional or unusual. The pursuit of God's true essence is the realm of the preacher or commentator with a religious or political commitment.

The intellectual purpose that guides this chapter is one that seems appropriate to the material and the larger themes of this book. It is to illustrate the several faces of God that appear in the Hebrew Bible. Political episodes described in the Bible reveal different and shifting sides of the Almighty without an explicit ordering of priorities or doctrinal clarity.[15] The episodes considered here are those dealing with the nature of God as supreme authority and the actions of God (or the prophets who spoke for him) at crucial points of regime creation, the criticism of elites, the selection and change of leaders.

I AM THE LORD YOUR GOD

God is concerned with his authority. In this he resembles other leaders who must assure their position before they can use its power.[16] His monopoly of the title God and the prohibitions against dealing with other gods or misusing his name appear prominently in the first of the Ten Commandments.

> I am the Lord your God . . .
> You shall have no other god to set against me
> You shall not make a carved image . . .
> You shall not bow down to them or worship them . .
> You shall not make wrong use of the name of the Lord your God . . .[17]

God's jealousy, or insecurity, appears in several forms. He demanded that his people listen to all his words and not even mention the names of other gods.[18] In one of Moses' final speeches, he detailed curses spread over 53 verses of text that the Israelites and their descendants would suffer for lack of compliance with God's laws. They include starvation, thirst, dysentery, military defeat, locusts, "and sickness and plague of every kind not written down in this book of the law, until you are destroyed."[19]

There are several puzzles concerned with the nature of God's power. Especially problematic are assertions of his omniscience and omnipotence alongside the reality that is described. The creator of the world could perform many wondrous deeds. The powers ascribed to other gods were no match for him. Yet individuals have free will and thwart the Almighty's law. Perhaps God limited himself in order to test his people in the use of freedom. He may have given people free will to heighten the appreciation of whatever loyalty he received from them.[20] The loyalty that he received, however, was never enough and never lasted. God struggled continuously with his people and the individuals he chose to be their leaders. God seemed to lose more often than he won. Perhaps he erred in the recipe used to create the creatures said to be made in his image or erred in his choice of the Israelites. Could not the Almighty have chosen a better people? A rabbinical interpretation is that God chose a weak people in order to test himself and demonstrate his power.[21]

When he worked with Moses in order to obtain the freedom of the Hebrew slaves, God was concerned to demonstrate the superiority of his power. He instructed Moses in a number of tricks that would be more powerful than those of Egyptian magicians.[22] He told Moses how to turn his and Aaron's staffs into serpents, and the serpent from Aaron's staff swallowed those from the staffs of Egyptian magicians.[23] God hardened Pharaoh's heart, in order to assure himself additional opportunities to demonstrate his power: the plagues of increasing severity that struck the Egyptians but not the Hebrews and then the great demonstration of parting the waters for the fleeing slaves but drowning the Egyptians.[24]

God exhibited his power by the destruction that he imposed on wayward Israelites. Yet God seemed to be as dependent on his people as they were on him. He never liquidated them. There was always a remnant to be saved and provided another opportunity. Was this God's continuing hope that his people would be faithful sooner or later, a mockery of his power, a self-imposed limit on his power that signified his mercy or his commitment to Israel, or a demonstration of chronic tension between an omnipotent God and the people he made to be free?

God took actions that would have been unnecessary if he truly was omnipotent. Some episodes even suggest that the Almighty was a model of Israelite pragmatism. He coped with stressful situations. When the Israelites set out across the desert, he guided them in a roundabout way. He explained that the shortest route would lead the Israelites to encounter the Philistines, but "they may change their minds when they see war before them, and turn back to Egypt."[25] God seemed to recognize that he should not or could not simply make the Israelites brave and the Philistines weak.

There is a curious feature in the demands that God and Moses made to Pharaoh. They did not insist on the freedom of the slaves but asked that they be allowed a vacation so they might go into the desert and worship. Why not be more forthright? Was it necessary for an omnipotent God to deceive the Pharaoh? If the Almighty was concerned to harden the Pharaoh's heart so he could demonstrate his power, why did he not put all the cards on the table? Free the slaves completely, or else![26]

God was generous with his promises. He committed himself to provide the Israelites with extensive boundaries (in passages that seem to have been written into the Torah after David had already extended his empire) and went beyond medical science: "I will take away all sickness. . . None shall miscarry or be barren. . . I will grant you a full span of life."[27]

God used his power in support of justice.[28] The freeing of Hebrew slaves is a keystone of Israelite history. The fair treatment of the weak is a recurring theme. Some modern commentators find that justice or morality is the most important theme among the numerous issues that appear in the Holy Book.[29] The prophet Amos condemned ritual observance in the presence of exploitation

> When you present your sacrifices and offerings I will not accept them. . . Spare me the sound of your songs . . .Let justice roll on like a river and righteousness like an everflowing stream.[30]

During the period after the return from exile in Babylon, Nehemiah raged against the economic elite for taking advantage of the poor.

> Let us give up this taking of persons as pledges for debt. Give back today to your debtors their fields and vineyards, their olive-groves and houses, as well as the income in money, and in corn, new wine, and oil.[31]

The prophet Malachi spoke against "those who wrong the hired laborer, the widow, and the orphan, and who thrust the alien aside."[32]

As befitting a figure concerned with knotty problems of justice, God is a teacher as well as a lawgiver. On occasion he was willing to change his decisions. He bargained with earthly figures, seemingly to reach an acceptable balance between what he wanted and what he could achieve. Sometimes God could be persuaded by individuals who, at least at the moment, seemed more wise or just than he. Abraham challenged God's intention to destroy the evil city of Sodom, arguing specifically on the nature of justice: "Wilt thou really sweep away good and bad together? . . Shall not the judge of all the earth do what is just?"[33] Abraham began by obtaining God's agreement to pardon the city if he found 50 good men there. Then in stages the Lord agreed that he would save the cities if he found only 10 good men. This story shows either the flexibility of the Lord or an omniscient God's willingness to be teased when he knows all along the outcome of the bargaining.

When the Israelites made the golden calf while Moses was on Mount Sinai receiving the law, the Lord wanted to destroy them all and provide Moses with a new people to lead. Moses dissuaded him from rashness, by appealing to God's vanity, and by reminding him of a previous commitment:

> Why let the Egyptians say, "So he meant evil when he took them out to kill them in the mountains and wipe them off the face of the earth?" Turn from thy anger, and think better of the evil thou dost intend against thy people. Remember Abraham, Isaac and Israel, thy servants, to whom thou didst swear by thy own self: "I will make your posterity countless as the stars in the sky, and all this land, of which I have spoken, I will give to them, and they shall possess it for ever."[34]

Sometimes God overlooked his standards of justice and ruled like a short-tempered autocrat. He commanded that man shall not kill but demanded the killing of his people's enemies. He struck down the hapless Uzzah for the seemingly innocent action of putting out his hand to protect the Ark of the Covenant when it appeared in danger of falling.[35]

God's treatment of Moses adds to the case against him for a lack of justice. We saw in Chapter 3 that Moses was denied entry into the Promised Land for a seemingly trivial departure from God's instructions. Instead of only speaking to a rock in order to produce water, he struck it with the staff that God had told him to bring with him.[36] Against an interpretation of a trivial violation, a religious Jew would assert that God's punishment of Moses indicates that the offense was not unimportant.

Another case of God's doubtful justice concerns the treatment of Saul. The 13th chapter of *I Samuel* tells of the king's performance of a sacrifice prior to battle without waiting for the arrival of Samuel. The text appears to be less a report about Saul's lack of faith than a comment on Samuel's tardiness and Saul's sense of when a battle must start. For this, however, Samuel proclaimed that Saul must lose the Lord's blessing for himself and his family.[37] Religious commentators assert that Saul's downfall reflects the severity of his faults and his lack of suitability to be king.[38] Perhaps Saul's greatest problem was the fact that he preceded David. This may be sufficient explanation for Saul's guilt. Whatever Saul did, those who finally edited the *Book of*

Samuel had to justify the end of his kingdom in order to make way for David.[39]

Some writers find material in the Bible to soften God's message of cruelty toward Israel's enemies. One example is the story of the envoys to the Amorite king Sihon, cited for the principle that the Israelites should provide their antagonists with an alternative to war. Sihon refused the envoys' request to let the Israelites pass peacefully and was attacked only when he sent his own forces against them.[40] The *Book of Jonah* tells how the Lord has mercy even on the capital of Assyria on account of the repentance that he saw there.

Among the different faces of God is one that is modest and another that demands glory. Modesty is the theme of Nathan's response to David when the king suggested building a Temple: "Down to this day I have never dwelt in a house since I brought Israel up from Egypt; I made my journey in a tent and a tabernacle."[41] Haggai prophesied to those who returned from exile. His concern for a proper Temple has none of the modestly associated with Nathan.

> Go up into the hills, fetch timber, and build a house acceptable to me, where I can show my glory, says the Lord. . . when you would bring home the harvest, I blast it. Why? says the Lord of Hosts, Because my house lies in ruins, while each of you has a house that he can run to.[42]

Once the Temple was constructed, Haggai was not satisfied.

> Is there anyone still among you who saw this house in its former glory? How does it appear to you now? Does it not seem to you as if it were not there?[43]

There was a "dark side of God" revealed in the cruel testing of Abraham, who was led to the verge of sacrificing his son, and in the story of Job, who was tested by the loss of his property and his children.[44] A commentary on the *Book of Job* assembles the following epithets that scholars have employed to describe God as they perceive him in that book:

> blustering, buffoon, bully, childish, evil, inscrutable, insecure, irrelevant, irresponsible gambler, less clever than Satan, less than average human being with a great deal of power, majestic, petulant, small-minded king that everyone has to humor, thundering, wantonly cruel, weak.[45]

The prophet Ezekiel, one of the strangest characters of the Hebrew Bible, described a God called "profoundly neurotic" by a modern commentator.[46] This God made his people "offer by fire all their first-born, that I might horrify them; I did it that they might know that I am the Lord."[47]

God worked through his prophets in creating regimes, limiting the authority of their leaders, and ending those that proved wayward. One story tells how the prophet Samuel warned the Israelites when they demanded a king.

> This will be the manner of the king that shall reign over you: he will take your sons, and appoint them unto him . . . And he will take your daughters . . . And he will take your fields . . . And ye shall cry out in that day because of your king whom ye shall have chosen you; and the Lord will not answer you in that day.[48]

Samuel chose Saul as the first king and then proclaimed his failure and indicated that God had chosen David in his place. Nathan condemned David for his adultery with Bathsheba and the contrived death of her husband, counseled David against constructing a Temple, and was instrumental in the selection of Solomon over Adonijah when David was about to die. The prophet Elijah condemned Ahab and Jezebel for introducing foreign gods to the kingdom of Israel and for killing the landowner Naboth. Elisha implemented the curse against Ahab's dynasty that Elijah had declared. Elisha sent one of his company of prophets to anoint the military officer Jehu to be king. Jehu then carried out the prophet's mission by killing Ahab's son King Jeroboam as well as Jezebel and Ahab's 70 other sons.[49] Jeremiah spent most of his career challenging Kings Jehoiakim and Zedekiah for regimes that lacked justice, honored foreign gods, and pursued a foreign policy that threatened the nation.[50]

THE POLITICAL ROLES OF GOD

The episodes about God described here reflect the work of anonymous compilers and editors who worked with oral and written materials over the course of centuries. Scholars argue about which segments of text were compiled when and with what point of view.[51] Apparent in the biblical stories are different political roles or functions of God. Several of the roles assigned to God seem to have been written into the Bible in order to use his stature to legitimize a writer's perspective about the writer's regime. A believer might describe the same roles as different aspects of God's being.

1. *God as active intervener in politically relevant events, perhaps in conjunction with a human emissary.* Under this role it is possible to classify stories of the patriarchs and the Exodus. God is quoted as he spoke directly to Noah, Abraham, and Moses. He made covenants with Noah and Abraham, produced the plagues of Egypt, hardened the Pharaoh's heart toward the Israelites, provided the law to Moses, and helped Moses during the Exodus by producing food, military victory, and punishment for wayward Israelites. Commentators describe these stories as written during the time of David[52] or as late as the return from Babylonian exile.[53] Among the details of these materials that are most clearly contrived are provisions of a covenant with Abraham that describe the extent of the Promised Land as it was achieved during the reign of David and details of law provided by Moses that seem more relevant for the agriculture and commerce of settled communities than for the needs of a community on the way through the desert. A number of the laws are prefaced with the comment, "when you enter the land that is promised to you" and then proceed to indicate the proper way of dealing with field crops, fruit trees, hired hands, and the unfortunate who do not possess land.[54] Other laws deal with property ownership, the construction and selling of houses, and behaviors to be followed by residents of walled towns.[55]

2. *God as legitimator of counsel or condemnation offered to the kings by prophets who claimed to speak in his name.* Nathan chastised David for his adultery and counseled him against building a Temple (perhaps written later to justify the story that it was Solomon who built the Temple). Elijah condemned Ahab for the unjust way in which Naboth was killed, and his land taken by the king. Micaiah claimed to be speaking for God when he ridiculed the support of King Ahab's war plans that had been offered by 400 prophets employed by the court. Micaiah then revealed one vision of the king's death and another vision that told of a spirit enticing Ahab to attack by causing his prophets to lie.[56]

3. *God as legitimator of intervention by a prophet.* This is a conception of God that not only allows a prophet to offer counsel or condemnation but to take an active part in regime creation or change. Samuel asserted that he was acting for God when he selected and then renounced Saul as king and selected David in his place. Elisha asserted that the Lord spoke through him when he had Jehu anointed King of Israel and instructed him to kill King Jeroboam and the entire house of Ahab.

4. *God as legitimator of condemnation and threat.* This is a variant on two roles described above: it is a more active role than God as legitimator of counsel and less active than God as legitimator of intervention. It is a role claimed for God by a number of the prophets who were less assertive than Samuel or Elisha in actually taking steps to change regimes. Amos is a prominent early example. He appeared in a context of plenty, splendor, elegance, power, and self-satisfaction, tempered by the looming threat of Assyria. In this context Amos found exploitation of the poor and condemned ritual observance in the presence of corruption.[57]

For Amos Israel's being "chosen" was no guarantee of its security but an assurance of especially strict demands for proper behavior. The first lines of Amos 9 threaten complete destruction. God will "kill them to the last man . . . (and) wipe the kingdom off the face of the earth." Yet the final lines in the same verse promise that a remnant will be spared and restored. Some commentators argue that the first of these sentiments might have been expressed by the real Amos, while the second is a later addition of editors who could not accept the prospect of total destruction.[58] A traditional Jewish view is that the prophet threatened the destruction of the northern kingdom, which came to pass with the invasions of Assyria but promised to preserve a remnant of the people.[59]

5. *God as intervener via a third party as explained by a prophet.* The classic example appears in the *Book of Jeremiah*, where the prophet condemned the Israelites for the sins of idolatry, injustice, and seeking security in international alliances rather than in acceptance of God's law. He identified Babylon as the instrument of the Lord and predicted the total destruction of Judah and Jerusalem.[60] As in the case of other portions of the Hebrew Bible, scholars quarrel about who wrote the passages attributed to Jeremiah that describe in

gory detail the destruction of Jerusalem and when they were written. Traditional religious commentators assert that they were written by Jeremiah himself or expressed by him and written by his scribe Baruch. Secular scholars see in the same materials indications of later editings, when the actions of God that are described as the prophet's predictions had already occurred.[61] In such a view, the biblical Jeremiah is not uttering threats that will occur unless the Judeans reform their ways but is a figure contrived by later authors to express a view of Judean catastrophe that is linked to God's power and to a promise that God will revive the remnant of the people that remains.

WAS GOD ALMIGHTY?

Politics is pervasive in the Hebrew Bible, and there is no doubt about God's centrality. The Bible depicts him as creating the world, selecting the Israelites as his people and assigning them a land, choosing and guiding their leaders, providing the law, inspiring the prophets to keep the people and their leaders from wayward behavior and explain their punishments. Loud and mighty are the signs of God's power. He spoke from thunder and the whirlwind. He dealt in small tricks like turning a staff into a snake, intermediate tricks like producing food and water in the desert, and the larger feats of opening the waters for the Israelites and closing them upon the Egyptians, splitting the earth under Korah and his rebels, and using plagues and military defeats against other antagonists. He decided large issues of national planning (the generation of the slaves must die off before invading the Promised Land) and advised leaders on the small details of battle tactics.[62]

Can a secular reader accept this at face value? The material does not lend itself neatly to modern analysis. The ambiguities and contradictions in the biblical text render God's character elusive. There is material to suggest that God was imperfectly created, or created with several faces, rather than the creator of it all. A modern writer can hardly do better than Philo, who wrote that we can know that God exists but cannot know his character. A political scientist has applied the logic of game theory to God's traits of omniscience, omnipotence, immortality, and incomprehensibility. The exercise deserves a place along with all the other efforts to probe the character of the Almighty, but the author is left with what he calls divine mystery, unknowability, and enigma.[63]

The Bible claimed omnipotence for the Lord and demanded loyalty to the one God. Yet he allowed his rebellious people one opportunity after another to desist from wayward behavior. There are authoritarian traits in the regimes said to be created by God. But it was not a simple autocracy. At times, God responded positively to some of his people's complaints, and he bargained with his emissaries about the action that would be most just. Some modern scholars have described a "separation of powers" in the Israelite polity, where the king, the priests, and prophets competed with one another, with each claiming to derive power from God's laws.[64] Those laws elevated moral precepts above the actions that could be taken by human rulers. Individuals revered as the Lord's prophets did not hesitate to criticize the kings and other elites in the most severe terms. The Bible does not indicate that the prophets often swayed the rulers. Yet the collection of their works in sacred books indicates the value bestowed upon them by compilers of the Bible.

The Bible also provides a role for the people. What precise ideas lay behind the notion of covenant assemblies is not clear from a reading of the text. Yet the mass of the people were consulted at least ritually. In the case of an assembly described in the *Book of Ezra*, where the people are commanded to rid themselves of foreign wives and children, one is tempted to read in the text a lack of popular compliance.[65] This may not be a proclamation of civil rights in modern terms but may indicate the limits of one biblical regime.

God was said to be powerful beyond comprehension, but he also used tricks and cunning that seemed to belie a capacity to impose his will unilaterally. The staff that turned into a serpent, the plagues, and the parting of the sea were meant to make an impression of power. In case magic was not sufficient to achieve his ends, God also instructed Moses to tell Pharaoh that he wanted only a vacation for the slaves rather than freedom. If God was Almighty why all these other devices? Like creatures bound by human rules, the Almighty got his way by threat, bargaining, and subterfuge.

God could not overcome his people's lack of loyalty despite his reputation for being omnipotent. He threatened to abandon and destroy the Israelites. As described in the Bible composed by Israelites, however, God neither tired of the struggle nor decided to rid himself of the Israelites and choose another people.

* * *

The idea of God provided the Israelites with a framework of national history and destiny. They wrote that he created the universe and chose the Israelites for special treatment and testing. His existence gave purpose to the people and a source of explanation and hope amidst their travails. Within the framework of God-driven history, the Almighty's will was used to explain the selection of national leaders and the leaders' decisions. Insofar as God's call was claimed by the prophets, he ennobled the activity of regime critics. The idea of God also glorified the actions of legendary ancestors, whose stories seem to have been compiled and edited centuries after they were said to have occurred.

The ancient Israelites were more god-fearing than moderns. The problem of the Bible's writers was not to convince the people to believe in God but to limit them to one God.[66] The Israelites' concept of a single God, all-powerful and intangible, was especially attractive. It lent itself to explanations of success and failure, perhaps more readily for the interpreted past than the evolving present. The incorporeal nature of God and his inscrutability protected him from all challenge.

There was a persistent relationship between God and his people. During almost all of their ancient history, the Israelites were a small, poor, and weak people, fated to be located in a place that was important strategically to larger and more powerful empires. Despite numerous defeats and a destruction at the hands of the Babylonians that was almost total, a Judean regime lasted from the rise of Saul in about 1050 B.C.E. until the Romans reduced Judea to a province in their empire, destroyed Jerusalem, and wreaked havoc among the population during the period of 4 B.C.E. to 135 C.E. Prophets saw disasters as God's way of punishing his people for their sins and purifying the remnant that survived. After the end of the ancient country, the Judaic idea of God continued to be viable despite one crisis after another during an interminable Diaspora and, more recently, amidst the international and domestic problems of modern Israel.[67]

NOTES

[1] Max I. Dimont, *Jews, God and History* (New York: Signet Books, 1964), Chapter 1; and Brams, p. 176.

[2] Walter Beltz, *God and the Gods: Myths of the Bible*, translated by Peter Heinegg (Harmondsworth, England: Penguin Books, 1983).

[3] P. Kyle McCarter, Jr., "Aspects of the Religion of the Israelite Monarchy: Biblical and Epigraphic Data," in Patrick D. Miller, Jr., Paul D. Hanson, and S. Dean McBride, eds., *Ancient Israelite Religion* (Philadelphia: Fortress Press, 1987), pp. 137-56; David Noel Freedman, "`Who Is Like Thee Among the Gods?' The Religion of Early Israel," in Miller, Hanson, and McBride, pp. 315-36; and John Bright, *A History of Israel* (London: SCM Press Ltd., 1980), p. 101.

[4] Albrecht Alt, "The God of the Fathers," in his *Essays on Old Testament History and Religion*, translated by R. A. Wilson (Garden City, N.Y.: Doubleday & Company, 1967); and Daniel Jeremy Silver, *A History of Judaism*, Volume I (New York: Basic Books, 1974), Chapter 1.

[5] Michael Grant, *The Jews in the Roman World* (New York: Dorset Press, 1973), p. 14.

[6] *Genesis* 1:26. For explications, see Burton L. Visotzky, *Reading the Book: Making the Bible a Timeless Text* (New York: Anchor Books, 1991), Chapter 10.

[7] Ephraim E. Urbach, *The Sages: Their Concepts and Belief*, Translated by Israel Abrahams (Cambridge: Harvard University Press, 1987), p. 564f.

[8] Mordecai Zar-Kavod, "Introduction to Kohelet," in *The Five Scrolls* (Jerusalem: Mossad Harav Kook, 1973), Hebrew, p. 26.

[9] John L. McKenzie, S.J., *The Two-Edged Sword: An Interpretation of the Old Testament* (Garden City, N.Y.: Image Books, 1966), p. 104. For the development of the concept, God, both before and after the biblical period , but Jews as well as non-Jews, see Karen Armstrong, *A History of God: The 4,000-Year Quest of Judaism, Christianity and Islam* (New York: Ballantine Books, 1993).

[10] Gordon D. Kaufman, *The Theological Imagination: Constructing the Concept of God* (Philadelphia: The Westminster Press, 1981), pp. 15-16.

[11] Joan Chamberlain Engelsman, *The Feminine Dimension of the Divine* (Philadelphia: Westminster Press, 1979), Chapter 7.

[12] *Genesis* 12:10-20.

[13] Louis Ginzberg, *Legends of the Jews* (New York: Simon and Schuster, 1956), p. 101.

[14] See Steven J. Brams, *Biblical Games: A Strategic Analysis of Stories in the Old Testament* (Cambridge, Massachusetts: M.I.T. Press, 1980); Brams, *Superior Beings: If They Exist, How Would We Know?* (New York: Springer-Verlag, 1983); H. Mark Roelofs, "Hebraic-Biblical Political Thinking," *Polity* XX, 4 (Summer 1988), 572-97; and Roelofs, "Liberation Theology: The Recovery of Biblical Radicalism," *American Political Science Review* 82, 2, June 1988, pp. 549-66.

[15] See Martin Buber, *Israel and the World: Essays in a Time of Crisis* (New York: Schocken Books, 1963), especially "The Man of Today and the Jewish Bible" and "The Faith of Judaism"; and Gershom Scholem, *Sabbatei Sevi: The Mystical Messiah*, Translated by R. J. Zwi Werblowsky (Princeton: Princeton University Press, 1973), p. 117.

[16] Niccolo Machiavelli made this point. For a modern expression see Richard Neustadt, *Presidential Power: The Politics of Leadership* (New York: Wiley, 1976).

[17] *Exodus* 20:1-7.

[18] *Exodus* 23:13.

[19] *Deuteronomy* 28:15-68.

[20] Brams, *Biblical Games*, p. 34.

[21] Silver, Chapter 2.

[22] *Exodus* 4:1-9.

[23] *Exodus* 7:12.

[24] *Exodus* 10:1-2.

[25] *Exodus* 13:17.

[26] For the efforts of traditional Jewish commentators to deal with this curiosity, see Nehama Leibowitz *Studies in Shemot (Exodus)***.** Translated and adapted by Aryeh Newman (Jerusalem: The World Zionist Organization, 1981), pp. 94-95.

[27] *Exodus* 23:25-33.

[28] Paul D. Hanson, *The People Called: The Growth of Community in the Bible* (New York: Harper and Row, 1986).

[29] Nahum M. Sarna, *Understanding Genesis: The Heritage of Biblical Israel* (New York: Schocken Books, 1966); Paul D. Hanson, *The People Called: The Growth of Community in the Bible* (San Francisco: Harper & Row, 1986).

[30] *Amos* 5: 22-24.

[31] *Nehemiah* 5:10-11.

[32] *Malachi* 3:5.

[33] *Genesis* 18.

[34] *Exodus* 32:10-14.

[35] *II Samuel* 6.

[36] William H. Propp, "The Rod of Aaron and the Sin of Moses," *Journal of Biblical Literature* 107, 1, March 1988, pp. 19-26.

[37] *I Samuel* 13:5-14. Another episode dealing with Saul's faults seems more weighty. After a battle against the Amalekites, Saul did not destroy all of the enemy and their possessions as instructed, but spared the king and the best of the livestock, "everything worth keeping." When challenged by Samuel, Saul protested that he had taken the livestock in order to sacrifice to the Lord. This led Samuel to rage that the Lord desires not sacrifice but obedience. The prophet then renounced Saul once again and killed the Amalekite king with his own hands (I Samuel 15).

[38] Adin Steinsaltz, *Biblical Images: Men and Women of the Book* (New York: Basic Books, 1984).

[39] David M. Gunn, *The Fate of King Saul: An Interpretation of a Biblical Story* (Sheffield: Journal for the Study of the Old Testament Supplement Series, 14, 1984); Meir Shalev, *The Bible Now* (Jerusalem: Schocken, 1985), pp 65-73, Hebrew; John A. Sanford, *King Saul, The Tragic Hero: A Study in Individuation* (New York: Paulist Press, 1985); and Steinsaltz, Chapter XVI.

[40] *Numbers* 21:21. See David W. Weiss, *The Wings of the Dove: Jewish Values, Science, and Halacha* (Washington: Bnei B'rith Books, 1987), p. 17.

[41] *II Samuel* 7:6-7.

[42] *Haggai* 1:7-9.

[43] *Haggai* 2:3.

[44] Gunn, pp. 129-31.

[45] David Penchansky, *The Betrayal of God: Ideological Conflict in Job* (Louisville, KY: Westminster/John Knox Press, 1990).

[46] Northrop Frye, *The Great Code: The Bible and Literature* (San Diego: Harcourt Brace Jovanovich, 1983), p. 218.

[47] *Ezekiel* 20:26. The translation in the King James Bible is less explicit: "And I polluted them in their own gifts, in that they caused to pass through the fire all that openeth the womb, that I might make them desolate, to the end that they might know that I am the Lord." As in many other cases, the original Hebrew is not so clear as to solve the choice between versions.

[48] *I Samuel* 8:10-18.

[49] *II Kings* 9.

[50] For a comprehensive treatment of Jeremiah, see the introduction to John Bright, *Jeremiah: The Anchor Bible* (Garden City, N.Y.: Doubleday & Company, 1965).

[51] For works that illustrate items of biblical scholarship that are controversial, have explicit political perspectives, and provide citations to many other works in an extensive literature see Richard Elliott Friedman, *Who Wrote the Bible?* (New York: Harper and Row, 1987); and Norman K. Gottwald, *The Tribes of Yahweh: A Sociology of the Religion of Liberated Israel, 1250-1050 BCE* (Maryknoll, New York: Orbis Books, 1979).

[52] George E. Mendenhall, "The Nature and Purpose of the Abraham Narratives," in Patrick D. Miller, Jr., Paul D. Hanson, and S. Dean McBride, eds., *Ancient Israelite Religion* (Philadelphia: Fortress Press, 1987), pp. 337-56.

[53] John Van Seters, *Abraham in History and Tradition* (New Haven: Yale University Press, 1975); and Alt, "The Origins of Israelite Law," in his *Essays on Old Testament History and Religion*.

[54] For example, *Leviticus* 19:9,19,25; 25:23; *Deuteronomy* 14:28; 22:9; 24:19-21.

[55] *Deuteronomy* 19:14; 22:8; Leviticus 25:29.

[56] *I Kings*, 22.

[57] *Amos* 5: 22-24.

[58] See the note to Amos 9:8b-15 in *The New English Bible: Oxford Study Edition* (New York: Oxford University Press, 1976).

[59] See the commentary on Amos 9 by Amos Chacham in the volume, *The Twelve* (Jerusalem: Mossad Harav Kook, 1987), Hebrew. For a commentary that portrays Amos as threatening the end of God's covenant and the complete destruction of the people, see Gerhard F. Hasel, *The Remnant: The History and Theology of the Remnant Idea from Genesis to Isaiah* (Berrien Springs, Mich: Andrews University Press, 1974), Part V.

[60] *Jeremiah* 9:10; 19:8-9; 20:4-5.

[61] For an introduction to the scholarship on the *Book of Jeremiah*, see Bright, *Jeremiah: The Anchor Bible*.

[62] *II Samuel* 5:23.

[63] Brams, *Superior Beings*, pp. 170-71; see also Brams, *Biblical Games*.

[64] Stuart A. Cohen, *The Three Crowns: Structures of Communal Politics in Early Rabbinic Jewry* (Cambridge: Cambridge University Press, 1990).

[65] *Ezra* 10:44.

[66] John Baillie, *Our Knowledge of God* excerpted in John Hick, ed., *The Existence of God* (New York: Macmillan, 1964), pp. 204-210; and John Hick, *God and the Universe of Faiths: Essays in the Philosophy of Religion* (London: Macmillan, 1973), p. 84.

[67] For religious Jews' explanation of the Holocaust, see Menachem Friedman, "The Hasidim and the Holocaust," *Jerusalem Quarterly* 53, Winter 1990, pp. 86-114.

Part III
The Modern Relevance of Biblical Politics

The diversity of political episodes apparent in the Hebrew Bible has relevance both for readers of the Bible and observers of current events. Chapter 8 focuses the description of political variety in the Bible. It portrays the wide range of political principles that can claim biblical legitimacy. By implication, it challenges any who would claim that a particular institution, behavior, or policy enjoys biblical support.

Chapters 9 and 10 demonstrate that there is more to be read from biblical politics than confusion and contradiction with respect to modern concepts. They link the character of politics described in the Bible with a respect for different and even contrasting principles and a willingness to argue about the meaning of political events and the responses that are appropriate. These are traits to be admired in any community and contribute to the continued vitality of Judaism and the democracy that is Israel.

Chapter 8
The Bounded Principles of Biblical Politics

Uncounted heads of state, regime apologists, revolutionaries, theologians, philosophers, and preachers have justified their ideas and behaviors with selective and tendentious reading of the Hebrew Bible.[1] Examples range historically from those who defended a divine right of kings, to modern activists who would outlaw abortions and homosexual practices. Sentiments like those expressed by the Archbishop of York in the nineteenth century are still alive and contribute to Israeli nervousness about their own claims.

> This country of Palestine belongs to you and me, it is essentially ours. . . . It was given to the father of Israel. . . that land has been given unto us. It is the land from which comes news of our redemption. It is the land to which we turn as the fountain of all our hopes; it is the land to which we look with as true a patriotism as we do to this dear old England.[2]

An honest commentary on the politics in the Hebrew Bible should begin by conceding its variety and discouraging an excess of certainty in any of the norms that can find a basis somewhere in the text. The authors and compilers of the Bible were anything but consistently doctrinaire. They provide legitimacy to a wide range of norms, some on different sides of the same issue. The most prominent of the biblical heroes were immoral at times, yet that did not disqualify them from holding office or receiving praise as being favored of the Lord. *Job* and *Ecclesiastes* won acceptance into the biblical canon although their authors cast doubt on the justice of God himself, plus the worth of hard work, study, and righteous living.

The Bible portrays how individuals and the Israelite community responded to severe pressures. Consistency seems less valued than flexibility and pragmatism. The laws of God and Moses and the prophets' criticisms express piety, justice, and equity. There is also ambivalence, avarice, and dishonesty. Aaron's excuse for his role in making the golden calf (I threw the gold into the fire and out came a bull) reads like a bold faced lie. David became the founder of a holy dynasty despite his ambivalent behavior toward the Philistines and the Israelites and the sordid story of Bathsheba and Uriah.

Survival was a prime value for the Israelites. They did not take the Christian route of postponing gratification to a life after death or relying on a man-god who would put things right. Leaders coped within the opportunities available to them and paid the price of imperfect decisions. The Israelites were usually weak, but fragments of the nation survived beyond the biblical period. The Bible's condemnation of syncretism and doubtful alliances indicates that worldly leaders worked at the interface of lofty ideals and the opportunism of a weak people.

The label of *bounded principles* is appropriate for the political norms that find expression in the Hebrew Bible. The Bible associates a range of norms and behaviors with God and other major characters. Each range can be presented as a series of positions which represent the politically relevant principles that may claim biblical roots. The ranges reflect the diversity that appears in the Bible and warns that it is an unreliable source for legitimating specific behaviors or institutions. The Bible can be used to endorse not only those activities that resemble one of the points along one of its several continua but also many other activities within the same continuum.

A problem with the concept of bounded principles is the failure of the biblical text to define the outer bounds of the principles. Some readers might conclude from previous chapters that "anything goes" or that the variety of political principles that can claim some biblical legitimacy are without bounds. This chapter does not claim to define clearly the biblical boundaries on a number of political issues. It rests with indicating a considerable width for each category. There is no precision in this work. It is in the nature of interpreting the biblical text that some may find indications that legitimize principles more or less extensive than those indicated here.

The categories used to described the bounded principles are defined in terms that derive from modern discussions of politics. They do not fit neatly the stories, proclamations, and other materials of the Bible. As defined here, several continua are closely related to one another and even overlap. The categories concern biblical endorsements of authoritarian as opposed to responsive regimes, the certainty or flexibility of biblical law, biblical support or skepticism with respect to monarchical government, support for ethnocentrism or universalism, the certainty of the Lord's promise with respect to the Land of Israel, and the Bible's promise of historical progress.

POWER AND ITS LIMITS: AUTHORITARIAN OR RESPONSIVE?

God is portrayed as omnipotent. He created the world out of nothing. On several occasions he demonstrated greater power than other claimants to the title of god. He chose the Israelites as his people and granted them a covenant, plus laws that offered protections to the weak, and proclaimed that a king should rule.[3]

Modern political scientists are alert to a range of regime traits between poles of a spectrum that can be label totalitarian, authoritarian, autocratic, or dictatorial as opposed to responsive, constitutional, democratic, or populist.[4] Most regimes are mixed in their characteristics and cannot be placed at one point on a spectrum without conceding that certain features could place them elsewhere.

The polities that are described in the Bible are especially difficult to classify in modern terms on account of the incomplete and ambiguous descriptions that appear in episodes having political significance. The text does not specify clearly the extent or the limits of the political power assumed by the Almighty or allowed to the kings. A reader must infer from a variety of proclamations, laws, and stories that describe politically relevant events. The power spectrum extended from episodes that seem to indicate limited government and a concern for justice to those indicating an authoritarian God and autocratic human rulers.

God's covenant is an important element in the argument that the polity was limited. The covenants promise the people God's protection and other benefits, including a land. On several occasions God wreaked great punishments on the people for being wayward with respect to his laws. Yet God promised to preserve a remnant of Israel, and to "follow them unfailingly with my bounty . . . and . . . plant them in this land."[5] The Israelites seem to have copied the general idea of covenants from other ancient peoples, adding their own ethics represented by God's law.[6]

One problem for modern readers emerges in the variations between different covenants. In his initial covenants with Noah (that promised a freedom from further destruction like that which came with the flood) and Abraham (that promised many progeny and a land) the people were not required to follow God's law, and there were no clauses that threatened mass destruction for disobedience.[7] In contrast, the covenants associated with the Exodus, Joshua, and later books threatened dire consequences if the Israelites did not obey God's laws. The later covenants did not limit God. He, or those who claimed to speak for him, could forgive the peoples' transgressions or choose to punish them.[8] Would a modern court allow such a drastic and unilateral change in the terms of an agreement? As viewed by one scholar, the covenants were sensitive to the issue of inequality, but they rule out the notion of human initiative and reject the idea of human rights.[9]

The Bible's description of assemblies convened to ratify the covenants suggests that the people had a role in legitimating their regimes at points of crisis.[10] However, the assemblies included classic authoritarian elements. They were anything but opportunities for serious debate or reasoned decision by the masses. They featured a leader reading text said to be from God, with the people limited to affirming their acceptance.[11] On some occasions, the people were humiliated by being reminded of their sins and were told that God offered them the covenant because of his concern for them, not because they have earned it with their integrity or good behavior.[12] The people were told that they must accept the covenant with death or other severe punishment as the only alternative.[13] The covenants offered did not limit God. By implication, the covenants also failed to limit the person claiming to speak for God. It was up to God or those who claimed to speak for him to decide when to forgive the peoples' transgressions, when to punish them, and how to punish them.[14] A religious view is that the Almighty could not be expected to bargain.[15] On other occasions, however, God did bargain: with Abraham over the destruction of Sodom, and with Moses over the destruction of the Israelites after the incident with the golden calf.

One mass assembly in the presence of the priest Ezra reads more like farce than political opportunity. The people were summoned to stand in the cold rain while Ezra indicted them for marriages to foreign wives and demanded their confessions and their separation from improper spouses and children. On account of the rain and the time involved, Ezra appointed a commission to deal with individual cases. The report on the commission's work suggests only partial or symbolic treatment of a widespread problem.[16] Perhaps Ezra recognized the value of appointing a commission to deal with a problem that could not be solved.[17] Ezra's failure to impose his will on the people may count as an occasion of popular rebellion against a biblical regime that limited the power of the regime to penetrate personal space. To mix some often quoted verses of *Judges* (21:25) and *I Kings* (5:5): there was no king in Israel; each man sat under his vine and fig tree with his own wife and children!

Another case for limited government in the biblical polities focuses on the relations of prophets to kings. Yet here, too, it is possible to perceive a range of postures with respect to the prophets and kings. Several prophets stood up to kings as shrill critics. The list begins with Moses' confrontations with Pharaoh and proceeds through Samuel against Saul, Nathan against David, Elijah and Micaiah against Ahab, Elisha against Jehoram, and reaches a culmination in the stories of Jeremiah's encounters against Jehoiakim and Zedekiah. Along with these cases, however, there are indications that weaken the description of constitutionalism via prophetic criticism.

One problem with the notion of prophets as checks and balances against the kings is the dismal record of the prophets in dissuading the kings from any course of action or setting the government on its proper course. One exception to this record is the success of Nathan in dissuading David from building the Temple. Another concerns the prophet Elisha, who may be credited with ending the abominable dynasty of Ahab and Jezebel. Elisha chose Jehu to be anointed king and to implement a bloody purge of Ahab's regime. However, Jehu was not up to the Lord's high standards: "Jehu was not careful to follow the law of the Lord the God of Israel with all his heart; he did not abandon the sins of Jeroboam who led Israel into sin."[18]

Hosea, Amos, Isaiah, and Jeremiah had little success in dissuading the elites of their periods to live righteously or to choose the foreign policies that they demanded. The prophet Ezekiel offered detailed revisions of priestly legislation and practice. According to one scholar, "Wherever Ezekiel's program can be checked against subsequent events it proves to have had no effect."[19] Beyond the issue of the prophet's success in projecting the future, the *Book of Ezekiel* is troublesome to anyone who would link prophecy to the notion of limited government. A passage that God wants followers who are circumcised in heart (or mind) as well as body rings like a symbol of authoritarianism that could have been adopted by George Orwell.[20]

Another problem with the idea of limited government via prophets is the prophets' inability to protect themselves from angry kings and other officials. Against the stories of prophets who got away with sharp criticism, even if they did not succeed in changing the king's policies, are stories of prophets who suffered in the royal courts. Elijah fled to the desert in order to avoid the fate of other prophets killed on the orders of Queen Jezebel.[21] The prophet Micaiah was last seen being put in jail because of his unfavorable advice to Ahab.[22] Amos was sent out of the kingdom of Israel on account of his prophecies.[23] King Jehoiakim had Uriah killed for his prophecies.[24] Jeremiah was in and out of trouble during the regimes of Jehoiakim and Zedekiah. There is a rabbinical tale that King Manasseh had Isaiah sawn asunder because of his prophecies.[25]

Yet another problem in the analysis of prophecy is the question of who was to be accorded the status of a prophet. The Hebrew Bible includes several stories of dispute between individuals who claimed to be speaking for the Lord. Micaiah confronted 400 prophets in the court of Ahab who had given advice diametrically opposed to his own. Amos sought to distance himself from prophets by asserting that he was neither a prophet nor the son of a prophet.[26] During the reign of Hezekiah, Isaiah prophesied that the Assyrians would not destroy Jerusalem, while Micah prophesied that "Zion will become a plowed field, Jerusalem a heap of ruins, and the temple hill rough heath."[27] Jeremiah was characteristically uncharitable when he termed competing prophets "adulterers and hypocrites" and cursed them to suffer early and ignoble deaths.[28]

It was not without risk to assert one's status as a prophet. An unconvincing claimant could be condemned to death as a false prophet or ignored as a madman, but the test of true prophecy is never clearly specified. The compilers of the Bible accorded the status of prophet to some and denied it to others.[29]

Several occasions of popular discontent (murmurings) reported in the Hebrew Bible might be read as contributing to the definition of regime power and its limits. At one point during the wandering in the desert, God noted that the people had already challenged him ten times,[30] and this was not to be the last of it.

In response to some challenges, God told Moses to give the people what they wanted: more water and food and greater variety in their diet. In other cases, the response to murmurings was to demonstrate the shame of the people for acting audaciously and to punish the protesters. It is tempting to speculate that demands of Israelites in the wilderness for better conditions brought positive responses from God. The severest responses seemed to come when the Israelites went beyond protesting conditions of life in the wilderness and sought to replace God, or Moses as God's emissary. The episodes of the golden calf and Korah's rebellion produced mass slaughter of the protesters. There was also a killing of the Israelites who set off on an invasion of the Promised Land after the Lord had decided that the invasion be delayed.[31] However, the Bible nowhere makes clear the distinction between rebellions that were tolerable and those that were intolerable. A modern analyst has concluded that unpredictability is characteristic of totalitarian regimes. They are concerned to keep the people insecure, as well as dependent, and always guessing as to when the authorities will be violent.[32]

Constitutionalism is a way of limiting government by describing the powers of functionaries with institutionalized checks against officials who overstep their authority. The Bible provides several designations of officials and individuals with elevated status. The labels may suggest a division of labor and limited authority, but the terminology seems casual or haphazard.

Priests and Levites are mentioned frequently. However, the categories are used in different ways that have confounded scholarly efforts to sort them out and assign functions to the titles.[33] The Bible also mentions judges, elders, officers, heads of families, heads of the tribes who were chiefs of families,[34] district officers,[35] captains of units of a hundred, heads of clans, nobles, and governors of the people[36] but with little or no specification as to their powers. Scholars have tried, without much success, to describe Israelite regimes on the basis of lists of names or job titles. Some fill in the gaps by speculating about how the Israelite royal courts might have compared with the courts in other ancient countries.[37] As will be noted below, the Bible does specify qualifications and sets limits for the Israelite kings, but then it notes the failure of kings to abide by the provisions.

There is one passage that reads either like the author's effort to keep the people guessing about a mechanism that would control government or a simple lack of awareness about modern political concepts. Moses invited the tribes to choose men of wisdom, understanding and repute in what seems to be an election. Then without a comprehensible transition, Moses seemed to forget about popular selection: "So I took the heads of your tribes men of wisdom and repute and set them in authority over you. . ."[38]

Another passage that is cited in behalf of majority rule is also ambiguous and can be read to warn against the passions of a majority. The same passage also indicates that judicial proceedings were not always just: "You shall not be led into wrongdoing by the majority, nor, when you give evidence in a lawsuit, shall you side with the majority to pervert justice."[39]

LAW AND IMPLEMENTATION

The Bible includes an impressive range of laws, which on the whole seem designed to constrain the behaviors of officials and individuals. These laws figure in claims that biblical polities limited the authority of their rulers. Yet enforcement of these laws was problematic. The Bible leaves open the questions of which laws were actually enforced? When? Or in what conditions?

There are three major collections of law in the Torah, with some repetitions among them: *Exodus* 21-23, *Leviticus* 17-26, and *Deuteronomy* 12-28. Biblical laws include commandments and prohibitions for the people's oral expressions and behaviors with respect to the Lord and to one another. There are laws dealing with killing and theft, obligations and rights of debtors and creditors, and rules of judicial procedure. Requirements of religious ritual included sacrifice, practices to be conducted within the sanctuary, and the rights and practices of the priests. There are dietary laws; rules of cleanliness; sexual prohibitions; procedures of engagement, marriage, and divorce;

rights of women, widows, slaves, orphans, the poor, and foreigners. There are requirements for agricultural practice, a calendar of festivals, plus requirements and prohibitions that apply to the Sabbath and holy days.

There are positive assessments about the implementation of some laws pertaining to the support of the disadvantaged, like those which commanded that corners of the field be left unharvested and available for gleaning by the poor.[40] However, the Bible describes government officials that oppressed the poor[41] as well as priests who were scoundrels[42] and invokes curses against corrupt judges.[43] Notable for the lack of any indication that they were enforced are the laws concerning the sabbatical and jubilee years. These were far-reaching enactments in behalf of economic equality which required the cancellation of debt and servitude and the return of land to its original owners. Perhaps these should be viewed not so much as laws to be implemented as appeals to proper moral behavior[44] or as aspirations for a polity that would be more perfect than the present one.[45] They suggest the proclamation on behalf of happiness in the United States' Declaration of Independence.

Traditional Christian views of Jewish legalism emphasize pettiness along with inflexibility to the point of being inhumane. Paul is quoted as asking, "Is God concerned with oxen?"[46] Modern scholars emphasize the multifaceted nature of Jewish law and the concern of judges to weigh a number of legal provisions along with characteristics of the case at hand. The flexibility of administration that is attributed to biblical law is also a commentary on the pragmatic and non-doctrinaire character in much of the Bible and Judaic culture.

> Judaism was a . . . loosely structured phenomenon, full of inconsistency, tension, and even contradiction . . . (T)he Torah of Moses . . . was not necessarily . . . a coherent body of doctrine universally believed. It was more the centrality of a national symbol, which was acknowledged by all, but which meant different things to different groups.[47]

It is tempting to infer backwards to the biblical period and forward to later periods from what is known about the activity of the Pharisees and the rabbis who came after them. Their work began, according to the beliefs of the rabbis, with the written and oral Torah provided to Moses in Sinai. Then Moses initiated a process of commenting on the law, which became part of the oral Torah handed down and added to by subsequent generations. At various points these oral traditions were grouped together according to subject matter and written as in the Talmud. These writings, along with later commentaries, also became part of the legal corpus that was learned and added to by subsequent generations of rabbis. In the words of one modern scholar

> the halakhah (law) is oriented toward free decision-making on the part of the judges and religious authorities. The intention of the ancient halakhists (teachers of law) was to teach and to guide, rather than to legislate; to express opinions, rather than to hand down decisions. . . the . . . process took place in an atmosphere of free decision-making.[48]

The Hebrew word *torah* means "teaching" and "commentary" as well as "law."[49] The word is also defined as "basic assumption," "theory," a "system in science or research," and "step in learning a profession or a craft."[50] The priest Jose (first century C.E.) said that the Torah must be learned, that it is not something that can be inherited. It is to be studied time and again, with each learning capable of revealing further understanding.[51] Jewish legends say that the Lord studied his Torah more than one hundred times before presenting it to Moses on Mount Sinai, and that God spends three hours each day learning Torah.[52]

Some ancient rabbis identified rules of logic to be used in deciding which legal formulation was appropriate for particular cases. Others found mystical and secret messages in the Torah. There was argument and persuasion among rabbis but nothing so simple as the victory of the side with the most votes. The weight of individual rabbis in the arguments reflected their reputations for learning, wisdom, and piety. The culture of the ancient rabbis and that of their successors down to the twentieth century provided for inspirations and insights into the Lord's purposes. They did not settle disputes by majority rule, and they were not members of a debating society or seminar at a western university; those are developments from the Greek culture that was anathema to many of the ancient rabbis.[53]

By one view, the fair treatment of the weak is the essence of biblical justice and the cornerstone of Judaic law.[54] The freeing of Hebrew slaves is a landmark of Israelite history. Elijah, Amos, and Jeremiah are prominent among the prophets who condemned the exploitation of the poor by the well-to-do. However, several notions of *justice* contribute to ambiguity. They include respect, legality, love and charity, sacred virtue and secular honesty, equity and good law, strict law and severity, clemency and rigor, sincerity, integrity, innocence, social well-being, and veneration.[55]

PRO- AND ANTI-MONARCHICAL

The *Book of Deuteronomy* calls on the Israelites to appoint as king the man chosen by God.[56] However, the final passage in the *Book of Judges* is a classic expression of individual freedom, unfettered by loyalty to a monarchy: "In those days there was no king in Israel, and every man did what was right in his own eyes."[57]

The Bible's perspective on the Israelite monarchy can be treated along with the themes of power and its limits or law and implementation. However, the prominence of the Israelite kings and the criticism of them justifies this separate consideration.

There were unsuccessful efforts to establish Israelite monarchies before the well-known selection of Saul as king. When Gideon was asked to establish a dynasty, his refusal stressed the simple, stateless character of the ideal theocracy described in the *Book of Judges*: "I will not rule over you, nor shall my son; the Lord will rule over you."[58] Gideon's son Abimelech was not self-effacing. He offered himself as king to the elders of Shechem. He also hired "idle and reckless men" and killed his 70 brothers. When Jotham heard that Abimelech had become king of Shechem, he climbed to the top of Mount Gerizim and shouted out a story of how the trees chose a king among themselves. The olive and fig trees and the grape vine refused the invitation because they had more honorable functions. It was only the despicable thorn bush that accepted the invitation. And the thorn bush threatened destruction with fire if its rule was not accepted.[59] We read that God had Abimelech killed, but only after he had ruled for three years.[60]

It is not only that the Israelites were unprepared for a king or other institutions of a state during the period of Judges. They were not a unified community. The nation building begun by Moses in the wilderness was not yet complete. The *Book of Judges* reports competition and fighting between the Israelite tribes as well as cooperation against common enemies under the leadership of charismatic but temporary leaders.[61]

The utility of temporary leaders reached the limits of its usefulness as the Philistines began moving from their coastal cities toward the upland Israelites. The people demanded a king who could defend them effectively. Socio-economic developments among the Israelites also contributed to a situation where temporary rule was inadequate. There was a growth of population and an increase in wealth that required more permanent government in order to protect land-holdings and trade. The same developments may have increased the efficiency of the economy and freed some individuals to serve full-time as officials.[62]

A biblical story tells how the prophet Samuel warned the Israelites that a king would take for himself their sons, daughters, and fields.[63] His speech is a key feature of the theme that the monarchy was a undesirable change from the idealized polity of charismatic and temporary leaders.

The *Book of Deuteronomy* sets limits on the Israelite kings. The king would be an Israelite man chosen by God; he must not acquire too many horses or wives, great quantities of silver or gold for himself, nor cause the people to go back to Egypt; he must not become prouder than his fellow-countrymen; he must read from God's law and not depart from it.[64]

Much of the text in *Samuel*, *Kings*, and *Chronicles* describes how the kings in Judah and Israel failed to abide by these provisions. Should these texts be viewed as the ethical preoccupation of biblical writers and their concern to constrain the kings? Or as their inability to limit the kings in keeping with biblical legislation and ethical norms? The answer seems to be "both," even though that is not made clear by the Bible.

Saul's reign deteriorated along with his sanity. David and Solomon come in for great praise by the writers of the Bible but also were condemned for personal failings. After the reign of Solomon, the quality of Israelite kings declined more or less consistently. The Bible portrays Jeroboam as a traitor and Rehoboam as a fool. Ahab is a fool in the way he ignores the good advice of Micaiah and evil for his treatment of Naboth. Josiah is praised for his religious reforms. However, Josiah's reforms had limited success, and he did not heed advice against taking part in the battle that ended his life.[65]

ETHNOCENTRISM AND UNIVERSALISM

The Israelites' status as the God's chosen people and numerous episodes indicating their special treatment support the assertion that the Bible is ethnocentric. However, other materials express universalistic sentiments.

The God of the Hebrew Bible chose a people and stuck with them through one period of waywardness and punishment after another. In the eyes of some commentators, this is the principal theme in a Bible that is marked by numerous perspectives and doctrines.[66] Some couple the themes of the chosen people and God's concern for justice and morality by noting the weakness of the Israelites. They focus on God's rescue of the Israelites from slavery, and his concern for them in the context of powerful and rapacious neighbors.[67] Other commentators contrast God's ethnocentrism with his traits of justice and mercy. God was not always just with respect to every last Israelite. What he did to hapless Israelites, however, is nothing compared to what he proclaimed against those who caused problems for Israel.

The classic enemies were the Amalekites. They were among the peoples who did not want to share land with the Israelites and served time and again as the symbols of hostile foreigners. The *Book of Exodus* notes that God resolved to "blot out all memory of Amalek from under heaven."[68] In a story involving Samuel and Saul, we read that God demanded that the Amalekites be destroyed completely, along with all their possessions: "men and women, children and babes in arms, herds and flocks, camels and asses."[69]

The writers and compilers of different books express conflicting views with respect to ethnocentrism and universalism. *Ezra* and *Nehemiah* take strong postures in behalf of Judaic purity.

> The land which you are entering and will possess is
> a polluted land, polluted by the foreign population

> with their abominable practices, which have made it unclean from end to end. Therefore, do not give your daughters in marriage to their sons, and do not marry your sons to their daughters, and never seek their welfare or prosperity.[70]

Rabbi Meir Kahane quoted passages like this in behalf of his proposals to forbid sexual relations between Israeli Jews and non-Jews, to deprive non-Jews of civil rights, and to expel them from Israel.[71]

In contrast to the *Books of Ezra* and *Nehemiah*, the story of the Moabite Ruth emphasizes the openness of Judaism to newcomers. Not only was Ruth welcomed into a Judaic family, but she is described as the great grandmother of King David.[72] Jonah describes God's mercy for the Assyrians.[73] Some portions of *Isaiah* are universalistic (nation shall not lift up sword against nation, neither shall they learn war any more),[74] while other sections are ethnocentric-centric.

> Israel will prevail over the nations.[75] . . .
> For that nation and kingdom that will not serve thee shall perish; Yea, those nations shall be utterly wasted.[76]

Numerous rabbis have sought to square the ethnocentric and the universal themes in the Hebrew Bible. It is common to say that the Jews have a special mission by virtue of being the chosen people. They are subject to heightened scrutiny and discipline by God and are meant to be an example that will attract the rest of the world to his law.[77]

THE ELUSIVE NATURE OF THE PROMISED LAND

The *Book of Genesis* couples the promise of the land with a prediction of alienation from it: "The Lord said to Abram, 'Know this for certain, that your descendants will be aliens living in a land that is not theirs. . . '"[78] The *Book of Joshua* describes the total conquest of the Land by the Israelites yet indicates that foreigners remained among them. The *Book of Judges* reinforces the image of an incomplete conquest and describes foreigners who continued to threaten the Israelites.[79] Especially after the split between Israel and Judah, the Israelites were chronically threatened by more powerful empires. There were exiles after conquests by Assyria and Babylon and later by Rome after the end of the period described in the Hebrew Bible. There were also voluntary migrations. Jews went abroad to serve in foreign armies or imperial governments and in search of other opportunities.[80] The *Book of Jeremiah* reports that the prophet was taken to Egypt along with a group of Judeans after Jerusalem fell to the Babylonians.[81]

The *Books of Ezra* and *Nehemiah* describe the return of Babylonian exiles, but they seem to have relied on wish more than reality. Most of the exiles may have remained in Babylon, and most of the world's Jews may have lived in the Diaspora during the latter period of the Second Temple.[82] One estimate is that one million Jews lived in Judea during the reign of Herod, while four million lived in Syria, Asia Minor, Babylon, and Egypt.[83] Another estimate is that only 10 or 20 percent of the Jews actually lived in Judea during the lifetime of Jesus.[84]

HISTORICAL PROGRESS AGAINST CYCLICAL PROMISE AND FAILURE

A number of commentators find a biblical theme of development toward greater perfection as represented by the fulfillment of God's law. It appears in the progression from Abraham's acceptance of God, to the acquisition of national consciousness during the exodus, the development of monarchy, and laws that seem to have been formulated during the monarchical period and later. An explicitly progressive view of history appears in Isaiah's prophecy that there will be an end of days when there will be peace among nations[85] and in Jeremiah's vision beyond the imminent destruction of Jerusalem by the Babylonians, to a time when God will provide a new covenant that would assure the security of a rebuilt Israel.[86] Christian commentators see a further progression to the coming of Jesus and doctrines of the New Testament.[87]

Israelites' progressive view of history is contrasted with a cyclical view of nature that emphasizes the repetition of birth, death, and regeneration. The Bible condemns cultic prostitution and other fertility rites linked by pagans to the seasonal cycles. However, a larger notion of cycles can be found in the Bible's account of history and stands in contrast to the theme of unilateral development.

The Bible's cycles appear in the successive promise of God's rule, and the failure of the people to live according to it. The theme begins with the Creation and the Fall brought about by Eve's eating the forbidden fruit. Promise and failure also appear in the Exodus and the numerous rebellions that occurred in the desert and again in the waxing and waning of Israelite fortunes along with their adherence to God's law and their waywardness during the period of Judges. The monarchy was ordained by God, revered for seeing to the people's defense, and criticized for its failings of justice and righteousness. Two kings who appeared toward the end of the Davidic dynasty, Hezekiah and Josiah, were praised for returning to the way of the Lord. Yet their reforms did not last. It was Jeremiah's task to identify Babylon as God's instrument for ending the Israelite monarchy and to predict that God would punish Babylon, revitalize Israel, and provide it with a new covenant.

For those who would doubt the cyclical theme in the Hebrew Bible, the third chapter of *Ecclesiastes* offers its sublime poetry. The same passage provides a fitting closing to this chapter. It expresses the contingency or relativism of postures that can claim biblical legitimacy: "For everything its season, and for every activity under heaven its time . . . to plant and to uproot . . to pull down and to build . . to tear and to mend . ."[88]

* * *

The final chapters of this book depart from the biblical period and develop linkages between the Bible and Judaism over the ages and modern Israel. They show the positive side of what some may see as biblical confusion or a mixture of different and contradictory norms. Jews continue to express many of the ideals that appear in the Bible, and they show a willingness to accept dispute about religious doctrines as well as the personalities and issues of current politics. Modern Israel has been threatened with national destruction and is a hot-house of conflicting perspectives. It is healthy for Jewish vitality and Israeli democracy that people admit the value of diverse norms, conclude that conditions may determine the relevance of principles, see good and bad in the same actions, and honor critics who resemble biblical prophets in how they censure elites.

NOTES

[1] See, for example, Leo Strauss and Joseph Cropsey, eds., *History of Political Philosophy* (Chicago: Rand McNally, 1963).

[2] Quoted in Neil Asher Silberman, *Digging for God and Country: Exploration, Archeology, and the Secret Struggle for the Holy Land 1799-1917* (New York: Anchor Books, 1990), p. 86.

[3] *Deuteronomy* 17:14-20.

[4] Charles H. McIlwain, *Constitutionalism, Ancient and Modern* (Ithaca, N.Y.: Cornell University Press, 1947); J. Ronald Pennock and John W. Chapman, eds., *Constitutionalism* (New York: New York University Press, 1977); John Patrick Kirscht, *Dimensions of Authoritarianism: A Review of Research and Theory* (Lexington: University of Kentucky Press, 1967); and Amos Permutter, *Modern Authoritarianism: A Comparative Institutional Analysis* (New Haven: Yale University Press, 1981).

[5] See Ernest W. Nicholson, *God and His People: Covenant and Theology in the Old Testament* (Oxford: Clarendon Press, 1986). This example of God's continuing commitment appears in *Jeremiah* 32.

[6] George E. Mendenhall, *The Tenth Generation: The Origins of the Biblical Tradition* (Baltimore: Johns Hopkins University Press, 1973).

[7] The covenant made with Noah in behalf of all living creatures appears in *Genesis* 9; the covenant with Abraham in behalf of his descendants appears in *Genesis* 15 and 17. *Genesis* 17 includes only the requirement of circumcision.

[8] See, for example, *Leviticus* 26:40-45; *Joshua* 24:19.

[9] Lionel Kochan, *Jews, Idols and Messiahs: The Challenge from History* (Oxford: Basil Blackwell, 1990), p. 15.

[10] Hayim Tadmor, "'The People' and the Kingship in Ancient Israel: The Role of Political Institutions in the Biblical Period," *Journal of World History*, Vol. XI, No. 1-2, 1968, pp. 1-23.

[11] See, for example, *Exodus* 19:7-19; *Joshua* 24:16,22.

[12] *Deuteronomy* 8:2; 9:5-6.

[13] *Deuteronomy* 30:15; *Joshua* 24:20.

[14] See, for example, *Leviticus* 26:40-45; *Joshua* 24:19.

[15] Abba Hillel Silver, *Where Judaism Differs: An Inquiry into the Distinctiveness of Judaism* (New York: Collier Books, 1989),Chapter 2.

[16] *Ezra* 10:44. For another reading of the biblical episode, see John Bright, *A History of Israel*, (London: SCM Press, Ltd., 19080), p. 388.

[17] J. Maxwell Miller and John H. Hayes, *A History of Ancient Israel and Judah* (Philadelphia: The Westminster Press, 1986), p. 474.

[18] *II Kings* 10:31.

[19] Moshe Greenberg, "The Design and Themes of *Ezekiel*'s Program of Restoration," in James Luther Mays and Paul J. Achtemeier, *Interpreting the Prophets* (Philadelphia: Fortress Press, 1987), pp. 215-36.

[20] *Ezekiel* 44:9.

[21] *I Kings*, 18, 19.

[22] *I Kings* 22:28.

[23] *Amos* 7:10-17.

[24] *Jeremiah* 26:20-23.

[25] Ephraim E. Urbach, *The Sages: Their Concepts and Belief*, Translated by Israel Abrahams (Cambridge: Harvard University Press, 1987), p. 559.

[26] *Amos* 7:14.

[27] *Micah* 3:12.

[28] *Jeremiah* 23:14; 28:16-17; 29:21-23.

[29] See Urbach, p. 564f.

[30] *Numbers* 14:19-23.

[31] *Numbers* 14:1-45.

[32] Hannah Arendt, *The Origins of Totalitarianism* (New York: Meridian Books, 1958).

[33] For example, Rodney K. Duke, "The Portion of the Levite: Another Reading of *Deuteronomy* 18:6-8," *Journal of Biblical Literature*, 106, 2, June 1987, pp. 193-201.

[34] *I Kings* 8:1.

[35] *I Kings* 20:14.

[36] *II Chronicles* 23:1-2,20.

[37] Tryggve N.D. Mettinger, *King and Messiah: The Civil and Sacral Legitimation of the Israelite Kings* (Lund, Sweden: Lieber Laeromedel, 1976).

[38] *Deuteronomy* 1:13-15.

[39] *Exodus* 23:2. See Joel Roth, *The Halakhic Process: A Systemic Analysis* (New York: Jewish Theological Seminary of America, 1986), especially Chapters 5-7.

[40] Joachim Jeremias, *Jerusalem in the Time of Jesus: An Investigation into Economic and Social Conditions during the New Testament Period* (London: SCM Press, Ltd., 1969), p. 132.

[41] *Ecclesiastes* 5:8.

[42] *I Samuel* 2:12-17.

[43] *Proverbs* 24:23-25.

[44] Nahum M. Sarna, *Exploring Exodus: The Heritage of Biblical Israel* (New York: Schocken Books, 1987), Chapter VIII. See also E. W. Heaton, *The Hebrew Kingdoms* (Oxford: Oxford University Press, 1968), p. 223.

[45] Leon Epsztein, *Social Justice in the Ancient Near East and the People of the Bible* (London: SCM Press Ltd, 1986), p. 134. On the comparison of Israelite implementations of law with other ancient societies in the region, see A. Leo Oppenheim, *Ancient Mesopotamia: Portrait of a Dead Civilization* (Chicago: University of Chicago Press, 1977), pp. 158, 231-32.

[46] John L. McKenzie, S.J., *The Two-Edged Sword: An Interpretation of the Old Testament* (Garden City, NY: Image Books, 1966), p. 56. See *I Corinthians* 9:9.

[47] Philip S. Alexander, "Jewish Law in the Time of Jesus: Towards a Clarification of the Problem," in Barnabas Lindars SSF, ed., *Law and Religion: Essays on the Place of Law in Israel and Early Christianity* (Cambridge, England: James Clarke & Co., 1988), pp. 44-58.

[48] Gedaliah Alon, *The Jews in Their Land: In the Talmudic Age* (Cambridge: Harvard University Press, 1989), p. 28.

[49] Martin Sicker, *The Judaic State: A Study in Rabbinic Political Theory* (New York: Praeger, 1988), p. 18.

[50] Abraham Even-Shoshan, *The New Dictionary* (Jerusalem: Kiriyat Sepher, 1980), p. 1441, Hebrew.

[51] Leo Baeck, *Judaism and Christianity* (New York: Atheneum, 1970), p. 46.

[52] Simon Rawidowicz, *Studies in Jewish Thought* (Philadelphia: The Jewish Publication Society of America, 1974), Chapter 12.

[53] On the nature of Jewish lawmaking as it relates to the Bible, see Roger Brooks, *The Spirit of the Ten Commandments: Shattering the Myth of Rabbinic Legalism* (New York: Harper and Row, 1990).

[54] Paul D. Hanson, *The People Called: The Growth of Community in the Bible* (New York: Harper and Row, 1986).

[55] Leon Epsztein, *Social Justice in the Ancient Near East and the People of the Bible* (London: SCM Press Ltd, 1986), pp. 48, 66. For an attempt to find principles in Jewish law that are equivalent to modern conceptions of human rights, see Haim H. Cohn, *Human Rights in Jewish Law* (New York: KTAV Publishing House, 1984).

[56] *Deuteronomy* 17:14-20.

[57] *Judges* 21:25.

[58] *Judges* 8.

[59] *Judges* 9:7-15.

[60] *Judges* 9.

[61] *Judges* 12 and 20.

[62] Israel Finkelstein, "The Emergence of the Monarchy in Israel: The Environmental and Socio-Economic Aspects," *Journal for the Study of the Old Testament*, 44, June 1989, pp. 43-74.

[63] *I Samuel* 8:10-18.

[64] *Deuteronomy* 17:14-20.

[65] *II Chronicles* 35.

[66] Martin Buber, "The Man of Today and the Jewish Bible " and "The Faith of Judaism" in his *Israel and the World: Essays in a Time of Crisis* (New York: Schocken Books: 1963).

[67] For example, Nahum M. Sarna, *Exploring Exodus: The Heritage of Biblical Israel* (New York: Schocken Books, 1987), Introduction.

[68] *Exodus* 17:14.

[69] *I Samuel* 15:3.

[70] *Ezra* 9:11-12.

[71] Rabbi Meir Kahane, "Forty Years" (Brooklyn, New York: The Institute of the Jewish Idea, 1983).

[72] *Ruth* 4:13-22. Against the view that the Book of *Ruth* was written as a polemic against the ethnocentricism of *Ezra* is another explanation from a traditional Jewish perspective: that the central character of *Ruth* separated herself completely from her Moabite background, and therefore did not present the threat to Judaism that *Ezra* saw in the people of the land who were not completely Jewish. See the commentary of Fibal Melzar on the Book of *Ruth* in *The Five Scrolls* (Jerusalem: Mossad Harav Kook, 1973), p. 3, Hebrew. See also Harry M. Orlinsky, "Nationalism-Universalism and Internationalism in Ancient Israel," in his *Essays in Biblical Culture and Bible Translation* (New York: KTAV Publishing House, Inc., 1974), pp. 78-116.

[73] McKenzie, p. 231.

[74] *Isaiah* 2:4.

[75] *Isaiah*, 54:3-4.

[76] *Isaiah*, 60:12.

[77] Leo Baeck, *Essence of Judaism* (New York: Schocken Books, 1948).

[78] *Genesis* 15:6-14.

[79] See *Joshua* 10:40 and 23:9-13, and *Judges* 2:20-21.

[80] See, for example, *Jeremiah* 44:11-12.

[81] *Jeremiah*, Chapters 42-43.

[82] D. S. Russell, *The Jews from Alexander to Herod* (Oxford: Oxford University Press, 1967), Chapter VII.

[83] Chaim Potok, *Wanderings* (New York: Ballantine Books, 1978), p. 263.

[84] Samuel Sandmel, *Judaism and Christian Beginnings* (New York: Oxford University Press, 1978), p. 17.

[85] For example, *Isaiah* 2:4.

[86] *Jeremiah* 32:38-40.

[87] Paul D. Hanson, *Old Testament Apocalyptic* (Nashville: Abingdon Press, 1987).

[88] *Ecclesiastes* 3:1-8.

Chapter 9
Biblical Politics and Jewish Vitality

The Israelites aspired to rule themselves but usually found themselves ruled by others. This combination led them to compose a Holy Book that has much to say about politics and portrayed the diversity of behaviors and norms encountered in a turbulent history of several hundred years. Judaism developed as a religion with political traits. For an ancient Jew this observation may have been not at all striking. It is the modern secular Jew (and non-Jew), who thinks in terms of politics and religion as categories of behavior that are best kept separate.

This chapter is not a detailed introduction to Judaism as much as a discussion of political elements that Judaism seems to have inherited from its ancient roots. It begins with a brief portrayal of politics in the abstract, proceeds to review some of the material in previous chapters and associate it with continuing themes in what has been termed the *Judaisms* of past and present. The chapter concludes by reviewing two books by modern Jewish novelists that deal with David. These reflect the continuing appeal of biblical themes for Jewish culture. And especially as they are contrasted with pietistic Jewish legends, they illustrate the vast range of Jewish perspectives that emerge from Holy Scripture.

ON POLITICS AND JUDAISM

"Politics" does not lend itself to crisp definition. It includes elements of attaining and using power in a situation of competing groups, ideals, or interests; organizing supporters, pursuing tactics against antagonists; seeking the control of governments or other important bodies; and using power in order to implement goals. It is conventional to use "politics" in reference to activities that occur within the public forums of states. However, politics also occurs in private organizations and communities that are not autonomous governmentally, like religious congregations. Perhaps the prime political reality is a recognition of differences in desires or perspectives about a problematic situation and an effort to cope with those differences.

Problem-solving via politics is ideally non-violent, with an important role for persuasion. Von Clausewitz's epigram that war is "a political instrument, a continuation of political commerce, a carrying out of the same by other means" suggests that violence occurs when the usual conduct of politics does not achieve results that are acceptable to the participants.[1] Similar is an epigram attributed to Mao Tse Tung that politics is war without violence, while war is politics with violence.[2] Even in modern democracies violence is likely to be somewhere, to be used against citizens who will not pay their taxes or obey other rules voluntarily.[3]

This chapter and the next continue the themes developed in the discussion of politics in the Hebrew Bible. They emphasize the diversity of Judaic themes and practices and the coupling of politics with diversity. This chapter focuses on the diversities of Judaism and the cultures of Jews. The next chapter describes the diversity of political views and practices that have legitimacy in modern Israel, noting that Israelis quarrel loudly about Judaism and much else that is relevant to them.

No one who reads the Hebrew Bible, the works of the rabbis, or the myriad of commentaries on them can approach the subject of Judaism (historic or modern) casually. For every assertion of its essence there are sure to be experts who will quarrel. It is also not clear where religious doctrine ends and the cultural traits of Jews (religious and secular) begin.

With all appropriate reservations about the numerous principles of Judaism, it appears that politics has a place among them. Politics may be integral to any doctrines that are so diverse and a people who have developed so many sub-cultures over such a span of time and place. Perhaps the concern for politics derives from the centrality of a nation's history in Judaism, the perpetual concern as to how Jews will view their history and deal with the varieties of themselves as well as with powerful outsiders and foreign perspectives.

Persuasion appears at several points in the biblical polities and post-biblical Judaism. The great prophets viewed themselves as independent of the kings and sought to persuade the people and their rulers. The rabbinical sages quarreled and won adherents to their position from among their fellow sages by the power of their arguments.[4] Rabbinical students continue to learn from arguments on points of doctrine and the application of law. Disputes between ancient rabbis about the contents of the Passover service are included in the *Haggadah* that families recite prior to the festive meal. After the meal, it is traditional for participants to argue about the significance of different elements in the service and in the story of Exodus. From what we know about the compilation of the Hebrew Bible, it included some politics. The canonized version evolved over the ages among scholars who argued about the appropriateness of different versions and may have offered changes in order to make certain texts more acceptable to their colleagues.[5]

The Hebrew Bible is frequently cited as an example of revealed truth, but its truth is plural and open to dispute. Ancient and modern rabbis assert that a complete Torah (oral and written) was provided to Moses in Sinai and that they only add commentaries on their understanding of Torah. These claims should be viewed as statements of faith and doctrine. Scholars make a persuasive case that the written and oral Torah changed over the course of ancient history. A modern rabbi writes that the approaches used to interpret the Bible are too many to summarize and that the oral Torah serves "the function of keeping the canonical written Bible a fluid text through endless commentary and interpretation."[6] A related view is that the Hebrew Bible reflects numerous streams in the evolution of ancient Judaism and that rabbinical Judaism has continued the evolution in a plurality of streams.[7]

Numerous disputes are left unresolved in the Hebrew Bible. Different positions are expressed explicitly or implicitly. It is as if the editors agreed to disagree on a number of points. Commentators try to persuade one another of their interpretations. The final text both glorifies and condemns the monarchies of the Israelites. Some books and verses put the emphasis on ethnocentrism, while others express God's concern for Israel's neighbors and the roles that converts and their descendants have played in Israel. Different conceptions of God's covenant with his chosen people are contradictory: some are unconditional, while others threaten that God will abandon and destroy his people if they do not obey his laws.

Politics in ancient Israel was sacred business, concerned with the destiny of God's people. Kings and prophets differed about what God expected of them and how they should behave with respect to his doctrines. There was also politics concerned with worldly issues: who would be king, who would be a member of the king's retinue, and whether the king would pay tribute to this or that foreign power. At times there was an overlap between sacred and worldly politics, as when the prophets joined the disputes about paying tribute or who should be king and argued that the fate of God's chosen people was in the balance.

The politics described in the Bible could be as bloody as politics in modern Lebanon. We should remember the rabbinical story of King Manasseh having the prophet Isaiah sawed through on account of unwanted prophecies, court figures who wanted to eliminate Jeremiah, and the death penalty enacted against the prophet Uriah who spoke out like Jeremiah.

As he is described in the Hebrew Bible, even the Lord is political. At times he is flexible and tolerant of different conceptions of what is right. He changes his mind in response to argument. God proclaimed ideals but in some cases could be satisfied with what was attainable.

Struggle is a prominent feature of the Hebrew Bible. The people at its center struggle continuously for their security and their faith in the midst of hostile foreign powers and temptations to be like other people. God himself struggles with his wayward people. It is a short step from the prophets' struggle with the peoples' chronic misbehavior to the statement that appears in the apocryphal *Second Book of Esdras*: "The truth is, no man alive is innocent of offense. It is through thy mercy towards those with no store of good deeds to their name that thy justice and kindness, O Lord, will be made known."[8] From this it is another short step to the Christian doctrine of original sin and another step to the need for a Savior to intervene with God for the people. Jews have not taken these steps. For them, the choice between good and evil and the ambiguities remain a matter of struggle for each generation and individual.

Since the biblical period there have been changes in the Jews' rituals, doctrines, communal governance, issue agendas (i.e., the problems that Jews argue about), and styles of politics. Studies of Jewish communal government in different periods and countries show varieties of self rule, dependence and autonomy from Gentle authorities. Jews continue to quarrel about biblical issues described in the previous chapter: the justice of God, the propriety of authoritarian or responsive leadership, the centrality of the Promised Land and the value of a Diaspora existence, and the relative weight of Jewish doctrines that are ethnocentric or universal. Some Jewish writers have been nonpolitical or even anti-political. They have urged Jews to refrain from contact with the governments of the Gentiles and to concentrate on their own inner spirituality.[9]

The character of biblical politics seems to have been particularly suitable to the subsequent history of the Jews. From their first appearance in the Promised Land they have had to accommodate themselves to foreign neighbors and outsiders more powerful than themselves. Several scholars have characterized the Hebrew Bible and Judaism as providing provocative questions and a lack of final answers. Gabriel Josipovici writes that "Christianity expresses profound desires and suggests that these can eventually be fulfilled. The Hebrew Bible refuses that consolation."[10] Aaron Wildavsky made a similar point about Moses' leadership in the desert.

> (there was not) a series of successful solutions but rather a set of perennial problems that may be mitigated from time to time but can never be resolved. (In his search for the ideal style of leadership) Moses moves through several political regimes, seeking but never finding the ideal balance among them. In the same way, Jews are commanded to seek God, though they will never find him; the journey is as important as the destination.[11]

Jewish communities in ancient times, both in the Promised Land and the Diaspora, began the process of finding in the Bible the themes that served their needs. Lionel Kochan adapts a Talmudic passage, based on a phrase in Deuteronomy, to his own study of Jewish communities in Berlin and London: "'The Torah is not in heaven,' but it is in Berlin and London, as much and as little as anywhere else."[12]

The assertion of diversity in the Hebrew Bible and Judaism may be too flaccid or trivial a theme. It is an obvious point that has been made by numerous others. Yet it is crucial to understanding Jewish vitality in the presence of its diversity and the implications of that diversity for modern Israel.

With hardly less vitality and creativity than their biblical ancestors, the Jews of the modern world have adapted to a variety of cultures and have developed numerous perspectives about themselves and their surroundings. According to the prominent and politically involved American rabbi Abba Hillel Silver:

> In the Bible and Talmud the doctrines of Judaism are nowhere presented in the unified form of a treatise. They are broadly diffused in prophetic utterances, legal codes, history, poetry, precept, parable, and drama. . . Men enamored of compact systems will have difficulty in grasping the essence of Judaism . . . Judaism is no more the product of any one country than it is the product of any one age. . . It is the emergent spiritual way of life of a historical people. . . It possesses the unity not of a system but of a symphony.[13]

Gershom Scholem wrote that Judaism contains such a variety of doctrines that:

> There is no way of telling *a priori* what beliefs are possible or impossible within the framework of Judaism. . . . The "Jewishness" in the religiosity of any particular period is not measured by dogmatic criteria that are unrelated to actual historical circumstances, but solely by what sincere Jews do, in fact, believe, or, at least, consider to be legitimate possibilities.[14]

It only begins the categorization of modern Judaism to speak of three major streams of Judaism (Orthodox, Conservative, and Reform). Within the liberal wing of North American Jewry, the Reconstructionists fit themselves in the spectrum among Conservative and Reform congregations. "Conservative" and "Reform" Judaism are relevant mostly to North America, where they describe most of the Jews. A survey of Israeli Jews used the terms "ultra-Orthodox," "Orthodox," "traditional," and "secular." It found 10 percent of the population within each of the "ultra-Orthodox" and "Orthodox" categories, 29 percent "traditional," and 51 percent secular.[15] Israelis who consider themselves "traditional" are typically from North African or Asian backgrounds. Many of them observe kashrut and Sabbath and wear kipot (yarmulkes) but are not as rigorous about observances as those who consider themselves Orthodox.

Numerous ultra-Orthodox communities of Jerusalem, Bnei Brak, New York, London, Melbourne, and Antwerp signify their varieties by distinctive clothing and their insistence on adhering to their own rabbis' rulings with respect to law and custom.[16] Individual rabbis continue the age-old tradition that each scholar learns the Torah and other sources. They view disagreement as natural, as something that will contribute to the greater understanding of each scholar. The label of Jewish humanist is available to individuals who identify as Jews but shy away from all conventional religious doctrines or even renounce them explicitly. Failures to live according to God's word appear to Jewish humanists as understandable in the face of attractive cosmopolitan cultures.

It seems accurate to speak of Judaism not as a unitary religion but as a variety of sects, plus many Jews who would not admit to any doctrinal loyalties. Jacob Neusner claims to identify eight varieties of "Judaisms" in a book entitled, *Death and Birth of Judaism*, but he seems to identify at least *ten* varieties: that which preceded the Judaism of the dual Torah (written and oral), which Neusner dates from the fourth century C.E.; the Judaism of the dual Torah; Reform, Orthodox, and Conservative Judaisms; Zionism; Jewish socialism; American Judaism; Israeli Judaism; and a Judaism of "reversion" which advocates a fresh encounter with the Judaism of the dual Torah.[17]

In the commonalty that is Jewishness, ethnicity may be more important than any shared doctrines. The perception of peoplehood that Jews and Gentiles share about Jews sets the community apart from others. Yet the ethnicity of Jews has its own mysteries. It stretches across peoples who differ on obvious racial characteristics as well as language and other cultural traits.

Jewish ethnicity has proved useful for community survival, insofar as it allows diversity of doctrine. While individual sectarian leaders may be outspoken in their intolerance of ideas they consider to be foreign, the community has been willing to accept as Jews individuals of widely variant beliefs and practices (as well as non-beliefs and a failure to practice any conventional rituals). A Christian historian of Christianity expressed his admiration of Jews for inter-communal tolerance without the warring factionalism of Christian sects: "Countless varieties of Christianity have fought about matters of doctrine and interpretation, with each claiming to be a universal faith, more advanced doctrinally than tribal Judaism."[18]

Thirty years ago the editors of *Commentary* magazine asked a number of distinguished rabbis and other Jewish thinkers to address questions about the concept of the chosen people, Jewish law, and the interface between Judaism and politics. The responses cannot be taken as a representative picture of Jewish thinking. None of the respondents reflected the traditions of Kabbalah or other forms of mysticism, charisma, pietism, messianism, wonder rabbis who practice healing, and those who pursue hidden meanings via *gematria*. Such movements have waxed and waned among rabbis from ancient times to the present. Even the more conventional ultra-Orthodox were not well represented in *Commentary*'s survey. Despite these limitations, however, the survey reveals a great variety among the rabbis and other scholars.[19]

The survey revealed contrasting statements about the chosen people. Some rabbis demanded significant change: "the revision of the ethnocentric impetus in our tradition should be the first item on the agenda," according to a Conservative rabbi;[20] and "the best way . . . to answer the charge that the chosen-people doctrine has been `the model' for theories of national and racial superiority is to eliminate that doctrine from the Jewish liturgy," according to the founder of Reconstructionism.[21] Others ascribed to an assertion by a Conservative rabbi that "the essence of Judaism is the affirmation that the Jews are the chosen people; all else is commentary."[22]

Several of the respondents indicated that a number of the biblical commandments are anachronistic and that individuals learned in the Torah are entitled to decide how to observe them or whether to observe them. A number of Orthodox rabbis asserted that they accepted every word of the Torah (i.e., the Pentateuch, or Genesis through Deuteronomy) as revealed from God. However, they said that their interpretations of the written commandments depended on the oral Torah or the commentaries made by rabbis.[23]

Some of the rabbis added to the picture of diversity by stressing that Judaism encourages doubt or skepticism. According to an Orthodox rabbi

> I do teach that Judaism encourages doubt even as it enjoins faith and commitment. A Jew dare not live with absolute certainty, not only because certainty is the hallmark of the fanatic and Judaism abhors fanaticism, but also because doubt is good for the human soul, its humility, and consequently its greater potential ultimately to discover its Creator.[24]

A well-known Conservative rabbi wrote that Jews await the messiah but should resist the claim that the messiah has arrived. He noted the long list of false messiahs ("from Jesus to Shabbethai Zevi to Karl Marx and Leon Trotsky").[25]

A number of respondents to *Commentary*'s survey wrote about the inevitable interface between Judaism and politics: "Judaism is deeply concerned with the condition of the *polis*. Consequently, Judaism has something to say on all political matters which involve moral judgments."[26] Several rabbis expressed the view that Judaism must reject certain political doctrines, but would not necessarily support any policy or practice of a secular state: ". . . whereas Judaism rules out some political viewpoints, it does not entail an absolute and unalterable commitment to any positive viewpoint."[27] Several participants in *Commentary's* anthology wrote that a practicing Jew could not support a totalitarian regime which elevated itself above the individual's capacity to search out the truth and express it. Once freedom of conscience was assured, however, the rabbis conceded that Jews would probably argue among themselves as to whether current circumstances justified one or another option with respect to economic policy or social services.

Some rabbis stressed that *Judaism was not so diverse as to be open to all perspectives*. They anchored themselves in the words of the Torah or wrote that it was necessary to rely on those who are learned in the Torah in order to discern the Jewish approach to an issue. Yet even Orthodox rabbis conceded the different schools in rabbinical tradition. There is no monopoly of wisdom. It is desirable to engage in consultation in order to seek God's will and not one's own.[28]

The diversity among learned Jews appears strikingly in the acerbic nature of some rabbinical arguments. Just as the Hebrew Bible as finally compiled seems to have a tolerance for diversity along with individual episodes that are anything but tolerant, so modern Judaism has numerous intolerant figures amidst its great variety of communities and leaders. Some rabbis of Orthodoxy's right wing describe rabbis affiliated with Conservative, Reform, and Reconstructionist movements as beneath contempt. They also direct serious criticism to rabbis who claim to be Orthodox. The work of the Orthodox rabbi quoted above as saying that he teaches doubt was described by another rabbi as an example of modern Orthodoxy. The critic referred to the treatment of Jewish law (halacha) by this school as "dangerous and even ludicrous . . . crude misunderstandings of the . . . material . . . glaring misuses of . . . generalities . . . semantic legerdemain . ."[29]

A spokesman of modern Orthodoxy has sought to find a place between one extreme that he described as the chaos of Jewish movements that depart too greatly from historic roots and another extreme of the ultra-Orthodox right wing that is too quick to pin the label of heresy on scholars who propound divergent views. This rabbi defends what he calls *finite pluralism*. It is *pluralist* insofar as it admits of more than a single valid solution to individual problems. It is *finite* insofar as it must base its argument on the Torah and the prior work of recognized sages. The process is more important than the conclusions. A scholar who bases his conclusion on such materials may be in error but should be able to maintain his membership in the Orthodox community. Outside the community would be one who would

> seek to advance an anti-halachic position, and legitimate it by invoking either science or psychology or the *Zeitgeist* . . . (Such) a person is, in this open and democratic society, free to advocate his position. But he is not morally at liberty to claim membership in the Orthodox Jewish community.[30]

An anthology organized under the heading of Jewish fundamentalism describes numerous differences of doctrine and political style within the Israeli Orthodox community.[31] A partial list of political parties and movements provides one insight into the plurality of orthodoxy in Israel: National Religious Party, Agudat Israel, Degel Hatorah, SHAS (Association of Sephardi Observants of the Torah), Gush Emunim, and Neturei Karta. Members of all these groups would insist that they are strictly religious and are likely to accuse others of being lax on one or another item of importance. The groups differ from one another on their interpretation and acceptance of the label "Zionist," their concern for the Land of Israel as a possession of prime importance, their openness to secular education, and their views about redemption and messianicism. Within some of these groups are further divisions no less contentious. The Chabad or Lubavitcher community has moved in and out of alliances with other "heredim" (ultra-Orthodox), reflecting differences with respect to the proselytizing of Jews and the status to be accorded its Rebbe. Commentators differ in their assessment of SHAS: is it a religious party whose appeal is largely ethnic (to Jews of North African and Asian origins) or a movement that differs from other Orthodox religious parties on religious doctrines? Other insights into the plurality of Judaism come from assessments that the leadership of SHAS is more willing than that of other religious parties to give up part of the Land of Israel for the sake of peace, while the voters of SHAS tend to be stridently nationalist and not inclined to territorial concessions.

In practical terms, there are no simple and unambiguous boundaries to differentiate the various streams of Judaism. It is possible to use indicators like membership in synagogues that affiliate formally with one or another movement, to ask individual Jews how they define themselves or about their observance of various commandments. Sociologists who work in this field identify commandments dealing with dietary practices and Sabbath observance as critical indicators that discriminate between the Orthodox and the non-Orthodox.[32] For scholars identified with the ultra-Orthodox, however, these would only begin to distinguish the truly observant Jews from the wayward. And like the biblical prophets, modern Jewish commentators lament individuals who observe the letter of many commandments but do not behave in ways that are just or righteous.

Prominent among the issues that produce argument among contemporary Jewish scholars is the appropriate separation of the community from non-Jews. This is a continuation of the different perspectives on foreign gods, cultures, and living in the Promised Land or the Diaspora that are apparent in the Bible itself.

Sex also figures among the topics of Jewish dispute. A recent book documents numerous varieties of eroticism and asceticism in the writings of rabbis and Jewish intellectuals at various periods from the Bible, the Talmud, medieval Europe, eighteenth-century Hasidism, the European Jewish Enlightenment, Israeli, and American communities. It shows that Jewish perspectives on sex often paralleled those of their Gentile neighbors, along with Jews' tendencies to write extensively about the subject and to justify their perspectives.[33]

The vitality among Jews reflects a diversity that is more than *Judaism.* From the time when the Enlightenment began to spread outward from western Europe at about the period of the French Revolution, Jews in increasing numbers have left the isolation of communities where the learning was traditionally Jewish. The experience produced a multiplication of secular cultural and political as well as religious perspectives as Jews were exposed to and participated in the events of numerous lands.[34]

The wealth of the American Jewish community supports both an impressive amount of learning and a great deal of sophisticated publication on religious issues by some Jews as well as stylish sports and social facilities that are the sole linkage of other Jews to their community.[35] Some intellectuals ponder the marginal status of American Jews among their middle- and upper-income Gentile neighbors.[36] Others worry about assimilation and the threat of disappearance.[37] A special concern is intermarriage, with perhaps 50 percent or more of new couples having only one Jewish partner. Orthodox leaders worry about other signs of assimilation: an increase in Orthodox Jewish women who pursue professional careers, divorce in Orthodox families, the introduction of secular subjects to a Jewish curriculum, the pursuit of secular higher education, the availability of radio and television, and pressures to keep up with a materialistic life style that compete with the outlays of money and time necessary for Jewish education and a Jewish life style. In this perspective, insularity is a virtue or even vital to Jewish survival. The greatest strength of Orthodoxy may be its *irrelevance* to cosmopolitan values.[38]

Some words written about Diaspora and Judean communities of 2,000 years ago have their parallels in what some Diaspora Jews and Israelis express about one another today:

> While the Jews of Judea . . . tended to be poor, backward, obscurantist, narrow-minded, fundamentalist, uncultured and xenophobic, the Diaspora Jews were expansive, rich, cosmopolitan, well-adjusted to Roman norms and to Hellenic culture, Greek-speaking, literate and open to ideas.[39]

Secular as well as religious leaders of Diaspora communities have sent their money and given political support to Israel in their national governments. Some see Israel as the means to preserve Jews and even Judaism or as essential to Jewish identity. With the exception of community leaders in Asia and North Africa, however, Diaspora Jews have not led mass movements to settle in the Promised Land. Some figures have reacted against the image that Israel is *the* center of world Jewry. They point to the numerical preponderance of Diaspora communities that has prevailed since biblical times as well as to the intellectual and religious vitality in the Diaspora.

A distinctive outlying view is that Judaism is more suited to a Diaspora existence than to independent statehood. Where the state is not explicitly Jewish, Jews do not have to accommodate the ethnocentric elements of religious doctrine with the need to rule a population that is ethnically heterogeneous. Jews can thrive among the Gentiles without dealing with the complexities of ruling them according to Jewish norms.[40]

There have been demonstrations of unity in Diaspora communities alongside disputes about competing world views and priorities. In the United States, metropolitan federations of Jewish organizations cooperate in raising money and allocating it among competing needs. At the national level in the United States, an organization of presidents of major Jewish organizations seeks to present a united political front on Jewish issues. Unity has been most impressive when Israel has been threatened by its neighbors. Disunity has been prominent when Israel's actions could be interpreted as threatening its neighbors, or as frustrating efforts at reaching international accommodation. There have been additional disagreements about the destiny of

Russian Jewish migrants, with some Diaspora organizations competing with Israel in efforts to attract them, each to their own homeland.

No discussion of Jewish responses to events should proceed without reference to the Holocaust. It destroyed 40 percent of the world's Jews and virtually erased what had been the world's greatest concentration of Jews in Europe. The official records of the Nazis and the tales of victims read like Jeremiah's prophecies of Jerusalem's destruction and Josephus' report of the havoc during the revolt against Rome.

One response to the Holocaust has been to compare it to previous Jewish catastrophes and to identify the Nazis as agents of God who were used to punish his wayward people. But which sins warranted such a punishment? The very question flaunts a problem that cannot be resolved authoritatively, especially during the first generations when the wounds of many victims are still fresh. Ultra-Orthodox commentaries about the Holocaust reveal soul searching on account of European rabbis who failed to advocate flight in time for their congregants to avoid the Nazis alongside a tendency to blame the Zionist and Reform movements for provoking God.[41]

Jews also quarrel about the messages of God that might be perceived in other recent events. Insofar as Israel's survival and gains in the 1948 war of independence and then its victory in 1967 came so soon after the Holocaust, the proximity has been seen as signs of the messiah's arrival. One group sought to ease the messiah's path. It stole explosives from an Israeli military depot and planned the destruction of Moslem holy places that have been on the Temple Mount since the Middle Ages.[42] Other groups of religious Jews, including Jerusalem's Neteuri Karta and the followers of the Satmar Rebbe, see the secular Jewish state as an abomination that should not have been declared prior to the messiah's arrival. The followers of the Lubavitcher Rebbe take a slightly different position. They are active in seeking affiliates among Israel's Jews and in Israeli politics, but their late Rebbe directed his extensive network from New York. He waited for the messiah there, without traveling to Israel.

Some secular Jews are also be attracted to messianic visions. Pragmatists accuse them of wanting to force the end with bold but unwise actions.[43] Israel's election of 1992 was fought partly in these terms. Secular candidates of the Labor Party charged that secular candidates of Likud were out of step with reality and would bring about a catastrophic war by trying to force a solution to Israel-Arab problems by seeking permanent control of the territories occupied in the 1967 war.

David Hartman, a well-known American rabbi who moved to Israel, expresses his distrust of messianicism: "whenever Jews sought to act on the basis of their messianic hope, the result was invariably catastrophic."[44] This recalls some advice attributed to Rabbi Yohanan Ben Zakkai. He had his own problems with messianic Jews who rebelled against the Romans in the expectation of God's help.

> If you are planting a tree and hear that the messiah has arrived, finish planting the tree and then greet the messiah.

Gershom Scholem's treatment of messianicism in Judaism resembles the treatment of bounded principles in Chapter 8 of this book. That chapter focused on contrasting political norms that are apparent in the Hebrew Bible. Scholem described messianicism as one pole in contrasting Jewish modes of dealing with difficult conditions: as an irrepressible quest after redemption that has emerged in Judaism as a way of dealing with catastrophe. Scholem saw messianicism as anti-existential, a polar opposite to a this-worldly pragmatism that is also apparent in Judaism.[45]

To follow this insight of Scholem, the next chapter will discuss Israeli pragmatism, or coping. Here it should be mentioned in the context of different ways that Jews have used for dealing with historical problems and opportunities. Coping appears as an option to be preferred by pragmatists concerned to minimize threat and avoid cataclysm. To be contrasted with this is the expectation of an otherworldly, messianic solution that aspires to a complete and rapid solution to vexing problems. Messianicism is also grounded in Jewish tradition. The application of labels is made complicated by the negative connotation associated with messianicism. Often each side in a Jewish or Israeli dispute will claim the mantle of pragmatism and accuse the opposition of unrealistic and even dangerous messianicism.

THE VARIETIES OF DAVID IN THE BIBLE AND LITERATURE

The diversities in the Hebrew Bible and in the cultures of modern Jews find a striking illustration in the treatments of David provided by two Jews who have written extensively on Jewish themes and who know the ancient sources well. The focus of their work is David, who represents in himself so many sides of the Holy Book. He is adulterer, killer, and penitent; musician, composer of pious poetry and military leader; an example of personal virtue and tragedy; a man of lascivious greed and cruelty, a cunning plotter who becomes a venerated king but cannot control his own family; a rural innocent raised to prominence in a story to rival that of Cinderella; a love object (perhaps bisexual) whose life is detailed until he becomes senile and impotent; a provider of care for a mentally ill king and a bandit chief who offers to fight with a foreign king against his own people; the creator of an empire and dynasty that acquired mythic status. He lives a full life, is passionate, fallible, and must accept the consequences of his mistakes. His story reflects the history of the Israelites: enjoyment of God's grace, falling into sin and disfavor, repentance and reconciliation, together with a psychological realism unparalleled elsewhere in the Hebrew Bible or the New Testament.

The richness of David's story has attracted a long history of scholarship and literature.[46] The selective use of his stories over the years suggests that the biblical episodes are more useful as a mirror of later realities than as a portrayal of orthodox morality. Insofar as the biblical sources can support such a wide variety of interpretation and extrapolation, what a writer portrays is likely to say as much about the writer as about the Bible.[47] Numerous modern authors have expanded on biblical episodes about sex, violence, and personal weakness in high places.[48] Here the focus is on two books that have received attention by critics and scholars on account of their political commentary as well as their elaboration on the Bible's sex and violence.[49]

Stefan Heym's *The King David Report* [50]and Joseph Heller's *God Knows*[51] portray biblical politics from widely different perspectives. Heller's book resembles others that he has written to mock the officious character of honored regimes.[52] Heym's book is more daring. It describes the writing of David's history by his successors to justify their own positions by emphasizing the positive and eliminating or glossing over the negative aspects of David's stories. Viewed as a portrayal of how the Bible may have been written, Heym's book parallels several academic efforts that are described in Chapter 2 of this book.[53] The book is also autobiographical. Heym wrote as an East German who had returned home after spending the Nazi period in the United States. He was alternatively lionized and threatened by the East German regime. His experiences resemble those of Ethan who is the central figure in *The King David Report.*[54] (Since the re-unification of Germany, an aged Heym has been elected to the German Bundestag and has been alternatively lionized as a Jewish survivor and condemned as a communist.)

Both Heym and Heller expand on biblical episodes that mock simple portrayals of the Bible's morality. Heym's expansions on the Bible are more sharply focused on statecraft than sex, while Heller's are more sexual than political and occasionally scatological.

While the Bible begins with the awesome story of God the Creator, Heller begins his book with Abishag taking off her clothes, laying on top of David, and taking "gentle possession of me with her small arms and legs and with her tiny plump belly and fragrant mouth . . ."[55] Abishag appears in only four verses in *I Kings 1*, and another 11 verses in *I Kings 2*, but she is prominent throughout Heller's book. Heller's Bathsheba is barely second to David in importance, while the biblical Bathsheba appears only in two chapters of *II Samuel* , two chapters of *I Kings*, and has a brief mention in *Psalms*.

The principal theme as well as the opening scene of Heym's book is the assignment offered by Solomon to Ethan the Ezrahite to compose *The One and Only True and Authoritative, Historically Correct and Officially Approved Report on the Amazing Rise, God-fearing Life, Heroic Deeds, and Wonderful Achievement of David the Son of Jesse, King of Judah for Seven Years and of Both Judah and Israel for Thirty-three, Chosen of God, and Father of King Solomon* (i.e., *The King David Report*).

When Ethan proceeds to accumulate information about David's life by interviewing surviving witnesses, Solomon's courtiers make it clear that the whole truth is neither necessary nor desirable. Ethan's mission is to write positively, to portray David in a way that will glorify Solomon's family background and provide moral uplifting for the Israelite population. Yet it is inevitable that Ethan learns some unpleasant details about David. Passages to be included in the *Report* are vetted before a Commission comprised of the king's advisors. It includes Nathan the prophet and Zadok the priest. They are wise men who can ponder the various sides of an issue. Another member is Benaiah, the king's aide who carried out the death sentences on Adonijah and Joab[56] and shows little tolerance for subtleties.

Ethan writes in a way to emphasize the piety and the glory of David and to leave some of the messier parts vague. When he cannot control his curiosity or his pen, he is provided with guidance by Commission members. Often there are arguments. Eventually the courtiers' patience wears thin, or they see an opportunity to ingratiate themselves before Solomon by accusing Ethan. Eventually they charge him with slander, subversion, calumny, innuendo, perversion of the mind, and literary high treason. Benaiah was the heavy. He demanded a sentence of death and rebutted Ethan's defense by the assertion that, "We can read . . . even between the lines."[57]

There is no doubt that Heller and Heym add numerous details to the biblical stories about David. It is less clear that they depart from the range of characterizations that appear in the Hebrew Bible itself and in well-established traditions of secular and religious scholarship. Heym's portrayal of a *Report* on King David that will satisfy King Solomon and his courtiers may not be too different from the cleaning up of David's image that is apparent in *Chronicles*. *Samuel* and *Kings* present a wide range of behaviors. The heavy concentration of sex amidst Heller's politics has its origins in biblical stories of Bathsheba, Amnon's rape of Tamar, Absalom's use of David's concubines, and Solomon's many wives. Heller and Heym represent one pole of literary embellishment. At another extreme are the Jewish traditions, noted in Chapter 4, that seek to make David a model of piety.

* * *

The study of Jewish historiography, or how Jewish historians have dealt with the subject of their people, is a thriving field of intellectual activity.[58] As might be expected, it is a field of academic research replete with different perspectives and sharp criticism between the practitioners. Experts have distinguished an American and an Israeli school of Jewish historiography and have subdivided the Israeli school into Jerusalem and Tel Aviv elements, focused on academics affiliated with the Hebrew University and Tel Aviv University. The schools and individual historians differ in the importance they assign to the Diaspora or to the Zionist enterprise in Israel as dominant features in modern Jewry. They also differ in their emphasis of Jewish suffering through history or a contrary stress on Jewish strength and survival through periods of general persecution when Gentiles as well as Jews, peasants as well as town dwellers, suffered from poverty and depredations.[59]

This book does not deal systematically with Jewish historiography. However, it offers the historical observation that political diversity in the Bible reflects the people's capacity to deal with different views under turbulent conditions. This chapter has added to the picture of Jewish diversity by describing briefly the variety of Jewish religious and secular movements and examining the liberties that two modern authors have taken with the ancient text. The implication is that Jewish exploration of diverse norms and behaviors has something to do with the people's capacity to survive and thrive. The anachronism of the Jews and their imminent assimilation has been proclaimed by outsiders and feared by insiders, but it has not occurred. Numerous Jews have reached the heights of modern civilizations that proclaim their adherence to secular and universal values. Yet the Jews remain a distinctive people. Some of them insist that they should remain isolated and parochial.[60]

Religious faith attracts its followers by the mysteries it presents and its way of dealing with them. Among the mysteries of Judaism are the laws that are said to have been received in their completeness from God and provide a way for dealing with all of life's contingencies in the modern age. The specifics require learning not only the original laws as written in Torah but also how they are explored in subsequent books of the Bible and rabbinical commentaries composed since then. The peoplehood or ethnicity of the Jewish nation admits individuals who show no concern for their religiosity or even ridicule episodes that are prominent in Holy Scriptures. There is enough here to occupy for a lifetime both those who believe and those who are skeptical but are intrigued by the continued vitality of the Jewish enterprise.

Judaic doctrines and ideas expressed about Jewish themes by secular individuals may be most fascinating for those who are attracted by the traits of complexity, ambiguity, subtlety, principles that appear contradictory to one another, the weighing of law against problematic conditions, and the assertion of fine distinctions. It is not a field for those who aspire to clear, systematic, simple, or unambiguous arrangements of spiritual, social, or political ideas.

NOTES

[1] Carl Von Clausewitz, *On War* (London: Penguin Books, 1968), p. 119.

[2]Barlett's *Familiar Quotations* includes a quotation by Mao, "War cannot for a single minute be separated from politics" from a lecture he gave in 1938.

[3] A. D. Lindsay, *The Modern Democratic State* (New York: Oxford University Press, 1943), Chapter 8.

[4] Stuart A. Cohen, *The Three Crowns: Structures of Communal Politics in Early Rabbinic Jewry* (Cambridge: Cambridge University Press, 1990).

[5] Norman K. Gottwald, *The Hebrew Bible: A Socio-Literary Introduction* (Philadelphia: Fortress Press, 1985), Chapter 3.

[6] Burton L. Visotzky, *Reading the Book: Making the Bible a Timeless Text* (New York: Anchor Books, 1991, pp. 226-27.

[7] Giovanni Garbini, *History and Ideology in Ancient Israel* (New York: Crossroad Publishing Company, 1988).

[8] *II Esdras* 8:35-36.

[9] Robert M. Seltzer, *Jewish People, Jewish Thought: The Jewish Experience in History* (New York: Macmillan, 1980), Chapter 16.

[10] Gabriel Josipovici, *The Book of God: A Response to the Bible*, (New Haven: Yale University Press, 1988), p. 89.

[11] Aaron Wildavsky, *The Nursing Father: Moses as a Political Leader* (University, Alabama: University of Alabama Press, 1984), p. 6.

[12] Lionel Kochan, *Jews, Idols and Messiahs: The Challenge from History* (Oxford: Basil Blackwell, 1990), p. 39. On the selective commentary practices by early Greek diasporas, see John J. Collins, *Between Athens and Jerusalem: Jewish Identity in the Hellenistic Diaspora* (New York: Crossroad, 1986). For a collection of literary essays based on the same passage used by Kochan, see Jason P. Rosenblatt and Joseph C. Sitterson, Jr., *"Not in Heaven:" Coherence and Complexity in Biblical Narrative* (Bloomington: Indiana University Press, 1991).

[13] Abba Hillel Silver, *Where Judaism Differs: An Inquiry into the Distinctiveness of Judaism* (New York: Collier Books, 1989), pp. 2-6.

[14] Gershom Scholem, *Sabbatei Sevi: The Mystical Messiah*, Translated by R. J. Zwi Werblowsky (Princeton: Princeton University Press, 1973), p. 283.

[15] *The Jerusalem Post,* January 17, 1992, p. 1B.

[16] For an insight into one of the multifaceted branches of ultra-orthodox Judaism, see Jerome R. Mintz, *Legends of the Hasidim: An Introduction to Hasidic Culture and Oral Tradition in the New World* (Chicago: University of Chicago Press, 1968); and Tamar El-Or, *Educated and Ignorant: On Ultra-orthodox Women and Their World* (Tel Aviv: Am Oved, 1992). Hebrew.

[17] Jacob Neusner, *Death and Birth of Judaism: The Impact of Christianity, Secularism, and the Holocaust on Jewish Faith* (New York: Basic Books, 1987)..

[18] Paul Johnson, *A History of Christianity* (NY: Atheneum, 1976), Part One.

[19] *The Condition of Jewish Belief: A Symposium Compiled by the Editors of Commentary Magazine* (New York: Macmillan, 1966).

[20] Jacob B. Agus, *The Condition . . .*, p. 12.

[21] Mordecai M. Kaplan, *The Condition*, p. 121.

[22] Arthur Hertzberg, *The Condition*, p. 90.

[23] Eliezer Berkovits, *The Condition*, p. 24.

[24] Emanuel Rackman, *The Condition*, p. 179.

[25] Hertzberg, *The Condition*, pp. 90-97.

[26] W. Gunther Plaut, *The Condition*, p. 169.

[27] Emil L. Fackenheim, *The Condition*, p. 57.

[28] Rackman, *The Condition*, p. 181.

[29] Chaim Dov Keller, "Modern Orthodoxy: An Analysis and a Response," in Reuven P. Bulka, ed., *Dimensions of Orthodox Judaism* (New York: KTAV Publishing House, 1983), pp. 253-71.

[30] Norman Lamm, "Pluralism and Unity in the Orthodox Jewish Community," in Bulka, pp. 272-78.

[31] Laurence J. Silberstein, ed., *Jewish Fundamentalism in Comparative Perspective: Religion, Ideology, and the Crisis of Modernity* (New York: New York University Press, 1993).

[32] Even in biblical times there was no absolute demarcations around the concept of "Jew." See Jonathan Z. Smith, *Imagining Religion: From Babylon to Jonestown* (Chicago: University of Chicago Press, 1982), Chapter 1.

[33] David Biale, *Eros and the Jews: From Biblical Israel to Contemporary America* (New York: Basic Books, 1992).

[34] A sample of the relevant literature appears in Ezra Mendelsohn, *On Modern Jewish Politics* (New York: Oxford University Press, 1993);

Jonathan Frankel, *Prophecy and Politics: Socialism, Nationalism, and the Russian Jews, 1862-1917* (Cambridge: Cambridge University Press, 1981); Zvi Gitelman, ed., *The Quest for Utopia: Jewish Political Ideas and Institutions Through the Ages* (Armonk, NY: M.E. Sharpe, Inc., 1992); and Eli Lederhandler, *The Road to Modern Jewish Politics: Political Tradition and Political Reconstruction in the Jewish Community of Tsarist Russia* (New York: Oxford University Press, 1989).

[35] For a commentary by a well-known scholar of Judaism that emphasizes the lack of learning among most Jews, see Jacob Neusner, *American Judaism: Adventure in Modernity* (Englewood Cliffs, N.J.: Prentice-Hall, 1972). For the variety of commentaries on the Bible by American Jewish writers who are not biblical scholars, see David Rosenberg, ed., *Congregation: Contemporary Writers Read the Jewish Bible* (San Diego: Harcourt, Brace, Jovanovich, 1987).

[36] For example, Marshall Sklare, Joseph Greenblum, and Benjamin B. Ringer, *Not Quite at Home: How an American Jewish Community Lives with Itself and Its Neighbors* (New York: The American Jewish Committee, 1969).

[37] For findings that reveal continued high Jewish identity and affiliation, even among Jews who are not overtly religious, see Calvin Goldscheider, "Ethnicity, American Judaism, and Jewish Cohesion," in Goldscheider and Neusner, pp. 194-211.

[38] Bulka, Chapters 5 and 6.

[39] Johnson, *A History of Christianity*, p. 11. On the parallels and differences between Israeli and American Judaisms, or Jeweries, see Charles S. Liebman and Steven M. Cohen, *Two Worlds of Judaism: The Israeli and American Experiences* (New Haven: Yale University Press, 1990).

[40] A. B. Yehoshua, "The Golah as a Neurotic Solution," *Forum: On the Jewish People, Zionism and Israel*, Spring/Summer, 1979, #35,

pp. 17-36. See also Chaim Bermant, *The Jews* (London: Weidenfeld and Nicolson, 1977).

[41] Menachem Friedman, "The Hasidim and the Holocaust," *Jerusalem Quarterly* 53, Winter, 1990, pp. 86-114.

[42] Ehud Sprinzak, "Fundamentalism, Terrorism, and Democracy: The Case of Gush Emunim Underground," Washington: The Wilson Center, Occasional Paper, September 16, 1986 (mimeo).

[43] Ehud Sprinzak, *The Ascendance of Israel's Radical Right* (New York: Oxford University Press, 1991).

[44] David Hartman, *A Living Covenant: The Innovative Spirit in Traditional Judaism* (New York: Free Press, 1985), p. 288.

[45] Gershom Scholem, "Toward An Understanding of the Messianic Idea in Judaism," in Scholem, *The Messianic Idea in Judaism and Other Essays on Jewish Spirituality* (New York: Schocken Books, 1971), pp. 1-36.

[46] For example, Robert Davidson, *The Courage to Doubt: Exploring an Old Testament Theme* (London: SCM Press, 1983), Chapter 10; James W. Flanagan, *David's Social Drama: A Hologram of Israel's Early Iron Age* (Sheffield, England: Almond Press, 1988); Randall C. Bailey, *David in Love and War: The Pursuit of Power in 2 Samuel 10-12* (Sheffield, England: JSOT Press, 1990); Walter Brueggemann, *David's Truth: In Israel's Imagination and Memory* (Philadelphia: Fortress Press, 1985); and Susan Nidith, *Underdogs and Tricksters: A Prelude to Biblical Folklore* (San Francisco: Harper & Row, 1987); David M. Gunn, *The Fate of King Saul: An Interpretation of a Biblical Story* (Sheffield: Journal for the Study of the Old Testament Supplement Series, 14, 1984); Meir Shalev, *The Bible Now* (Jerusalem: Schocken, 1985), Hebrew; Yehuda Kil, *The Book of Samuel* (Jerusalem: Mossad Harav Kook, 1981), (Hebrew); Yehuda Kil, *The Book of Kings* (Jerusalem: Mossad Harav Kook, 1981), Volume I, He-

brew; Yehuda Kil, *The Book of Chronicles* (Jerusalem: Mossad Harav Kook, 1986), (Hebrew).

[47]On the selective use of the biblical materials about David over the ages, see Raymong-Jean Frontain and Jan Wojcik, ed., *The David Myth in Western Literature* (West Lafayette, Indiana: Purdue University Press, 1980).

[48] See, for example, Torgny Lindgren, *Bathsheba,* Translated from the Swedish by Tom Geddes (New York: Harper & Row, 1989); R. V. Cassill, *After Goliath* (New York: Ticknor & Fields, 1985); Ari Ibn-Zahav, *David and Bathsheba*, translated by I. M. Lask (New York: Crown Publishers, 1951); Laurence Chinn, *The Unanointed: A Novel* (New York: Crown Publishers, 1958); and Malachi Martin, *King of Kings* (New York: Simon and Schuster, 1980). For a more general review of literary embellishments on biblical themes, see Sol Liptzin, *Biblical Themes in World Literature* (Hoboken, NJ: KTAV Publishing House, 1985).

[49] There is no claim here that Jews are more liberal, expansive, or varied in their biblical interpretation than non-Jews. However, they hardly seem to be less liberal, expansive, or varied than others. For a comparison of Heller and Heym's books with the more simple piety characteristic of works concerned with biblical figures produced by Mormons, see Ira Sharkansky and Jay Zollinger, "Contrasting Treatments of Biblical Heroes," *Sunstone*, forthcoming. A textbook on the psychology of religion remarks on the preponderance of Jews among psychoanalysts who have explored the Bible for its psychological meanings. David M. Wulff, *Psychology of Religion: Classic and Contemporary Views* (New York: John Wiley & Sons, 1991), p. 288.

[50] Stefan Heym, *The King David Report: A Novel* (New York: G.P. Putnam's Sons, 1973).

[51]Joseph Heller, *God Knows* (New York: Alfred A. Knopf, 1984).

[52] Most notable are *Catch 22* (New York: Dell, 1955) and *Good as Gold* (New York: Pocket Books, 1979).

[53] For example, Richard Elliott Friedman, *Who Wrote the Bible?* (New York: Harper and Row, 1987).

[54] Peter Hutchinson, *Stefan Heym: The Perpetual Dissident* (Cambridge: Cambridge University Press, 1992); Hutchinson, "Problems of Socialist Historiography: The Example of Stefan Heym's *The King David Report,*" *The Modern Language Review*, Vol. 81, January 1986, pp. 131-38; also see reviews by Alvah Bissie, *The Nation*, January 19, 1974; Gerda Hess, *Library Journal*, November 1, 1973; and Charles Dollin, *Best Sellers*, October 1, 1973. For serious treatments of other Heym books, see R. W. Fisher, "The State Against Stefan Heym: Fact and Fiction in Heym's *The Queen Against Defoe*," *German Life and Letters*, Vol. 45, 1992, pp. 94-107; Peter J. Graves, "Authority, the State, and the Individual: Stefan Heym's Novel *Collin*," *Forum for Modern Language Studies*, Vol. 23, October 1987, pp. 341-50; Nancy A. Lauckner, "Stefan Heym's Revolutionary Wandering Jew: A Warning and a Hope for the Future," in Margy Gerber, ed., *Studies in GDR Culture and Society, 4: Selected Papers from the Ninth New Hampshire Symposium on the German Democratic Republic* (Lanham, Md.: University Press of America, 1984); and M. Dorman, "The State Versus the Writer: Recent Developments in Stefan Heym's Struggle Against the GDR's Kulturpolitik," *Modern Languages: Journal of the Modern Language Association*, Vol. 62, September 1981, pp. 144-52.

[55] Heller, p. 3.

[56] *I Kings* 2:25-34.

[57] Heym, pp. 243-44.

[58] See, for example, Nathan Rotenstreich, *Tradition and Reality: The Impact of History on Modern Jewish Thought* (New York: Random House, 1972; Hayim Yerushalmi, *Zakhor: Jewish History and Jewish*

Memory (Seattle: University of Washington Press, 1982); Lionel Kochan, *The Jew and His History* (London: Macmillan, 1977); and Seltzer.

[59] Norman F. Cantor, *The Sacred Chain: The History of the Jews* (New York: Harper Collins, 1994), especially the Prologue.

[60] For a Jewish response to the Arnold J. Toynbee's assertion of their being a dried remnant of past glory, see Maurice Samuel, *The Professor and the Fossil* (New York: Alfred A. Knopf, 1956). For a pessimistic Jewish conclusion, see Cantor, Ch.12.

Chapter 10
The Hebrew Bible and Israeli Politics

Israel is the only place where Jews dominate a national polity. Like other components of world Jewry, the Israeli state exhibits wide diversity, especially in comparison to its small size and population (slightly larger than New Jersey and about half the size of Holland, with about 5.25 million people).

This chapter is no more a comprehensive introduction to Israeli politics than the last chapter was a comprehensive survey of Judaism. Both are selective essays, seeking to bring together several themes of political culture apparent in the Hebrew Bible and modern Judaism. This chapter highlights those elements of Israeli politics that seem to emerge from Jewish history, including the continuing prominence and legitimacy of shrill criticism directed against political and economic elites. It describes how Israeli policymakers have dealt with their quandaries and the prominence of the official State Comptroller among regime critics. The conclusion offers the idea of "coping" as a summary of skills that may have been acquired over the centuries and illustrates its use by Israeli policymakers in the especially vexatious setting of Jerusalem.

Israel is not an easy country to describe. Even the obvious issue of region is elusive. Israel is located in the Middle East but has not been welcomed by its neighbors. Many Israeli are European in origins and culture and feel uncomfortable in the Middle East even while their Zionism prescribes a Middle Eastern location. Israel has been called communal, criminal, endangered, excessively self-centered, self-critical and self-righteous, hyper-active, imperialist, indecisive, morally congested, statist, turbulent, and uncertain. That some of these traits are the opposites of others does not keep them from existing simultaneously, but it does invite explanation.

Compared to what? is one of the first issues to be addressed in describing a country. As in other items addressed here, it is not a simple question to answer. On the trait being of rich or poor, a developing or developed country, Israel exists in the mid-range between the major categories. On the economic indicator of gross national product per capita, it ranks among the poorest of the First World or among the most well-to-do of the Third World. Gross National Products per capita for a group of countries in 1989 were (in U.S. dollars) Switzerland: $27,510; Sweden: $21,900; United States: $21,213; Italy: $14,940; United Kingdom: $14,580; Spain: $9,471; *Israel*: *$9,438*; Taiwan: $7,390; Greece: $5,286; South Korea: $4,920; Portugal: $4,323; South Africa: $2,253; Mexico: $2,170; Malaysia: $2,099; Chile: $1,890; Colombia: $1,139.[1]

Israel also exists on the edges of conventional definitions of politics. Procedurally it is a democracy in the manner of electing officials, providing access to the voting booths for all citizens, and transferring power after an election. Israeli politics shows both the positive and negative sides of Jewish familiarity with diversity. Alongside freedom to criticize public policy in the sharpest terms, there is an indecisiveness that hinders policymaking. An electoral system of proportional representation is appropriate in a disputatious culture, but it contributes to government that dithers rather than decides clearly. There have been 10 or more political parties in each Knesset as the result of national elections. No party has ever won a majority. Each government has included several parties, with major decisions waiting on the satisfaction of competing partners in the coalition.

Israel's polity is problematic by virtue of the religious or ethnic element. Jews are assured a better deal than non-Jews in competing for major elective office and political appointments and as beneficiaries of public service. Thus, Israel is less than an *egalitarian* democracy. The United States, Great Britain, Germany and Japan are also less than egalitarian by virtue of how they have treated ethnic or racial minorities and the differentials in political access and public services between the wealthy and poor. The dissonance between democratic ideals and reality is more prominent in Israel's case because it is explicit about proclaiming itself a *Jewish state*.

Being a Jewish state does not mean a *religious* state. More accurately, it means that Israelis quarrel a great deal about religion and how much Judaism they should allow in the state realm. There are usually several rabbis sitting in the Knesset, typically as representatives of religious parties that have receive together about 12 percent of the vote in recent elections. The rabbis in the Knesset during 1990 illustrated the complexity and disputes in Judaism. Some expressed rage and others laughed as, in opposition to their proposal to strengthen the laws against pornography, a secular member read from the *Song of Songs*: "thy neck shall be as a tower of ivory. . . thy breasts shall be as clusters of the vine . . ."[2]

To some observers, political disputes about religious issues in Israel are the stuff of shrill fanaticism. Upon investigation, however, they seem instead to combine elements of noisy theatrics with a willingness to compromise. Religious parties were especially well placed during the period of 1977-84. They held enough seats in the Knesset to topple the government, and the ruling Likud Bloc coupled an inclination to support religiosity along with its prominent nationalism. Religious politicians demanded the cessation of abortions and post-mortems, archaeological digs (which they accused of despoiling ancient Jewish graves), as well as Sabbath flights of El Al Israel Airlines, plus the further liberalization of the Army's policy of exempting religious women from service, the definition of *who is a Jew?* according to religious law, and more money for religious institutions. On several of these issues, the religious parties won only symbolic victories. El Al ended its Sabbath flights, but other Israeli airlines expanded theirs and hired some of the personnel laid off by El Al. The religious parties did not succeed in changing the Law of Return, which evades an explicit definition of *who is a Jew?* and allows the immigration of non-Jewish relatives of Jews. The clearest victory of religious parties seemed to be in the pragmatic politics of money. They argued that funding for their institutions had been lower than for comparable secular institutions, and they won increased allocations for religious schools and housing in religious neighborhoods.[3]

It is also difficult to describe Israel's political economy in conventional terms. It has a prominent element of socialism, with a large percentage of economic management in public hands. Yet while the formal structure of government is centralized, controls are compromised by numerous bodies that have considerable independence from one another. There are three public sectors. That of the Labor Federation (Histadrut) sometimes cooperates and sometimes competes with that of the government as well as that of the World Zionist Organization (representing Israeli and Diaspora Jewry). Major banks, industries, service providers, and most of the country's agriculture are formally owned or affiliated with the Labor Federation or the World Zionist Organization. In addition, several hundred hospitals, universities, orphanages, schools, museums, theaters, orchestras, sports associations, and other bodies are established as independent not-for-profit institutions, receive government funds, and seek donations from overseas Jews.

Israel provides room for entrepreneurialism as well as socialism, reflecting the co-existence of communal and individual themes throughout Jewish history. Free enterprise adds to liberty as well as to chaos.[4] The formal rules require the approval of many projects by government ministries, but the reality is that entrepreneurial organizations and individuals achieve in practice more autonomy than they are supposed to exercise.[5]

The related traits of adversity, ambiguity, instability, threat, turbulence, uncertainty, and weakness have been with the people of Israel from biblical times. The modern version has included several conventional military encounters and uncounted terrorist incidents since 1948, plus an Arab boycott on those who would invest or trade with the Jewish country. Israel's small size and population and economic problems add to the uncertainty by rendering the country dependent on other countries for economic assistance, military technology, and political support in international forums. On several occasions Israel has suffered from changing political priorities in European or North American countries that had been its patrons.

The Gulf War of 1991 included some 20 missile attacks on Israel, even though it was not a participant in the hostilities. Post-war efforts by the United States to bring Israel, Palestinians, Jordan, Syria, and Lebanon to peace negotiations have offered both promise and threat. The promise associated with this continuing process is peace and the reduction of economic costs reflecting permanent anticipation of war. The threat is having to give up territories occupied since 1967 as well as to question perspectives and policies built on the assumption of unrelenting Arab intentions of destroying the Jewish country.

Changes in what had been the Soviet Union have produced the largest wave of immigration since the early 1950s. The population increased by some 10 percent during 1989-92. Newcomers have felt that they have not been well served, and native job-seekers have had to compete with immigrants for employment. The United States government took advantage of the problems involved in the absorption of the immigrants and the international negotiations by making loan guarantees concerned with immigrant integration contingent on Israel's postures in the negotiations. United States Secretary of State James Baker was quoted in the American and Israeli press during March 1992 as saying "Fuck the Jews" in connection with Israel's request for loan guarantees and the tendency of American Jews not to vote for Republican presidential candidates. While Israelis conceded that they frequently express similar sentiments about Jews, the statement by a highly placed Gentile raised Israeli fears of yet another bout with anti-Semitism.

The election campaign that culminated in June 1992 helped to focus current problems. Major issues were the government's posture with respect to international negotiations and its inability to absorb immigrants without high levels of unemployment. The electorate showed once again, as it had at every previous national election, that it could not choose clearly between policy alternatives and give a majority to any of the parties. The result was a period of negotiations between potential partners to the governing coalition from the center, right, and left of the political spectrum, as well as religious parties, and a blurring of the postures that the parties had presented to the voters.

MORAL CONGESTION

All countries may have problems that some of its officials or residents consider to be moral quandaries. A country may be destined to have a high incidence of difficult issues by virtue of unsettled boundaries; hostile neighbors; populations that are heterogeneous and antagonistic on traits of religion, ethnicity, or culture; or a regime that does not enjoy a high degree of legitimacy.[6] These traits seem likely to invite violence by the regime in order to defend itself or its supporters. *When to use violence? How much to use?* These questions are likely to involve difficult moral choices. The openness and self-criticism of a democratic polity may be necessary for the issues to be manifest in debates involving officials and citizens. Authoritarian regimes may encounter just as many, if not more, issues with moral implications than democracies. However, their issues may be kept below the threshold of the troublesome because of the discipline and fear that comes from the center of government.

The incidence and seriousness of Israel's problems may be judged by the country's prominence in the international media. Most noticeable is a high incidence of wars and lesser conflicts. The professionally skilled, well-equipped, and active military provides both the means of self-defense and an organization trained to raise numerous difficult questions of which targets to strike under which conditions. The Israeli state is strong not only militarily but also with respect to its control of the country's economic resources.[7] The economic power of the state together with the socialist doctrines that are prominent components of Zionism help explain the tendency to discuss issues of social justice and to encounter the problems associated with policies of *redistribution*.[8]

Israel and the PLO signed an accord in September 1993 to provide Palestinian autonomy in Jericho and Gaza. Negotiations to implement the accord had slipped behind the timetable, but they seemed to be moving toward a successful conclusion when Baruch Goldstein, M.D., a religious Jew, killed some 30 Moslems during their prayers in Hebron's Tomb of the Patriarchs. The violence that erupted throughout the occupied territories and Arab communities within Israel produced numerous additional casualties. According to surveys taken within a week of the killings, 76 percent of Israeli Jews condemned the killings in Hebron. Yet 52 percent expressed opposition to dismantling the controversial settlement of religious Jews in the center of Hebron. Statements put out by organizations of settlers in the occupied territories lamented the violence but explained Goldstein's actions against the background of numerous cases of Palestinian violence against Jews since the Israeli-Palestinian accord had been signed. Meanwhile, tens of thousands of other Israelis demonstrated against the violence, and 7 out of 15 Cabinet members indicated their support for dismantling some Jewish settlements.[9]

The noise of dispute among Israel's Jews was not unusual. In this case, it reflected the numerous factions that have developed around the issue of expanding Jewish settlements throughout the Land of Israel. Settlement activities have been promoted by groups affiliated with Israel's left-wing secular parties as well as the National Religious Party and the more radical movement associated with the late Rabbi Meir Kahane. Baruch Goldstein was identified with the Kahane group, which had been banned from Israeli national elections on account of its anti-Arab racism.

Assertions that Israel's religious right supports Jewish settlements in the occupied territories are no more accurate than statements that secular Jews oppose them. A substantial number of secular Israelis support the Jewish settlements in the occupied territories, as shown by the 52 percent of the population that opposed dismantling the settlement in Hebron. While the National Religious Party is often identified with an aggressive posture toward settlement, a faction of that party supports territorial concessions for the sake of peace. Leaders of the ultra-Orthodox parties in the Knesset seem to be indifferent to the settlement issue or at least place it lower on their priorities than enacting measures on a religious agenda that includes prohibitions against non-kosher food and desecration of the Sabbath, budget allocations for religious schools, and housing for religious Jews.[10]

MANAGING THE QUANDARIES

Israel has been described both as having a high tolerance for dispute and as enjoying a high incidence of political consensus.[11] The consensus on being a beleaguered Jewish state may support the tolerance for dispute within the Jewish majority. Jewish history and culture have produced a polity that is skilled at pondering the many sides of difficult issues, and is open to severe self-criticism. Previous chapters of this book have described several moral quandaries apparent in the Bible. The story of David portrays how a man can be both pious and immoral. The *Book of Job* describes a good man wracked by suffering that seems to be undeserved and shows that even the Almighty may not answer important questions in a straightforward manner.[12] The prophet Jeremiah offered shrill social criticism. He dissented from regime policies and urged its soldiers to desert Jerusalem while it was under siege. Yet King Zedekiah offered Jeremiah refuge in the palace against courtiers who wanted to kill him.[13] The *Song of Songs* and *Ecclesiastes* demonstrates that authors and compilers of the Bible could be sensual, skeptical, and relativistic as well as devout. A people who could produce such a literature should not be blinded by faith in simple absolutes or incapacitated in the face of moral quandaries.

The conclusion of one commentary on the Hebrew Bible seems to be appropriate also for modern Israelis:

> The future belongs not to those who must have certainties, but to those who can live with uncertainty, who can calmly and self-confidently explore the heritage of the past, the problems of the present, and the opportunities for the future, without the crutches of rigid and doctrinaire ideology.[14]

The incidence of political violence is one measure of a country's capacity to deal with disputes. The issue is clouded by problems of concept and method: Which incidents of violence are political, and which are the activities of unstable individuals or ordinary criminals that may have been directed against a politician or given a patina of a political cause? How to measure the activities of state officials (military or police) that are described officially as actions to protect the society but which regime opponents describe as "state crimes."[15] In Israel's case, the issue is complicated further by questions of violence among Jews or between Jews and non-Jews and whether the violence occurred within Israel, *per se*, within Palestine prior to the establishment of the State in 1948, or after 1948 in territories occupied by Israel. In the framework of this book's concern with linkages between Jewish culture and Israeli politics, there is yet another thorny issue: whether the record should include political violence by non-Israeli Jews throughout history and wherever Jews have lived?

Nachman Ben-Yehuda has made an extensive review of political assassinations by Jews along with a sociological analysis of the phenomenon. He admits the difficulties in classifying individual cases as "political assassinations." He reports the public controversies that have erupted time and again in Israel as to whether individual cases were politically motivated, whether they were justified, or whether the perpetrators were dealt with in an appropriate manner. His data show 83 cases of assassinations and attempted assassinations, including killings of Jews by Jews for political reasons, during the pre-state period in Palestine. The number fell off considerably after 1948. He records only one case of Jews killing a Jew after 1948, and that was an incident traceable to a vendetta concerned with the victim's alleged collaboration with the Nazis in Europe. Ben-Yehuda concludes that once Israel was established, Israeli Jews came to rely on the institutions of the state to achieve justice among themselves. He concedes a lack of reliable comparative data but surmises that the incidence of political violence in Jewish history has been low in relation to other national experiences.[16]

One comparative indicator that supports Ben-Yehuda's conclusion is the incidence of murder reported in the Annual *Statistical Abstracts* of Israel and the United States. The Israeli murder rate was 1.97 per 100,000 population, while that of the United States was 9.8, with rates of 80.1 in Washington, D.C., 68.9 in New Orleans, 65.0 in St. Louis, and 59.3 in Detroit.[17]

Justifying "Moderate Physical Pressure"

The work of a Commission of Inquiry (Landau Commission) is symptomatic of the security problems facing Israel, the subtleties with which policymakers attempt to deal, and their inability to satisfy all critics. The Commission headed by retired Justice Moshe Landau of the Israeli Supreme Court was appointed by the Cabinet in 1987 to inquire into the investigative methods of the General Security Service. Ranking members of the Service had been accused of lying to a judicial inquiry about the use of physical pressure to extract confessions.

The *Report* of the Landau Commission accepted the need for the protection of the state against those who would destroy it.[18] Its most debated passages concern the techniques that interrogators can use to extract information from detainees. The Commission sanctioned the "use of moderate physical pressure," which it defended with principles of necessity and the balance of evils:

> A person may be exempted from criminal responsibility for an act . . . provided that he did no more than was reasonably necessary for that purpose and

that the harm caused by him was not disproportionate to the harm avoided.[19]

Torture is widely held to be outside the pale of moral integrity. Yet the concept is not without its problems. A dictionary definition is "severe . . . pain or suffering of body or mind."[20] But how much physical pain is severe? May not some degree of pain be administered when a detainee is thought to have information of life and death character? What about a captured terrorist who will not reveal if there is another bomb hidden in a crowded place? The Landau Commission was not so daring as to deal with the concept of torture head on, but it sought to define acceptable pressure.

1. Disproportionate pressure is inadmissible, and should never reach a level of physical torture, grievous harm to the subject's honor or deprivation of human dignity.
2. Officials must consider the use of less serious measures.
3. Physical and psychological means of pressure must be defined and limited in advance by binding directives.
4. There must be strict supervision of interrogators.
5. Superiors must react swiftly and firmly against deviations from what is permissible.[21]

The Commission admitted to going beyond what United States courts grant in the administration of justice. It noted that Israeli law allows the prosecution to submit some information to the judges who decide on innocence or guilt and pass sentencing that it keeps secret from the defendant and defense attorneys[22] and that Israeli courts admit the use of evidence that United States courts would exclude as tainted as a result of improper police behavior. The Commission also justified keeping secret certain sections of its *Report* in order to aid the state in combating those who would destroy it. These included specifications concerning degree of pressure allowed, the conditions under which it is permitted, and procedures for supervising interrogating officers.

The tendency to sharp criticism among Israel's elites did not spare the Landau Commission. The *Israel Law Review* published a special issue dedicated to the *Report*.[23] One contributor praised the Israeli government for dealing with "issues that virtually every government confronts, but almost no government discusses officially and openly."[24] Others made the point that it was not only a question of moderate pressure in the face of severe danger (e.g., slapping a suspect's face against the possibility of saving civilians from a terrorist's attack) and doubted that a policy of moderate physical pressure could co-exist with the quality of human rights they would identify with a truly enlightened country. One writer worried that the dynamics of a campaign against terror and other police actions would produce an escalation upward from moderate physical pressure.[25] Another wrote that torture during an investigation leaves the courts unable to evaluate the truth of a confession.[26] Against this, another commentator concluded that the moral ban against torture disappears for those who cause the need for physical pressure by planting bombs that must be located and disarmed. However, he would extend the doctrine of moderate physical pressure only to cases of imminent harm and not to cases where security forces sought to obtain convictions.[27]

One commentator described the explication of proper behavior for interrogators as "a search for the impossible." He conceded that there is dirty work required for the protection of society that does not lend itself to definitions of right and wrong that avoid all ambiguities.[28] Another wrote that there was a "smell of hypocrisy" about the principles that he was articulating but saw them as integral to the difficult balancing of contending norms. He would accept the morality of cruel practices under extraordinary circumstances. In contrast with the Landau Commission, however, he would not give them the support of explicit law. In his view, this subtle change would require the justification of individual cases that present the need for extraordinary action and tilt the game against those who would too easily engage in cruel practices.[29]

The Landau Commission's standard of moderate physical pressure has continued to trouble Israel's establishment. Five years after the publication of its *Report*, the policy of "moderate physical pressure" came under attack by prominent members of centrist as well as left-wing parties. The head of the Israeli Medical Association indicated that he would bring charges for violating professional ethics against physicians who facilitated the application of the policy by the General Security Services. Then there was a bus hijacking in Jerusalem that resulted in the death of two hostages. The event seemed to be the work of Moslem Fundamentalists opposed to the peace talks between Israel, the Palestinians, and Arab governments. With the reminder of terrorism, the issues left the items currently discussed in nation's media. The issue returned some months later, when a continuation of violence attributed to Moslem Fundamentalists opposed to the peace process led officials to advocate a temporary suspension of the restraints associated with the Landau Commission. This would mean an increase in the physical pressure employed by investigators of the security forces. It remained unclear how the problem of physical pressure would play itself out against the continued threat of Arab violence along with the prospect of peace.

An Aggressive State Comptroller

The State Comptroller (the supreme auditor, responsible to the Knesset) is a prominent source of moral reflection and shrill criticism from within the Israeli government establishment. The laws empowering Israel's State Comptroller are unusually broad in comparison to those dealing with parallel bodies in other countries. Israel's auditor is authorized to review government activities for their *moral integrity* as well as for the more conventional standards of legality, economy, efficiency, and effectiveness. Israel's State Comptroller was among the first government auditors to criticize not only the implementation of policy but the choice of major policy goals. Its reports have dealt with prominent issues of military research and development, a major restructuring of Israel's banks, police responses to terrorist episodes, and the allocation of resources for Arab education.[30]

More recently there has been a further development of activity into the field of "political auditing." This focuses on the activities of officials and citizen activists that are concerned directly with political advantage. It is an extension of audit traditions that involves the auditor in the thick of political conflict and threatens the auditor with the ire of elected officials.

An early expression of political auditing by Israel's State Comptroller was a 1986 report that was explicit in targeting the patronage activities of David Levy, the Minister of Housing and Construction. Levy was the head of a prominent faction in the Likud Bloc that dominated government coalitions from 1977 until 1992. The report concluded that there was no apparent need to fill the posts and that the individuals chosen were not qualified for their positions. According to the report, they were appointed because they were political allies of Levy, members of his family, or residents of his home town.[31] Another report criticized Likud Minister of Health Ehud Olmert for evading established procedures for purchasing hospital equipment. The report indicated that the head director of the company from which the equipment was purchased was active in Olmert's political party.[32]

The State Comptroller attracted considerable media attention by a 1991 report that focused on the activities of Interior Minister Aryeh Dery. Dery was the leading Knesset member of the Sephardi ultra-Orthodox party, known by its Hebrew acronym of SHAS, that had been a pivotal member of government coalitions. The State Comptroller's report focused on procedures initiated by Dery whereby funds budgeted for the general needs of low income municipalities or for municipal debt consolidation were allocated to religious schools affiliated with SHAS. In defense, Dery explained that he was following a policy of *compensatory discrimination*. He claimed that the ultra-Orthodox Sephardi community had been systematically deprived of state resources prior to the creation of his political party and that his actions were meant to make up for a lack of fair allocations in the past.

The State Comptroller did not accept Dery's explanation. The report concluded that the improper allocations were linked to the maneuvers of the SHAS political party and that the sums involved were especially high during 1988 when there were elections both for the Knesset and local authorities. With respect to Dery's allegations of past discrimination, the State Comptroller concluded that his allegations of discrimination had not been demonstrated by appropriate inquiries. The Comptroller went on to conclude that if discrimination were demonstrated, compensation for the discrimination must be provided by criteria clearly associated with principles of equality and not as Dery had done.[33]

Israel's State Comptroller has had a role in auditing party finance since 1966.[34] In recent years the Comptroller has gone beyond a routine application of the roles assigned to it by the statutes. The Comptroller has pointed out loopholes in existing laws and described how the parties and their supporters have exploited them in order to avoid what the State Comptroller considers to be the basic principles of the laws. The Comptroller published the names of individuals whose contributions to parties amounted to more than the equivalent to US $20,000[35] and later named individuals who contributed substantial sums to more than one party. The Comptroller articulated a view of proper citizenship which permits support for the program of one and only one political party.

> Contributions to a party are meant to express support for the ideology and the program of the party. The giving of contributions to a number of parties by one contributor, especially to parties of different ideologies, arouses wonder concerning the purpose of the contributor.[36]

In response to the State Comptroller's chastising, one of the individuals named in the report appeared on television. He defended his legal and moral rights and questioned the State Comptroller's right to criticize lawful activities that he pursued as a private citizen. He explained that he wanted to assure post-election access for his points of view in an election that seemed likely to be closely contested between the major parties.

The State Comptroller also criticized the Knesset for legislating retroactive increases in state support of the parties in order to compensate for overspending by the parties. According to the State Comptroller, "this legislation cut off the law from its moral basis and left it with only formal validity." [37]

This language recalls the prophet Amos who demanded righteousness rather than narrow compliance with religious law.

> Though ye offer me burnt offerings and your meat offerings, I will not accept them: neither will I regard the peace offerings of your fat beasts. Take thou away from me the noise of thy songs; for I will not hear the melody of thy viols. But let judgment run down as waters, and righteousness as a mighty stream. [38]

The biblical comparison between regime criticism in ancient and modern Israel raises the question of the auditor's effectiveness.[39] The biblical prophets earned the prestige of being included in sacred writings, but they were hounded and sometimes killed by the elites they criticized. Moreover, the Bible generally portrays the prophets as not producing changes in the behaviors that they condemned. Like the prophets, the present State Comptroller has been criticized by political elites as a meddler who goes beyond her legal mandate. However, her record of concrete accomplishments seems to be better than the prophets'. In accordance with the Comptroller's recommendations, the Knesset extended the regulations concerning political party financing to limit the magnitude of individual contributions. One target of the State Comptroller's reports, Aryeh Dery, resigned as Interior Minister in September 1993 when a criminal indictment was brought against him for the crimes of bribery, receiving things of value by deceit, violating trust, and filing false reports. When the Comptroller's first term of five years was about to expire in 1993, she won a second appointment with 78 Knesset votes in a body of 120 members.

COPING

According to one commentator, the essence of biblical wisdom was to cope.[40] And coping, rather than solving problems in a complete manner, seems to be the fate of modern Israel: to avoid grand illusions of meeting fully the demands of foreign or domestic protagonists. Its policymakers may have to be content with the limited achievements of "satisficing." This implies solutions that are less than optimal. It means choosing from partial and temporary options for problems that defy permanent solution.[41]

"Coping" has been used in various ways, often casually, to describe policymaking in difficult settings or to prescribe how policymakers should deal with vexing problems. Dictionary meanings include: contend, deal with, endure, fight successfully or on equal terms, handle, hold one's own, manage, struggle, subsist, survive, barter, weather. Daniel Patrick Moynihan used coping to convey good judgment or a capacity to anticipate developments that require action.[42] Several works of political science include coping in their titles or subtitles but do not provide any systematic discussion of the concept. The prominent use of the word seems designed to emphasize the difficulties encountered by officials or political activists.[43]

Psychologists have been more precise than political scientists in their use of "coping." Some have analyzed the coping behaviors of individuals under stress in ways that are suggestive politically. Formulations for what are labeled "active" as opposed to "passive" coping are similar to what others call "hardiness" as opposed to "helplessness" or "engaging" as opposed to "avoidance."[44] Coping by engagement (active coping or hardiness) suggests efforts to salvage something from a difficult situation; to keep a process going in the expectation of greater opportunities or holding off great losses; surveying options; maintaining the integrity and political assets of oneself and one's organization; changing the conceptions of oneself, an organization, or supporters in the face of conditions that are not likely to change in the short range; ranking priorities in order to achieve or preserve the more important at the expense of the less important. Policymakers who practice engagement coping accept the limitations of serious problems and adjust their aspirations accordingly. Where they do not see the possibility of an immediate and far-ranging solution, they seek opportunities to achieve marginal improvements.[45] Engagement coping may allow a resolution of issues in a way that keeps continued disputes on a low flame.

Avoidance coping (like that called passive coping or helplessness) suggests pointless emoting that involves loss of control and direction for oneself and potential allies, quixotic choice of options in an effort to *do something!* without taking account of likely costs and benefits, and frittering away resources in efforts that do not produce significant accomplishments.

Many Israelis, like their distant ancestors, have pursued what they perceive as vital interests amidst the threats and temptations that surround them. Those who practice engagement coping, whether or not they recognize that label, have chosen goals with a pragmatic eye as to what is feasible. This may mean an acceptance of something less than total victory in military encounter if that would provoke an international reaction that is too hostile for a small country to withstand. They have also steered a cumbersome middle course in issues beset with conflict between religious and secular Jews or between strident nationalists and cosmopolitans willing to compromise with Arab nationalism. Critics chastise the Israeli establishment for its helplessness in the face of challenge and its failure to plan and formulate policy rationally.[46] There is, to be sure, a great deal of noise in Israeli politics. There is avoidance coping by frenzied individuals. There is no lack of dispute between those who pose sharply different views of what is best for Israel and the Jews, collectively. If the more dominant pattern is one of engagement coping, its symptoms are that individuals of different perspectives accuse one another of being unrealistic in what they perceive or advocate.[47]

The Case of Jerusalem

An example of Israel's engagement coping appears in its policies with respect to Jerusalem. It has sought to maintain control over the city as its most prized possession, even at the loss of some attributes normally associated with sovereignty.[48]

The problem for policymakers is that Jerusalem is the epicenter of the Israeli-Arab conflict as well as being divided between Jewish and non-Jewish residents at proportions of about 70-30. Few of the world's countries and none of the great powers formally recognize Jerusalem as Israel's capital or even as an entirely Israeli city.[49] Survey results offer sobering findings about the feelings of Palestinian Jerusalemites.[50] Eighty-six percent answered "No," or "Not at all" when asked if they were satisfied with the services rendered by the Jerusalem municipality. Almost 90 percent chose "Palestinian state" when asked, "If confronted with a choice, which would you choose: Palestinian state, economic well-being, family and community, or religion?" Only 26 percent of the Palestinian respondents indicated their support for an open city where residents could move freely between Jewish and Palestinian sectors. Fifty-five percent responded to the same question by saying that the city should be divided east (Palestinian) and west (Jewish).

The Jerusalem municipality and Israeli ministries have gone to bizarre lengths of distorting or ignoring their own rules in order to accommodate hostile Palestinians.[51] Palestinians in neighborhoods of East Jerusalem that were annexed in 1967 have been allowed to operate businesses and practice professions on the basis of Jordanian licenses without having to apply for Israeli documents. The Jerusalem Municipality and the Israeli Ministry of Education and Culture gave up efforts to impose Israeli Arab curricula on the local schools. Schools financed by Israel offer Jordanian curricula and prepare students for Jordanian examinations that will permit their graduates to attend universities in Arab countries. Jordanian bank notes circulate freely in the Arab sections of the city, seemingly in violation of Israeli regulations about foreign currency.

National policymakers have said that the Jerusalem issue should be the last of the Israeli-Arab issues that is scheduled for resolution. They admit that Jerusalem's problems will be the most difficult to solve. They hope that goodwill and trust between Israelis, Palestinians, and other Arabs can grow as a result of other agreements that will come first. Israeli leaders do not want to make concessions on Jerusalem prior to settling the country's external borders, out of fear that further concessions on Jerusalem might be demanded as part of subsequent border negotiations. They also hope that the world's tolerance of Israel's control over Jerusalem will grow along with the continued development of the city and the Israelis' management of its affairs. Acceptance *de facto* of Israeli control over Jerusalem may be the most the regime can achieve if it cannot solve formally the problems of national borders and other outstanding issues. Israelis may not know for some time if they have acquired an operative title to Jerusalem or have been lucky in postponing a deluge.

During his long tenure from 1966 to 1993, Mayor Teddy Kollek acquired a reputation for openness to non-Jewish concerns that fits the description of engagement coping. However, he exhibited avoidance coping when a member of his coalition on the city council collaborated with a prominent Palestinian in proposing to divide the area of Jerusalem into separate Jewish and Palestinian municipalities. For the mayor, this was too much of a concession to Palestinian aspirations. That proposal differed only in degree from Kollek's own proposal to create Palestinian and Jewish boroughs in Jerusalem. The mayor announced that he would break off all contact with this council member and sought to remove his responsibility for the municipal transportation department.

The Jewish city council member who provoked the mayor's anger had been a prominent critic of Israeli policy for Jerusalem and made a point that is relevant to this discussion of coping. He documented the behaviors of city residents that indicated a minimum of economic and social contacts between Jewish and Palestinian sectors and thereby highlighted the limited success that Israeli policymakers could claim for their actions in Jerusalem. The city has remained under Israeli control, but the assertions of Israeli officials that it is *unified* or *united* are not accurate with respect to several conventional meanings of that term.[52] The issue illustrates that coping is a way of managing problems whose solution is elusive and may remain ambiguous. In keeping with the priorities of Israeli policy for Jerusalem, it has been more important to maintain control over Jerusalem than to assure a high level of economic and social integration among its residents.

Coping need not be quiet. Israel's democracy honors the diversity apparent in Jewish doctrines and culture by the range of shrill criticism directed against government policy. Chapter 1 notes the prophetic challenges coming from Yehoshafat Harkabi, Meron Benvenisti, and Yeshayahu Leibowitz, as well as the distinctions earned by those figures despite the sharpness of their views. Each of these figures criticized Israeli policies for not being sufficiently forthcoming with respect to the Arabs of Israel and the occupied territories.

The late Rabbi Meir Kahane was a shrill critic from the perspective of extreme nationalism. He also caused the Israeli polity to define the outer limits of political dispute that would be allowed without threatening the democratic character of the state. The task was difficult and the effort was clumsy. Kahane quoted biblical passages that revealed one pole of the Bible's ethnocentric-universalistic spectrum in behalf of his demand to curtail sharply the rights of non-Jews in Israel. When politicians sought to limit Kahane's involvement in legitimate politics, they came up against the demands of religious parties that nothing could be legislated against the Holy Book. Near the end of its summer session in 1986, the Knesset sat for 15 hours and enacted a law against racial incitement. In order to win the support of the religious parties, the law's framers excluded expression of religious doctrine from the definition of racist incitement. Later it became apparent that Kahane's political candidacy could be dealt with under the provisions of another law against racist political campaigns, even though the Rabbi's practice of citing Holy Scripture in support of his doctrines would cause some problems in prosecuting him under the law against racist incitement. The Electoral Commission banned Kahane's party from the election campaign in October 1988, and the Supreme Court rejected Kahane's appeal. Kahane was killed by an Arab on the streets of New York, but his movement continued. It became prominent again in 1994 when one of its followers massacred 30 Moslems in the mosque at Hebron's Tomb of the Patriarchs.

The activities of Jerusalem's Palestinians add to our appreciation of complexities in the description and assessment of coping. Until recently, an Israeli observer would likely conclude that the Palestinians provided one example after another of avoidance coping. A popular epigram is that they have never missed an opportunity to miss an opportunity. Almost none of the Palestinians living in formerly Jordanian Jerusalem accepted Israeli citizenship after 1967 and the right to vote in national elections that is linked with citizenship. Large majorities also refused the opportunity of local residents who are not citizens to vote in municipal elections. No more than 25 percent, and on one occasion less than 5 percent, of eligible Palestinians in the post-1967 sections of Jerusalem took advantage of the opportunity to vote in municipal elections between 1967 and 1993. By avoiding Israeli citizenship and the right of residents to vote in local elections, Palestinians lost opportunities to translate almost a quarter of the local population into significant leverage in local and national policymaking.

Some Palestinians in Jerusalem went further toward the extreme of avoidance coping via participation or support of violence. This Palestinian activity fit the description that terror is an expression of rage (and avoidance coping) by individuals who cannot mount successful, conventional assaults against their targets. Palestinian terror may have stiffened the resolve of Israelis against making concessions to Palestinians and added to Israel's support among Western democracies.[53]

The complexities of coping categories become evident when the perspective of analysis is changed. What looked like the avoidance coping of Palestinians when viewed from the Israeli perspective may have been engagement coping when viewed from the Palestinian perspective. They were giving up the opportunity to affect the conventional distribution of benefits within Jerusalem in order to maintain the unity of their community against the Israeli regime. Their posture held out the prospect of achieving control over Jerusalem, or part of it, plus the hinterland heavily settled with Palestinians to the north, east, and south of the city. The major organization that had practiced terror, the Palestine Liberation Organization (PLO), won the support of many Palestinians and numerous national governments.

Events of 1993 illustrated the pressures on the city's Palestinians, their ambivalence, and a shift in strategies. In September Israel and the PLO declared mutual recognition and signed an accord designed to lead through stages to an eventual settling of differences. This appeared to signal a change in coping by the Palestinian leadership, from a pursuit of an all-or-nothing posture with respect to Palestine that fit the model of avoidance coping, to an acceptance of partial success that fit the model of engagement coping.

In the run-up to the November municipal election, Jerusalem's Palestinians dithered between continuing their boycott of Israeli politics or departing from it in order to support the incumbent Teddy Kollek against an opponent who was identified with the more overtly nationalist (and anti-Palestinian) Likud Bloc. Among Jews, Kollek's reputation was that of supporting accommodation with Palestinians. Among many Palestinians, however, he was a smooth talking Israeli, whose actions were designed to maximize Israeli control over the city and its hinterland. Some 7 percent of the eligible Palestinians voted in the 1993 election. This was a higher percentage than voted in the election of 1989 but a lower incidence than voted in elections of 1969, 1978, and 1985. The Palestinian votes that Kollek received were not enough to overcome his disadvantages. A number of his former supporters among the city's Jews voted for his opponent or did not vote, due partly to Kollek's age and his own ambivalence with respect to continuing in office. Prior to the election he had announced that he was too old to run again, then gave in to pressures that came from the leaders of his political party.

The long run may demonstrate that Palestinians' manner of coping in Jerusalem will have enabled them to maintain their distance from the Israeli regime and preserve their community in readiness for the day when they will create their own political center in Jerusalem. If this happens, it will not necessarily negate the accomplishments of Israeli coping with respect to Jerusalem. That judgment will depend on subsequent Israeli actions and achievements in the same locale.

Coping is endless. Issues move from the agenda of high priority as policymakers find ways to deal with them, but they may only move to the agenda of issues to be dealt with more thoroughly at a later time. There is seldom a rest, as other issues compete for attention. Israel is caught in a situation made hostile both by outside enemies, perhaps becoming antagonists as peace moves across the Middle East, and its own domestic quarrels.

Israelis argue about whether things are getting better or worse or if the country has lost more than it has gained by each agreement reached with former enemies. The tenets of Judaism guide some Israelis but show no signs of solving the nation's problems once and for all times. Judaic doctrines are diverse. They are more likely to support argument than clear resolve with respect to contemporary options. Like politicians elsewhere, but under more pressure than many, the present generation of Israeli leaders must decide what is appropriate for their nation in the face of contemporary enticements and threats as well as from whatever inspirations they may receive from the Hebrew Bible.

NOTES

[1] *Statistical Abstract of the United States, 1992* (Washington: U.S. Government Printing Office, 1992), p. 831; *Statistical Yearbook, 1992* (Jerusalem: Central Bureau of Statistics, 1992), pp. 43, 197, 280.

[2] *Song of Songs* 7:5-8; a report about the different responses of the rabbis who were members of Knesset appears in *Ma'ariv,* November 21, 1990 (Hebrew).

[3] See the author's *What Makes Israel Tick? How Domestic Policy-makers Cope with Constraints* (Chicago: Nelson Hall, 1985), Chapter 4.

[4] See the author's *The Political Economy of Israel* (New Brunswick, NJ: Transaction Books, 1987).

[5] Daniel Elazar and Chaim Kalchheim, eds., *Local Government in Israel* (Lanham, Maryland: University Press of America, 1988); and Frederick A. Lazin, *Policy Implementation of Social Welfare in the 1980's* (New Brunswick, NJ: Transaction Books, 1987).

[6]An Israeli scholar has identified the Palestine Liberation Organization and South Africa as more beset with difficult problems than Israel. See Yehezkel Dror, *Policymaking Under Adversity* (New Brunswick, NJ.: Transaction Press, 1986).

[7]Sharkansky, *The Political Economy of Israel.*

[8] Dan Horowitz and Moshe Lissak, *Origins of the Israeli Policy: Palestine Under the Mandate* (Chicago: University of Chicago Press 1978).

[9] *Ma'ariv,* March 4, 1994. Hebrew.

[10] Ehud Sprinzak, *The Ascendance of Israel's Radical Right* (New York: Oxford University Press, 1991).

[11] Dan Horowitz and Moshe Lissak, *Trouble in Utopia: The Overburdened Polity of Israel* (Albany: State University of New York Press, 1989).

[12]See, for example, Moshe Greenberg, "Job," in Robert Alter and Frank Kermode, eds., *The Literary Guide to the Bible* (London: Fontana Press, 1987), pp. 283-304; and Harold S. Kushner, *When Bad Things Happen to Good People* (New York: Avon Books, 1981).

[13]Jeremiah 38.

[14] Robert Davidson, *The Courage to Doubt: Exploring an Old Testament Theme* (London: SCM Press, 1983), p. 213. Here Davidson is quoting A. M. Greeley, *Journeys*, G. Baum, ed. (New York, 1975), p. 202.

[15] See Jeffrey Ian Ross, ed., *Controlling State Crime: An Introduction* (New York: Garland Publishing, 1995), including this author's chapter, "A State Action May Be Nasty but Is Not Likely To Be a Crime."

[16] Nachman Ben-Yehuda, *Political Assassinations by Jews: A Rhetorical Device for Justice* (Albany: State University Press of New York, 1993).

[17] *Statistical Abstract of Israel, 1992* (Jerusalem: Central Bureau of Statistics, 1993), Table 21.14; *Statistical Abstract of the United States 1993* (Washington: U.S. Government Printing Office, 1994), Tables 300, 303.

[18] *Israel Law Review*. 1989, Spring-Summer, Volume 23, Numbers 2-3, p. 173.

[19] (*Israel Law Review*, 1989, p. 169; see also Menachem Hofnung, *Israel - Security Needs vs. The Rule of Law (*Jerusalem: Nevo Publishing Company, 1991), Hebrew.

[20] *The Oxford English Dictionary* (Oxford: Oxford University Press, 1992).

[21] *Israel Law Review, p.* 175.

[22] There are no juries in Israeli trials.

[23] *Israel Law Review,* 1989, Volume 23. Nos. 2-3.

[24] Alan M. Dershowitz, "Is It Necessary to Apply 'Physical Pressure' to Terrorists and to Lie About It?" *Israel Law Review,* 1989pp. 192-200.

[25] Mordechai Kremnitzer, "The Landau Commission Report - Was the Security Service Subordinated to the Law, or the Law to the 'Needs' of the Security Service?" *Israel Law Review,* 1989 pp. 216-79.

[26] Adrian A. S. Zuckerman, "Coercion and the Judicial Ascertainment of Truth," *Israel Law Review,* 1989 pp. 357-74.

[27] Michael S. Moore, "Torture and the Balance of Evils," *Israel Law Review,*1989 pp. 280-344.

[28] Zuckerman.

[29] Sanford H. Kadish, "Torture, the State and the Individual," *Israel Law Review,* 1989 pp. 345-56.

[30] Ira Sharkansky, "Israel's Auditor as Policy-maker," *Public Administration* (London), Spring1988; and Ira Sharkansky and James J. Gosling, "The Limits of Government Auditing: The Case of Higher Education," *Politeia* (South Africa), 1992, Vol. 11, No. 1, 2-15.

[31]State Comptroller,. "Appointment of Workers in Housing and Development Company." *Annual Report #37.* Jerusalem 1986. 235-44. Hebrew.

[32] State Comptroller, *Annual Report #42.* Jerusalem,1991. 297-302. Hebrew.

[33] State Comptroller, *Audit Report on the Provision of Support to Institutions by Local Authorities*, Jerusalem,1991, 125 pps. Hebrew.

[34]Nissim Mizrahi and Robert Schwartz, "The Audit of Political Party Financing and Election Financing in Israel " in Asher Friedberg, Benjamin Geist, Nissim Mizrahi, and Ira Sharkansky, eds, *State Audit and Accountability: A Book of Readings* (Jerusalem: Israeli State Comptroller, 1991), pp. 351-59.

[35] State Comptroller, *Annual and Special Reports: Selected Chapters,* Jerusalem, 1992. 312-16.

[36] State Comptroller, *Report on the Results of Expenditure Audit of Political Groups for the Period of the Election to the 13th Knesset: 1.1.92 to 31.7.92,.* Jerusalem, 1993. Hebrew.

[37] Mizrahi and Schwartz.

[38] Amos 5:22-24.

[39] For a review of biblical and rabbinical writings on financial control, see Zalman Bombach, "Financial Audit in the Period of the Bible," *Iyunim: State Control* #48, 1992, pp. 62-74. Hebrew.

[40] E. W. Heaton, *The Hebrew Kingdoms* (Oxford: Oxford University Press, 1968), Chapter IV.

[41] Herbert Simon, *Administrative Behavior: A Study of Decision-Making Processes in Administrative Organizations* (New York: Free Press, 1976).

[42] Daniel P. Moynihan, *Coping: On the Practice of Government* (New York: Vintage Books, 1975).

[43] For example, Deborah Pellow and Naomi Chazan, *Ghana: Coping with Uncertainty*, (Boulder, Colorado: Westview Press, 1986); Jeffrey Gale Williamson, *Coping with City Growth During the British Industrial Revolution* (Cambridge: Cambridge University Press, 1990).

[44] Jack T. Tapp, "Multisystems Holistic Model of Health, Stress and Coping," in Tiffany M. Field, Philip M. McCabe and Neil Schneiderman, eds., *Stress and Coping* (Hillsdale, N.J.: Lawrence Erlbaum Associates, Publishers, 1985), pp. 285-304. Some writers perceive active coping as leading to more effective adaptations to crises. See Rudolf H. Moos and Jeanne A. Schaefer, "Life Transitions and Crises: A Conceptual Overview," in Moos in Collaboration with Schaefer, eds., *Coping with Life Crises: An Integrated Approach* (New York: Plenum Press, 1986), pp. 3-28. Other researchers make the point that the literature has yet to confirm any strong linkage between types of coping and the outcomes of stressful situations. See Susan Folkman, "Personal Control and Stress and Coping Processes: A Theoretical Analysis." *Journal of Personality and Social Psychology*, 46, 1984, pp. 839-52.

[45] Richard E. Neustadt and Ernest R. May, *Thinking in Time: The Uses of History for Decision Makers* (New York: The Free Press, 1988).

[46] Yehezkel Dror is a prominent critic of non-rational decision-making both in Israel and internationally. See his *Public Policymaking Reexamined* (San Francisco: Chandler Publishing Company, 1968); *A Grand Strategy for Israel* (Jerusalem: Academon, 1989), Hebrew; and *Memorandum for the Israeli Prime Minister: I. Situation of the Nation* (Jerusalem: Academon, 1992), Hebrew.

[47] David Biale, *Power and Powerlessness in Jewish History* (New York: Schocken Books, 1987).

[48] See the author's *Governing Jerusalem* (Detroit: Wayne State University Press, 1996); and "Coping Strategies of Engagement and Avoidance: The Case of Jerusalem," *Policy and Politics*, Vol. 23, No. 2 (1995).

[49] Shlomo Slonim, "The United States and the Status of Jerusalem, 1947-1984," *Israel Law Review,* Vol. 19, No. 2, Spring 1984, pp. 179-252.

[50] Abraham Ashkenasi, "Opinion Trends Among Jerusalem Palestinians" (Jerusalem: Hebrew University, Leonard Davis Institute, 1990). On the larger issue of Jewish-Palestinian relations in Israel, see Sammy Smooha, *Arabs and Jews in Israel: Conflicting and Shared Attitudes in a Divided Society* (Boulder, Colorado: Westview Press, 1989).

[51] Meron Benvenisti, *Jerusalem: The Torn City* (Minneapolis: University of Minnesota Press, 1976); Uzi Benziman, "Israeli Policy in East Jerusalem After Reunification," in Joel L. Kraemer, ed., *Jerusalem: Problems and Prospects* (New York: Praeger, 1980), pp. 100-30; and Daniel Rubinstein, "The Jerusalem Municipality Under the Ottomans, British, and Jordanians," in Kraemer, pp. 72-99.

[52] Moshe Amirav, "Jerusalem: The Open-City Solution," *Jerusalem Post*, February 4, 1990, p. 4; and Amirav, "Toward Coexisting in the Capital," *Jerusalem Post*, October 18, 1990, p. 4.

[53]Martha Crenshaw, ed, *Terrorism, Legitimacy, and Power: The Consequences of Political Violence* (Middletown, Connecticut: Wesleyan University Press, 1983); and Brian Crozier, *A Theory of Conflict*, (London: Hamish Hamilton, 1974).

Bibliography

Ackroyd, Peter R., *Israel Under Babylon and Persia* (Oxford: Oxford University Press, 1970).

Ackroyd, Peter R., *Exile and Restoration: A Study of Hebrew Thought of the Sixth Century BC* (London: SCM Press, Ltd., 1968).

Aharoni, Yohanan, *The Land of the Bible: A Historical Geography* (Philadelphia: Westminster Press, 1979).

Aharoni, Yohanan, *Carta Atlas of the Biblical Period* (Jerusalem: Carta, 1974).

Alter, Robert, and F. Kermode, *The Literary Guide to the Bible* (Cambridge: Harvard University Press, 1987).

Alexander, Philip S. "Jewish Law in the Time of Jesus: Towards a Clarification of the Problem," in Barnabas Lindars, SSF, ed., *Law and Religion: Essays on the Place of Law in Israel and Early Christianity* (Cambridge, England: James Clarke & Co., 1988), pp. 44-58.

Almond, Gabriel A., and Sidney Verba, *The Civic Culture : Political Attitudes and Democracy in Five Nations* (Newbury Park, Calif. : Sage Publications, 1989).

Alon, Gedalyahu, *Jews, Judaism and the Classical World* (Jerusalem: The Magnes Press, 1977).

Alon, Gedaliah, *The Jews in Their Land: In the Talmudic Age* (Cambridge: Harvard University Press, 1989).

Alt, Albrecht, *Essays on Old Testament History and Religion*, translated by R. A. Wilson (Garden City, NY: Doubleday & Company, 1967).

Alter, Robert, *The Art of Biblical Narrative*(New York: Basic Books, 1981).

Alter, Robert, *The World of Biblical Literature* (New York: Basic Books, 1992).

Alter, Robert and Frank Kermode, *The Literary Guide to the Bible* (London: Fontana Press, 1989).

Anderson, Bernhard W.,*The Living World of the Old Testament* (Essex, England: Longman, 1988).

Arendt, Hannah, *The Origins of Totalitarianism* (New York: Meridian Books, 1958).

Ashkenasi, Abraham, "Opinion Trends Among Jerusalem Palestinians" (Jerusalem: Hebrew University, Leonard Davis Institute, 1990).

Baeck, Leo, *Judaism and Christianity* (New York: Atheneum, 1970).

Bailey, Randall C. *David in Love and War: The Pursuit of Power in 2 Samuel 10-12* (Sheffield, England: JSOT Press, 1990).

Baillie, John, *Our Knowledge of God* excerpted in John Hick, ed., *The Existence of God* (New York: Macmillan, 1964), pp. 204-210.

Barak, Gregg, *Crimes by the Capitalist State: An Introduction to State Criminality*, (Albany: State University of New York Press).

Baron, Salo W., and Joseph L. Blau, *Judaism: Postbiblical and Talmudic Period* (Indianapolis: Bobbs-Merrill, 1954).

Barton, John, *Oracles of God: Perceptions of Ancient Prophecy in Israel after the Exile* (London: Darton, Longman and Todd, 1986).

Beltz, Walter, *God and The Gods: Myths of the Bible*, translated by Peter Heinegg (Harmondsworth, England: Penguin Books, 1983).

Ben-Yehuda, Nachman, *Political Assassinations by Jews: A Rhetorical Device for Justice* (Albany: State University Press of New York, 1993).

Benvenisti, Meron, *Jerusalem: The Torn City* (Minneapolis: University of Minnesota Press, 1976).

Benvenisti, Meron, *The Shepherds' War: Collected Essays (1981-1989)* (Jerusalem: The Jerusalem Post, 1989).

Benvenisti, Meron, *The Sling and the Club: Territories, Jews and Arabs* (Jerusalem: Keter Publishing House, Ltd., 1988), Hebrew.

Benvenisti, Meron, *The West Bank Data Project: A Survey of Israel's Policies* (Washington: American Enterprise Institute for Policy Research, 1984).

Benziman, Uzi, "Israeli Policy in East Jerusalem After Reunification," in Joel L. Kraemer, ed., *Jerusalem: Problems and Prospects* (New York: Praeger, 1980), pp. 100-30.

Berger, Peter L.*The Sacred Canopy: Elements of A Sociological Theory of Religion* (New York: Anchor Books, 1967).

Bermant, Chaim, *The Jews* (London: Weidenfeld and Nicolson, 1977).

Biale, David, *Eros and the Jews: From Biblical Israel to Contemporary America* (New York: Basic Books, 1992).

Biale, David, *Power and Powerlessness in Jewish History* (New York: Schocken Books, 1987).

Bickerman, Elias J.,*The Jews in the Greek Age* (Cambridge: Harvard University Press, 1988).

Blenkinsopp, Joseph, *Gibeon and Israel: The Role of Gibeon and the Gibeonites in the Political and Religious History of Early Israel* (Cambridge: Cambridge University Press,1972).

Blenkinsopp, Joseph, *A History of Prophecy in Israel: From the Settlement in the Land to the Hellenistic Period* (Philadelphia: The Westminster Press, 1983).

Bloom, Harold, *The American Religion: The Emergence of the Post-Christian Nation* (New York: Simon and Schuster, 1992.

Bloom,Harold,*The Book of J* (New York: Vintage Books, 1990), p. 35.

Bola, Menachem, *The Book of Jeremiah* (Jerusalem: Mossad Harav Kook, 1983), Hebrew.

Bombach, Zalman, "Financial Audit in the Period of the Bible," *Iyunim: State Control* #48, 1992, pp. 62-74. Hebrew.

Brams, Steven J. *Biblical Games: A Strategic Analysis of Stories in the Old Testament* (Cambridge, Massachusetts: M.I.T. Press, 1980).

Brams, Steven J. *Superior Beings: If They Exist, How Would We Know?* (New York: Springer-Verlag, 1983).

Bright, John, *Covenant and Promise: The Prophetic Understanding of the Future in Pre-Exilic Israel* (Philadelphia: The Westminster Press, 1976).

Bright, John, *A History of Israel* (London: SCM Press Ltd., 1980).

Bright, John, *Jeremiah: The Anchor Bible* (Garden City, NY: Doubleday & Company, 1965).

Brooks, Roger, *The Spirit of the Ten Commandments: Shattering the Myth of Rabbinic Legalism* (New York: Harper and Row, 1990).

Brueggemann, Walter, *David's Truth: In Israel's Imagination and Memory* (Philadelphia: Fortress Press, 1985).

Brueggemann, Walter, "The Book of Jeremiah: Portrait of the Prophet," James Luther Mays and Paul J. Achtemeier, eds., *Interpreting the Prophets* (Philadelphia: Fortress Press, 1987), 113-29.

Buber, Martin, *Israel and the World: Essays in a Time of Crisis.* (New York: Schocken Books: 1963).

Bulka, Reuven P., ed., *Dimensions of Orthodox Judaism* (New York: KTAV Publishing House, 1983).

Burnett, Alan D.,and Peter J. Taylor, eds., *Political Studies from Spatial Perspectives: Anglo-American Essays on Political Geography* (New York: John Wiley & Sons, 1981).

Callaway, Joseph A.,"Ai(et-tell): Problem Site for Biblical Archaeologists," in Perdue et al, pp. 87-99.

Cantor, Norman F., *The Sacred Chain: The History of the Jews* (New York: Harper Collins, 1994).

Carroll, Robert P., "Prophecy and society," in Clements, pp. 203-25.

Cassill, R. V., *After Goliath* (New York: Ticknor & Fields, 1985).

Chacham, Amos, *The Book of Job* (Jerusalem: Mossad Harav Kook, 1984), Hebrew.

Chacham, Amos, *The Twelve* (Jerusalem: Mossad Harav Kook, 1987), Hebrew.

Chinn, Laurence, *The Unanointed: A Novel* (New York: Crown Publishers, 1958).

Cingranelli, David Louis, *Ethics, American Foreign Policy, and the Third World* (New York: St. Martin's Press, 1993).

Cingrannelli, David Louis ed., *Human Rights: Theory and Measurement* (New York: St. Martin's Press, 1988).

Clausewitz, Carl Von, *On War* (London: Penguin Books, 1968).

Clements, R. E., ed., *The World of Ancient Israel: Sociological, Anthropological and Political Perspectives* (Cambridge: Cambridge University Press, 1989).

Coats, George W., *Moses: Heroic Man, Man of God* (Sheffield. England: Sheffield Academic Press, 1988).

Cohen, Stuart A., *The Three Crowns: Structures of Communal Politics in Early Rabbinic Jewry* (Cambridge: Cambridge University Press. 1990).

Cohn, Haim H., *Human Rights in Jewish Law* (New York: Ktav Publishing House, 1984).

Collins, John J., *Between Athens and Jerusalem: Jewish Identity in the Hellenistic Diaspora* (New York: Crossroad, 1986).

Coote, Robert B. and Mary P. Coote, *Power, Politics, and the Making of the Bible: An Introduction* (Minneapolis: Fortress Press, 1990).

Crenshaw, James L,. "A Living Tradition: The Book of Jeremiah in Current Research" in Mays and Achtemeier, pp. 100-12.

Crenshaw, James L., *Ecclesiastes: A Commentary* (London: SCM Press Ltd., 1988).

Daiches, David, *Moses: The Man and His Vision* (New York: Praeger. 1975).

Dart, John, *The Jesus of Heresy and History: The Discovery and Meaning of the Nag Hammadi Gnostic Library* (San Francisco: Harper and Row, 1988).

Davidson, Robert, *The Courage to Doubt: Exploring An Old Testament Theme* (London: SCM Press, 1983).

Dershowitz, Alan M., "Is It Necessary to Apply 'Physical Pressure' to Terrorists and to Lie About It?" *Israel Law Review,* 1989. Spring-Summer. Volume 23, Numbers 2-3, pp. 192-200.

Dever, William G., and W. Malcolm Clark, "The Patriarchal Traditions," in John H. Hayes and J. Maxwell Miller, eds., *Israelite and Judaean History* (London: SCM Press Ltd., 1977), pp. 70-148.

Dimont, Max I., *Jews, God and History* (New York: Signet Books, 1964).

Dorman, M., "The State Versus the Writer: Recent Developments in Stefan Heym's Struggle Against the GDR's Kulturpolitik," *Modern Languages: Journal of the Modern Language Association*, Vol. 62, September 1981, pp. 144-52.

Dror, Yehezkel, *A Grand Strategy for Israel* (Jerusalem: Academon, 1989), Hebrew.

Dror, Yehezkel, *Memorandum for the Israeli Prime Minister: I. Situation of the Nation* (Jerusalem: Academon, 1992), Hebrew.

Dror, Yehezkel, *Policymaking Under Adversity* (New Brunswick, NJ.: Transaction Press, 1986).

Dror, Yehezkel, *Public Policymaking Reexamined* (San Francisco: Chandler Publishing Company, 1968).

Duke, Rodney K., "The Portion of the Levite: Another Reading of *Deuteronomy* 18:6-8," *Journal of Biblical Literature*, 106, 2, June 1987, pp. 193-201.

El-Or, Tamar, *Educated and Ignorant: On Ultra-orthodox Women and Their World* (Tel Aviv: Am Oved, 1992), Hebrew.

Elazar, Daniel J., and Stuart A. Cohen, *The Jewish Polity: Jewish Political Organization from Biblical Times to the Present* (Bloomington, Indiana: Indiana University Press, 1985).

Elazar, Daniel J., *American Federalism: A View from the States* (New York: Harper & Row, 1984).

Elazar, Daniel J., "The Book of Joshua as a Political Classic," *Jewish Political Studies Review*, Vol. 1, No. 1-2, 1989, pp. 93-150.

Elazar, Daniel J., and Chaim Kalchheim, eds., *Local Government in Israel* (Lanham, Maryland: University Press of America, 1988).

Emmerson, Grace I., "Women in Ancient Israel" in R. E. Clements, ed., *The World of Ancient Israel: Sociological, Anthropological and Political Perspectives* (Cambridge: Cambridge University Press, 1989), pp. 371-94.

Engelsman, Joan Chamberlain, *The Feminine Dimension of the Divine* (Philadelphia: Westminster Press, 1979).

Epsztein, Leon, *Social Justice in the Ancient Near East and the People of the Bible* (London: SCM Press Ltd, 1986).

Falk, Marcia, *The Song of Songs: A New Translation and Interpretation* (San Francisco: Harper, 1990).

Finkelstein, Israel, "The Emergence of the Monarchy in Israel: The Environmental and Socio-Economic Aspects," *Journal for the Study of the Old Testament*, 44, June 1989, pp. 43-74.

Fishbane, Michael ,"Sin and Judgement in the Prophecies of Ezekiel," in James Luther Mays and Paul J. Achtemeier, eds., *Interpreting the Prophets* (Philadelphia: Fortress Press, 1987), pp. 170-87.

Fisher, R. W., "The State Against Stefan Heym: Fact and Fiction in Heym's *The Queen Against Defoe*," *German Life and Letters*, Vol. 45, 1992, pp. 94-107.

Fishkin, James S., *The Limits of Obligation* (New Haven: Yale University Press, 1982).

Flanagan, James W., *David's Social Drama: A Hologram of Israel's Early Iron Age* (Sheffield, England: Almond Press, 1988).

Folkman, Susan, "Personal Control and Stress and Coping Processes: A Theoretical Analysis," *Journal of Personality and Social Psychology*, 46, 1984, pp. 839-52.

Fox, Michael V., "The Meaning of *Hebel* for Qohelet," *Journal of Biblical Literature*, 105, 3, September 1986, pp. 409-27.

Frankel, Jonathan, *Prophecy and Politics: Socialism, Nationalism, and the Russian Jews, 1862-1917* (Cambridge: Cambridge University Press, 1981).

Freedman, David Noel, *The Unity of the Hebrew Bible* (Ann Arbor: University of Michigan Press, 1991).

Freedman, David Noel, "'Who Is Like Thee Among the Gods?' The Religion of Early Israel," in Miller, Hanson, and McBride, pp. 315-36.

Fretheim, Terence E., *Deuteronomic History* (Nashville: Abingdon Press, 1983).

Fried, Charles, "Difficulties in the Economic Analysis of Rights," in Gillroy and Wade.

Friedman, Menachem,"The Hasidim and the Holocaust," *Jerusalem Quarterly* 53, Winter 1990, pp. 86-114.

Friedman, Richard Elliott, *Who Wrote the Bible?* (New York: Harper and Row, 1987).

Frontain, Raymong-Jean, and Jan Wojcik, ed., *The David Myth in Western Literature* (West Lafayette, IN: Purdue University Press, 1980).

Frye, Northrop, *The Great Code: The Bible and Literature* (San Diego: Harcourt Brace Jovanovich, 1983).

Garbini, Giovanni, *History and Ideology in Ancient Israel* (New York: Crossroad Publishing Company, 1988).

Georges-Abeyie, Daniel E. "Piracy, Air Piracy, and Recurrent US. and Israeli Civilian Aircraft Interceptions" in Barak, pp. 129-44.

Gershom, Scholem, *The Messianic Idea in Judaism and Other Essays on Jewish Spirituality* (New York: Schocken Books, 1971).

Gillroy, John Martin and Maurice Wade, eds. *The Moral Dimensions of Public Policy Choice: Beyond the Market Paradigm* (Pittsburgh: University of Pittsburgh Press, 1992).

Ginzberg, Louis, *The Legends of the Jews* (Philadelphia: The Jewish Publication Society of America, 1911).

Girard, Rene, *Job: The Victim of His People*, translated by Yvonne Freccero, (Stanford: Stanford University Press, 1987).

Girard, Rene, "'The Trail Trodden by the Wicked': *Job* as Scapegoat," in Harold Bloom ed., *The Book of Job* (New York: Chelsea House Publishers, 1988), 103-34.

Gitelman, Zvi, ed., *The Quest for Utopia: Jewish Political Ideas and Institutions Through the Ages* (Armonk, NY: M.E. Sharpe, Inc., 1992).

Glatzer, Nahum N., ed., *The Dimensions of Job: A Study and Selected Readings* (New York: Schocken Books, 1969).

Goldingay, John, "The Stories in Daniel: A Narrative Politics," *Journal for the Study of the Old Testament* 37, February 1987, pp. 99-116.

Goldscheider, Calvin, "Ethnicity, American Judaism, and Jewish Cohesion," in Goldscheider and Neusner, pp. 194-211.

Goldscheider, Calvin, and Jacob Neusner, *Social Foundations of Judaism* (Englewood Cliffs NJ: Prentice–Hall, 1990).

Good, Edwin M., *Irony in the Old Testament* (Philadelphia: The Westminster Press, 1965).

Good, Edwin M., *In Turns of Tempest: A Reading of Job* (Stanford: Stanford University Press, 1990).

Gordis, Robert, *Koheleth: The Man and His Work: A Study of Ecclesiastes* (New York: Schocken Books, 1968).

Gottwald, Norman K., *The Tribes of Yahweh: A Sociology of the Religion of Liberated Israel, 1250-1050 BCE* (Maryknoll, NY: Orbis Books, 1979).

Gottwald, Norman K., *The Hebrew Bible: A Socio-Literary Introduction* (Philadelphia: Fortress Press, 1985).

Grant, Michael, *The Jews in the Roman World* (New York: Dorset Press, 1973).

Grant,Robert M., with David Tracy, *A Short History of the Interpretation of the Bible* (Philadelphia: Fortress Press, 1984), p. 28.

Graves, Peter J., "Authority, the State, and the Individual: Stefan Heym's Novel *Collin*," *Forum for Modern Language Studies*, Vol. 23, October 1987, pp. 341-50.

Greeley, Andrew M., *Myths of Religion* (New York: Warner Books, 1989).

Greenberg, Moshe, "*Job*," in Robert Alter and Frank Kermode, eds., *The Literary Guide to the Bible* (London: Fontana Press, 1987), pp. 283-304.

Greenberg, Moshe, "The Design and Themes of *Ezekiel*'s Program of Restoration," in James Luther Mays and Paul J. Achtemeier, *Interpreting the Prophets* (Philadelphia: Fortress Press, 1987), pp. 215-36.

Gunn, David M.*The Fate of King Saul: An Interpretation of a Biblical Story* (Sheffield: Journal for the Study of the Old Testament Supplement Series, 14, 1984).

Hacham, Amos, *The Book of Isaiah* (Jerusalem: Mossad Harav Kook, 1984), Hebrew.

Halligan, John M. "The Role of the Peasant in the Amarna Period," in David Noel Freedman and David Frank Graf, eds., *Palestine in Transition: The Emergence of Ancient Israel* (Sheffield, England: The Almond Press, 1983), pp. 15-24.

Halpern, Baruch, *The Emergence of Israel in Canaan* (Chico, CA.: Scholars Press, 1983).

Halpern, Baruch, *The First Historians: The Hebrew Bible and History* (San Francisco: Harper & Row, 1988).

Hanson, Paul D., *The People Called: The Growth of Community in the Bible* (New York: Harper and Row, 1986).

Hanson, Paul D., *Old Testament Apocalyptic* (Nashville: Abingdon Press, 1987).

Hare, R. M., *Essays on Political Morality* (Oxford: Clarendon Press, 1989).

Harkabi, Yehoshafat, *The Bar Kokhba Syndrome: Risk and Realism in International Relations*, Translated by Max D. Ticktin. Edited by David Altshuler (Chappaqua, NY.: Rossel Books, 1983).

Harkabi, Yehoshafat, *Israel's Fateful Hour*, translated by Lenn Schramm (New York: Harper & Row, 1988).

Hartman, David A., *Living Covenant: The Innovative Spirit in Traditional Judaism* (New York: Free Press, 1985).

Hasel, Gerhard F., *The Remnant: The History and Theology of the Remnant Idea from Genesis to Isaiah* (Berrien Springs, Mich: Andrews University Press, 1974).

Hayes, John H., *An Introduction to Old Testament Study* (Nashville: Abingdon Press, 1979), .

Hayes, A. D. H., "The Period of the Judges and the Rise of the Monarchy," in John H. Hayes and J. Maxwell Miller, eds., *Israelite and Judaean History* (London: SCM Press Ltd., 1977), pp. 285-331.

Heaton, E. W., *The Hebrew Kingdoms* (Oxford: Oxford University Press, 1968).

Heaton, Eric William, *The Old Testament Prophets* (London: Darton, Longman and Todd, 1977).

Heller, Joseph, *God Knows* (New York: Dell Publishing Company, 1984).

Herrmann, Siegfried, *A History of Israel in Old Testament Times* (London: SCM Press, Ltd., 1975).

Herrmann, Siegfried, *Israel in Egypt* (London: SCM Press, Ltd., 1973).

Heschel, Abraham J.,*The Prophets* (New York: Harper & Row, 1962).

Heym, Stefan, *The King David Report: A Novel* (New York: G.P. Putnam's Sons, 1973).

Hick, John, *God and the Universe of Faiths: Essays in the Philosophy of Religion* (London: Macmillan, 1973).

Hofnung, Menachem, *Israel - State Security Against the Rule of Law 1948-1991* (Jerusalem: Nevo Publisher, 1991), pp. 110-37. Hebrew.

Holtz, ed., Barry W. *Back to the Sources: Reading the Classic Jewish Texts* (New York: Summit Books, 1984).

Horowitz,Dan, and Moshe Lissak, *Origins of The Israeli Policy: Palestine Under the Mandate* (Chicago: University of Chicago Press 1978).

Horowitz, Dan, and Moshe Lissak, *Trouble in Utopia: The Overburdened Polity of Israel* (Albany: State University of New York Press, 1989).

Huntington, Samuel, *Understanding Political Development : An Analytic Study.* (Boston: Little, Brown: 1987).

Hutchinson, Peter, "Problems of Socialist Historiography: The Example of Stefan Heym's *The King David Report, The Modern Language Review*, Vol. 81, January 1986, pp. 131-38.

Hutchinson, Peter, *Stefan Heym: The Perpetual Dissident* (Cambridge: Cambridge University Press, 1992).

Ibn-Zahav, Ari, *David and Bathsheba*, translated by I. M. Lask (New York: Crown Publishers, 1951).

Jeremias, Joachim, *Jerusalem in the Time of Jesus: An Investigation into Economic and Social Conditions during the New Testament Period* (London: SCM Press Ltd., 1969).

Johnson, Paul, *A History of Christianity* (NY: Atheneum, 1976), Part One.

Josephus, *The Jewish War* (New York: Penguin Books, 1970).

Josipovici, Gabriel, *The Book of God: A Response to the Bible* (New Haven: Yale University Press, 1988).

Kadish, Sanford H., "Torture the State and the Individual," *Israel Law Review*, 1989. Spring-Summer. Volume 23, Numbers 2-3, pp. 345-56.

Kahane, Rabbi Meir, "Forty Years" (Brooklyn, New York: The Institute of the Jewish Idea, 1983).

Kaufman, Gordon D., *The Theological Imagination: Constructing the Concept of God* (Philadelphia: The Westminster Press, 1981).

Kaufmann, Yehezkel, *The Religion of Israel: From Its Beginnings to the Babylonian Exile* translated and abridged by Moshe Greenberg (Chicago: University of Chicago Press, 1960).

Keller, Chaim Dov, "Modern Orthodoxy: An Analysis and a Response," in Bulka, pp. 253-71.

Keren, Michael, *Ben Gurion and the Intellectuals: Power, Knowledge, and Charisma* (Dekalb, Illinois: Northern Illinois University Press: 1983).

Kil, Yehuda, *The Book of Chronicles* (Jerusalem: Mossad Harav Kook, 1986), Hebrew.

Kil, Yehuda, *The Book of Joshua* (Jerusalem: Mossad Harav Kook, 1970) (Hebrew).

Kil, Yehuda, *The Book of Kings* (Jerusalem: Mossad Harav Kook, 1981), Hebrew.

Kil, Yehuda, *The Book of Samuel* (Jerusalem: Mossad Harav Kook, 1981). (Hebrew).

Kirscht, John Patrick, *Dimensions of Authoritarianism: A Review of Research and Theory* (Lexington: University of Kentucky Press, 1967).

Koch, Klaus, *The Prophets: The Assyrian Period* (Philadelphia: Fortress Press, 1983).

Koch, Klaus, *The Prophets: The Babylonian and Persian Periods* (Philadelphia: Fortress Press, 1984).

Kochan, Lionel, *Jews, Idols and Messiahs: The Challenge from History* (Oxford: Basil Blackwell, 1990).

Kramer, Joel I., ed., *Jerusalem: Problems and Prospects (New York: Praeger, 1980).*

Kremnitzer, Mordechai, "The Landau Commission Report - Was The Security Service Subordinated to the Law, or the Law to the 'Needs' of the Security Service?" *Israel Law Review,* 1989, Spring-Summer, Volume 23, Numbers 2-3,pp. 216-79.

Kushner, Harold S., *When Bad Things Happen to Good People* (New York: Avon Books, 1981).

Lamm, Norman, "Pluralism and Unity in the Orthodox Jewish Community," in Bulka, pp. 272-78.

Lasswell, Harold D., *Who Gets What, When, How?* (New York: McGraw-Hill, 1936).

Lauckner, Nancy A., "Stefan Heym's Revolutionary Wandering Jew: A Warning and a Hope for the Future," in Margy Gerber, ed., *Studies in GDR Culture and Society, 4: Selected Papers from the Ninth New Hampshire Symposium on the German Democratic Republic* (Lanham, Md.: University Press of America, 1984).

Lazin, Frederick A., *Policy Implementation of Social Welfare in the 1980's* (New Brunswick, NJ: Transaction Books, 1987).

Lederhandler, Eli, *The Road to Modern Jewish Politics: Political Tradition and Political Reconstruction in the Jewish Community of Tsarist Russia* (New York: Oxford University Press, 1989).

Leibowitz Nehama, *Studies in Bamidbar (Numbers)* Translated and adapted by Aryeh Newman (Jerusalem: The World Zionist Organization, 1980).

Leibowitz Nehama, *Studies in Shemot (Exodus)* Translated and adapted by Aryeh Newman (Jerusalem: The World Zionist Organization, 1981).

Leibowitz, Yeshayahu, *On Just About Everything: Talks with Michael Shashar* (Jerusalem: Keter Publishing House, Ltd., 1988), Hebrew.

Lewis, C. S., *Reflections on the Psalms* (London: Fontana Books, 1961), p. 9.

Liebman,Charles S., and Steven M. Cohen, *Two Worlds of Judaism: The Israeli and American Experiences* (New Haven: Yale University Press, 1990).

Lijphart, Arend, *Democracies: Patterns of Majoritarian and Consensus Government in Twenty-one Countries* (New Haven: Yale University Press, 1984).

Lindgren, Torgny, *Bathsheba,* Translated from the Swedish by Tom Geddes (New York: Harper & Row, 1989).

Lindsay, A. D., *The Modern Democratic State* (New York: Oxford University Press, 1943) .

Liptzin, Sol, *Biblical Themes in World Literature* (Hoboken, NJ: KTAV Publishing House, 1985).

Mays, James Luther and Paul J. Achtemeier, eds., *Interpreting the Prophets* (Philadelphia: Fortress Press, 1987)

Mann, Thomas, *Joseph and His Brothers* (London: Penguin Books, 1978).

Martin, Malach, *King of Kings* (New York: Simon and Schuster, 1980).

McCagg, O. I., Jr., *A History of Habsburg Jews, 1670-1918* (Bloomington: Indiana University Press, 1989).

McCarter, P. Kyle, Jr., "Aspects of the Religion of the Israelite Monarchy: Biblical and Epigraphic Data," in Patrick D. Miller, Jr., Paul D. Hanson, and S. Dean McBride, eds., *Ancient Israelite Religion* (Philadelphia: Fortress Press, 1987), pp. 137-56.

McIlwain, Charles H., *Constitutionalism, Ancient and Modern* (Ithaca, NY.: Cornell University Press, 1947).

McKenzie, John L.S.J., *The Two-Edged Sword: An Interpretation of the Old Testament*, (Garden City, N.Y.: Image Books, 1966).

Medding, Peter Y., *The Founding of Israeli Democracy 1948-1967* (New York: Oxford University Press, 1990).

Melzar Fibal, *The Book of Ruth,* in Zar-Kavod, Mordecai, ed., *The Five Scrolls* (Jerusalem: Mossad Harav Kook, 1973) Hebrew.

Mendelsohn, Ezra, *On Modern Jewish Politics* (New York: Oxford University Press, 1993).

Mendenhall, George E., "Ancient Israel's Hyphenated History," in David Noel Freedman and David Frank Graf, eds., *Palestine in Transition: The Emergence of Ancient Israel* (Sheffield, England: The Almond Press, 1983).

Mendenhall, George E., "The Nature and Purpose of the Abraham Narratives," in Patrick D. Miller, Jr., Paul D. Hanson, and S. Dean McBride, eds., *Ancient Israelite Religion* (Philadelphia: Fortress Press, 1987), pp. 337-56.

Mendenhall, George E., *The Tenth Generation: The Origins of the Biblical Tradition* (Baltimore: Johns Hopkins University Press, 1973).

Mettinger, Tryggve N.D., *Solomonic State Officials: A Study of the Civil Government Officials of the Israelite Monarchy* (Lund: CWK Gleerup, 1971).

Meyers, Carol, "David as Temple Builder," in Patrick D. Miller, Jr., Paul D. Hanson, and S. Dean McBride, eds., *Ancient Israelite Religion* (Philadelphia: Fortress Press, 1987), pp. 357-76.

Miller, Patrick D., Jr., Paul D. Hanson, and S. Dean McBride, eds., *Ancient Israelite Religion* (Philadelphia: Fortress Press, 1987)

Miller, J. Maxwell, and John H. Hayes, *A History of Ancient Israel and Judah* (Philadelphia: The Westminster Press, 1986).

Mintz, Jerome R., *Legends of the Hasidim: An Introduction to Hasidic Culture and Oral Tradition in the New World* (Chicago: University of Chicago Press, 1968).

Moore, Michael S., "Torture And the Balance of Evils," *Israel Law Review*.1989. Spring-Summer. Volume 23, Numbers 2-3,pp. 280-344.

Moos, Rudolf H., and Jeanne A. Schaefer, "Life Transitions and Crises: A Conceptual Overview," in Moos in Collaboration with Schaefer, eds., *Coping with Life Crises: An Integrated Approach* (New York: Plenum Press, 1986), pp. 3-28.

Morrow, William, "Consolation, Rejection, and Repentance in *Job* 42:6," *Journal of Biblical Literature* 105, 2, June 1986, pp. 201-25.

Moss, Steven A., "Who Killed Goliath?" *The Jewish Bible Quarterly* XVIII, 1, Fall 1989, pp. 37-40.

Neusner, Jacob, *American Judaism: Adventure in Modernity* (Englewood Cliffs, NJ: Prentice-Hall, 1972).

Neusner, Jacob, *Death and Birth of Judaism: The Impact of Christianity, Secularism, and the Holocaust on Jewish Faith* (New York: Basic Books, 1987).

Neusner, Jacob, *Judaism and Scripture: The Evidence of Leviticus Rabbah* (Chicago: University of Chicago Press, 1986).

Neustadt, Richard, *Presidential Power: The Politics of Leadership* (New York: Wiley, 1976). .

Neustadt,Richard E., and Ernest R. May, *Thinking in Time: The Uses of History for Decision Makers* (New York: The Free Press, 1988).

Nibley, Hugh, *The World and the Prophets* (Salt Lake City: Deseret Book Company, 1987).

Nicholson, Ernest W., *God and His People: Covenant and Theology in the Old Testament* (Oxford: Clarendon Press, 1986).

Nickelsburg, George W. E., *Jewish Literature Between the Bible and the Mishnah* (Philadelphia: Fortress Press, 1981).

Niditch, Susan, *Underdogs and Tricksters: A Prelude to Biblical Folklore* (San Francisco: Harper & Row, 1987).

Noth, Martin A., *History of Pentateuchal Traditions,* translated by Bernhard W. Anderson (Englewood Cliffs, NJ: Prentice Hall, 1972).

O'Connor, Kathleen M., *The Confessions of Jeremiah: Their Interpretation and Role in Chapters 1-25* (Atlanta: Scholars Press, 1988).

Oppenheim, A. Leo, *Ancient Mesopotamia: Portrait of a Dead Civilization* (Chicago: University of Chicago Press, 1977).

Orlinsky, Harry M., "Nationalism-Universalism and Internationalism in Ancient Israel," in his *Essays in Biblical Culture and Bible Translation* (New York: KTAV Publishing House, Inc., 1974), pp. 78-116.

Overholt, Thomas W., *Prophecy in Cross-Cultural Perspective: A Sourcebook for Biblical Researchers* (Atlanta: Scholars Press, 1986)..

Penchansky, David, *The Betrayal of God: Ideological Conflict in Job* (Louisville, KY: Westminster/John Knox Press, 1990).

Pennock J. Ronald, and John W. Chapman, eds., *Constitutionalism* (New York: New York University Press, 1977).

Perdue, Leo G., Lawrence E. Toombs, and Gary Lance Johnson, eds., *Archaeology and Biblical Interpretation* (Atlanta: John Knox Press, 1987)

Permutter, Amos, *Modern Authoritarianism: A Comparative Institutional Analysis* (New Haven: Yale University Press, 1981).

Pope, Marvin H., *Job*, The Anchor Bible, (Garden City, NY: Doubleday, 1973).

Potok, Chaim, *Wanderings: History of the Jews* (New York: Fawcett Crest, 1978).

Powell, G. Bingham, Jr., *Contemporary Democracies: Participation, Stability, and Violence* (Cambridge: Harvard University Press, 1982).

Prickett, Stephen, *Words and The Word: Language, Poetics, and Biblical Interpretation* (Cambridge: Cambridge University Press, 1986).

Propp, William H., "The Rod of Aaron and the Sin of Moses," *Journal of Biblical Literature* 107, 1, March 1988, pp. 19-26.

Raitt, Thomas M., "Jeremiah in the Lectionary," in Mays and Achtenmeier, pp. 143-56..

Rawidowicz Simon, *Studies in Jewish Thought* (Philadelphia: The Jewish Publication Society of America, 1974).

Reich, Bernard, and Gershon R. Kieval, eds., *Israeli Politics in the 1990s: Key Domestic and Foreign Policy Factors* (Westport CT: Greenwood Press, 1991) .

Roelofs, H. Mark, "Hebraic-Biblical Political Thinking," *Polity* XX, 4 (Summer 1988), 572-97.

Roelofs, H. Mark, "Liberation Theology: The Recovery of Biblical Radicalism," *American Political Science Review* 82, 2, June 1988, pp. 549-66.

Rosenberg, David ed., *Congregation: Contemporary Writers Read the Jewish Bible*, (San Diego: Harcourt, Brace, Jovanovich, 1987).

Rosenberg, Joel, *King and Kin: Political Allegory in the Hebrew Bible* (Bloomington: University Press, 1986).

Rosenblatt,Jason P., and Joseph C. Sitterson, Jr., *"Not in Heaven" Coherence and Complexity in Biblical Narrative* (Bloomington: Indiana University Press, 1991).

Rosenblum, Nancy L., ed., *Liberalism and the Moral Life* (Cambridge: Harvard University Press, 1989).

Rotenstreich, Nathan, *Tradition and Reality: The Impact of History on Modern Jewish Thought* (New York: Random House, 1972).

Roth, Joel, *The Halakhic Process: A Systemic Analysis* (New York: Jewish Theological Seminary of America, 1986).

Rubinstein, Daniel, "The Jerusalem Municipality Under the Ottomans, British, and Jordanians," in Kraemer, pp. 72-99.

Russell, D. S., *From Early Judaism to Early Church* (London: SCM Press, Ltd., 1986).

Russell, D. S., *The Jews from Alexander to Herod* (Oxford: Oxford University Press, 1967).

Safire, William, *The First Dissident: The Book of Job in Today's Politics* (New York: Random House, 1992).

Samuel, Maurice, *The Professor and the Fossil* (New York: Alfred A. Knopf, 1956).

Sanders James A., "The Integrity of Biblical Pluralism," in Jason P. Rosenblatt and Joseph C. Sitterson, Jr., *"Not in Heaven" Coherence and Complexity in Biblical Narrative* (Bloomington: Indiana University Press, 1991), pp. 154-69.

Sanders, James A., "Isaiah in Luke," in James Luther Mays and Paul J. Achtemeier, eds., *Interpreting the Prophets* (Philadelphia: Fortress Press, 1987), pp. 75-85.

Sandmel, Samuel, *Judaism and Christian Beginnings* (New York: Oxford University Press, 1978).

Sanford, John A., *King Saul, The Tragic Hero: A Study in Individuation* (New York: Paulist Press, 1985).

Sarna, Nahum M., *Exploring Exodus: The Heritage of Biblical Israel* (New York: Schocken Books, 1987).

Sarna, Nahum M ., *Understanding Genesis: The Heritage of Biblical Israel* (New York: Schocken Books, 1966).

Sartori, Giovanni, *The Theory of Democracy Revisited* (Chatham, NJ.: Chatham House Publishers, Inc.: 1987).

Scholem, Gershom, *Sabbatei Sevi: The Mystical Messiah*, Translated by R. J. Zwi Werblowsky (Princeton: Princeton University Press, 1973).

Schonfield, Hugh J., *The Passover Plot* (London: Corgi Books, 1967).

Scott, R. B. Y., *Proverbs and Ecclesiastes* (Anchor Bible) (New York: Anchor Books, 1965).

Seltzer, Robert M., *Jewish People, Jewish Thought: The Jewish Experience in History* (New York: Macmillan, 1980).

Seters, John Van, *Abraham in History and Tradition* (New Haven: Yale University Press, 1975).

Shalev, Meir, *The Bible Now* (Jerusalem: Schocken, 1985), pp. 93-98 (Hebrew).

Sharkansky, Ira, *Ancient and Modern Israel: An Exploration of Political Parallels* (Albany: State University of New York Press, 1991), especially Chapter 4.

Sharkansky, Ira, "Israel's Auditor as Policy-maker." *Public Administration* (London), Spring 1988.

Sharkansky, Ira, *Regionalism in American Politics* (Indianapolis: Bobbs-Merrill, 1970).

Sharkansky, Ira, *The Political Economy of Israel* (New Brunswick, NJ: Transaction Books, 1987).

Sharkansky, Ira, *What Makes Israel Tick? How Domestic Policy-makers Cope with Constraints* (Chicago: Nelson Hall, 1985).

Sharkansky Ira, and James J. Gosling, "The Limits of Government Auditing: The Case of Higher Education." *Politeia* (South Africa), 1992, Vol. 11, No. 1, 2-15.

Sicker, Martin, *The Judaic State: A Study in Rabbinic Political Theory* (New York: Praeger, 1988).

Silberman, Neil Asher, *Digging for God and Country: Exploration, Archeology, and the Secret Struggle for the Holy Land 1799-1917* (New York: Anchor Books, 1990).

Silberstein, Laurence J., ed., *Jewish Fundamentalism in Comparative Perspective: Religion, Ideology, and the Crisis of Modernity* (New York: New York University Press, 1993).

Silver, Abba Hillel, *Where Judaism Differs: An Inquiry into the Distinctiveness of Judaism* (New York: Collier Books, 1989).

Silver, Daniel Jeremy, *A History of Judaism* (New York: Basic Books, 1974).

Simon, Herbert, *Administrative Behavior: A Study of Decision-Making Processes in Administrative Organizations* (New York: Free Press, 1976).

Sklare, Marshall, Joseph Greenblum, and Benjamin B. Ringer, *Not Quite at Home: How an American Jewish Community Lives With Itself and Its Neighbors* (New York: The American Jewish Committee, 1969).

Slonim, Shlomo, "The United States and the Status of Jerusalem, 1947-1984," *Israel Law Review,* Vol 19, No. 2, Spring 1984, pp. 179-252.

Smith, Morton, *Palestinian Parties and Politics that Shaped the Old Testament* (London: SCM Press, 1987).

Smith, Jonathan Z., *Imagining Religion: From Babylon to Jonestown* (Chicago: University of Chicago Press, 1982).

Smooha, Sammy, *Arabs and Jews in Israel: Conflicting and Shared Attitudes in a Divided Society* (Boulder, CO: Westview Press, 1989).

Sprinzak, Ehud, *The Ascendance of Israel's Radical Right* (New York: Oxford University Press, 1991).

Sprinzak, Ehud, "Fundamentalism, Terrorism, and Democracy: The Case of Gush Emunim Underground," Washington: The Wilson Center, Occasional Paper, September 16, 1986 (mimeo).

Steinberg, Milton, *As a Driven Leaf* (Behrman House, Inc., 1939).

Steinsaltz, Adin, *Biblical Images: Men and Women of the Book* (New York: Basic Books, 1984), .

Stern, Ephraim, "The Bible and Israeli Archaeology," in Leo G. Perdue, Lawrence E. Toombs, and Gary Lance Johnson, eds., *Archaeology and Biblical Interpretation* (Atlanta: John Knox Press, 1987), pp. 31-40.

Sternberg, Meir, *The Poetics of Biblical Narrative: Ideological Literature and the Drama of Reading* (Bloomington: Indiana University Press, 1987), pp. 64, 67.

Strauss, Leo, and Joseph Cropsey, eds., *History of Political Philosophy* (Chicago: Rand McNally, 1963).

Tadmor, H., "The Period of the First Temple, the Babylonian Exile and the Restoration," in H. H. Ben-Sasson, *A History of the Jewish People* (Cambridge: Harvard University Press, 1976), pp. 100-101.

Tadmor, Hayim, "'The People' and the Kingship in Ancient Israel: The Role of Political Institutions in the Biblical Period," *Journal of World History*, Vol. XI, No. 1-2, 1968, pp. 1-23.

Tapp, Jack T., "Multisystems Holistic Model of Health, Stress and Coping," in Tiffany M. Field, Philip M. McCabe and Neil Schneiderman, eds., *Stress and Coping* (Hillsdale, NJ: Lawrence Erlbaum Associates, Publishers, 1985), pp. 285-304. .

The Condition of Jewish Belief: A Symposium Compiled by the Editors of Commentary Magazine (New York: Macmillan, 1966).

Thompson , Thomas L., and Dorothy Irvin, "The Joseph and Moses Narratives," in John H. Hayes and J. Maxwell Miller, eds., *Israelite and Judaean History* (London: SCM Press Ltd., 1977), pp. 149-212.

Tomes, Roger, "The Psalms," in Stephen Bigger, ed., *Creating the Old Testament: The Emergence of the Hebrew Bible* (Oxford: Basil Blackwell, 1989), pp. 251-67.

Trible, Phyllis, *Texts of Terror: Literary-Feminist Readings of Biblical Narratives* (Philadelphia: Fortress Press, 1984). .

Tuchman, Barbara W., *Bible and Sword: England and Palestine from the Bronze Age to Balfour* (New York: Ballantine Books, 1956).

Unterman, Jeremiah, *From Repentance to Redemption: Jeremiah's Thought in Transition* (Sheffield: JSOT Press, 1987).

Urbach, Ephraim E., *The Sages: Their Concepts and Beliefs* (Cambridge: Harvard University Press, 1979).

Vaux, Roland de, *Ancient Israel*(New York: McGraw-Hill, 1961).

Visotzky, Burton L., *Reading the Book: Making the Bible a Timeless Text* (New York: Anchor Books, 1991).

von Rad, Gerhard, *God at Work in Israel*, translated by John H. Marks (Nashville: Abingdon, 1980).

Vos, Howard F., *Ezra, Nehemiah, and Esther* (Grand Rapids, MI: Zondervan Publishing House, 1987).

Waetjen, Herman C., *A Reordering of Power: A Sociopolitical Reading of Mark's Gospel* (Minneapolis: Fortress Press, 1989).

Walzer, Michael, *Obligations: Essays on Disobedience, War, and Citizenship* (Cambridge: Harvard University Press, 1970).

Walzer, Michael, *Just and Unjust Wars: A Moral Argument with Historical Illustrations* (New York: Basic Books, 1977).

Walzer, Michael, *Exodus and Revolution* (New York: Basic Books, 1985).

Weiss David W., *The Wings of the Dove: Jewish Values, Science, and Halacha* (Washington: Bnei B'rith Books, 1987).

Whitelam, Keith W., "The Former Prophets," in Stephen Bigger, ed., *Creating the Old Testament: The Emergence of the Hebrew Bible* (Oxford: Basil Blackwell, 1989), pp. 151-68.

Whitelam, Keith W., "Israel's Traditions in Origin: Reclaiming the Land," *Journal for the Study of the Old Testament* 44, June 1989, pp. 19-42.

Wildavsky, Aaron, *The Nursing Father: Moses as a Political Leader* (University: University of Alabama Press, 1984).

Wildavsky, Aaron, "What Is Permissible So That This People May Survive? Joseph the Administrator," *PS: Political Science and Politics* XXII, 4 December 1989, pp. 779-88.

Williams, James G., "Proverbs and *Ecclesiastes*," in Alter and Kermode, pp. 263-82.

Williamson, Ronald, *Jews in the Hellenistic World: Philo* (Cambridge: Cambridge University Press, 1989).

Wolfensohn, Abraham, *From the Bible to the Labor Movement* (Tel Aviv: Am Oved, 1975). Hebrew.

Wolfsfeld, Gadi,*The Politics of Provocation* (Albany: State University of New York Press, 1988).

Wulff, David M., *Psychology of Religion: Classic and Contemporary Views* (New York: John Wiley & Sons, 1991).

Yaniv, Avner, ed., *National Security and Democracy in Israel* (Boulder, CO: Lynne Rienner Publishers, 1993).

Yehoshua, A. B., "The Golah as a Neurotic Solution," *Forum: On the Jewish People, Zionism and Israel*, Spring/Summer, 1979, #35, pp. 17-36.

Yerushalmi, Hayim, *Zakhor: Jewish History and Jewish Memory* (Seattle: University of Washington Press, 1982).

Zar-Kavod, Mordecai, *The Five Scrolls* (Jerusalem: Mossad Harav Kook, 1973), Hebrew.

Zeitlin, Solomon, *The Rise and Fall of the Judean State,* Vol I: 332-37 (Philadelphia: Jewish Publication Society of America, 1962).

Zuckerman, Adrian A. S. "Coercion and the Judicial Ascertainment of Truth," *Israel Law Review,* 1989. Spring-Summer, Volume 23, Numbers 2-3, pp. 357-74.

Index

—C—

—D—

—E—

—F—

—G—

—H—

—I—

—J—

—K—

—N—

—O—

—P—

—R—

—S—